Tales of the Rails
In Georgia

Co-written, Compiled and Edited
By
Olin Jackson
B.A., M.Ed.

Published by Legacy Communications, Inc.
200 Market Place, Suite 100
Roswell, Georgia, 30075

Copyright, 2004
Legacy Communications, Inc.
All Rights Reserved

TO: HARRY E. GAINES
FROM: MARGARET BAGWELL SMITH 4-20-06

International Standard Book Number (ISBN):
1-880816-19-9

For additional copies:
Legacy Communications, Inc.
Post Office Box 127
Roswell, Georgia 30077-0127
Tel: (770) 642-5569

Dedicated To

Those brave railroad men – both past and present – who have worked long hard hours and often risked their lives in the pursuit of their profession.

Acknowledgements

The articles, facts and photographs on the pages which follow are a compilation of information carefully researched and painstakingly collected over a period of approximately twenty years. These articles on the history of some of the railroads in Georgia are not designed as nor intended to be a comprehensive history of this topic. They, rather, offer a glimpse of some of the more unusual and interesting portions of this history.

All research involved in the preparation of this book was conducted by skilled historians and dedicated writers/researchers of history. All material herein is, to the best our knowledge, factual and accurate.

Grateful appreciation is hereby extended to the following writers and researchers without whose assistance this book would not have been possible:

- Harry Bartlett
- Robert S. Davis, Jr.
- Dr. Caroline M. Dillman
- Rutherford "Ruddy" Ellis
- Mary H. Free
- Joe Griffith
- Grover & Ethelene Dyer Jones
- Alline Kent
- Frank Kyper
- Judy D. Lovell
- Deborah Malone
- Sara Hines Martin
- Sybil McRay
- Michael Miller
- Theron E. Ragsdale
- Gordon Sargent
- Gordon Sawyer
- Susan Sawyer
- John A. Shivers
- Carol Thompson
- Lorayne B. Weizenecker
- Travis Williams

Contents

Bartow County
The Battle Of Allatoona Pass 1
Kingston, GA: The Early Years 7
The Story Of A Community Called Etowah 13

Cherokee County
The Marker That Missed Its Mark 18

Cobb County
Camp McDonald & The Great Locomotive Chase 21
The Place Where Andrews' Raiders Slept 31

Crisp County
Riding The Rails On The SAM Shortline 35

Dawson County
Early Railroads In Lumpkin And Dawson Counties 41

Fannin County
The Blue Ridge Scenic Railway 48
The Railway Through Blue Ridge 52
The Last Days Of The Old "Hook & Eye?" 54

Floyd County
The Calhoun - Williamson Duel And The CR&C Railroad 60

Fulton County
The Old Roswell Railroad 67
The Day The Railroad Came to Roswell – Almost 70

Gwinnett County
The Southeastern Railway Museum 74

Habersham County
Hoyt Tench And The Old "TF". 76
Retracing The Route Of The Tallulah Falls RR. 81
The Tallulah Falls Disaster of 1921 85

Hall County
Remembering The Gainesville & Northwestern Railroad 90
The Railroad And The Early Days In Clermont 94
Last Ride Of Old #209 On The Gainesville Midland 98
Bandit Bill Miner & A North Georgia Railroad Robbery 100
The Day Belton, Georgia "Dried Up" 108

Monroe
Remembering *Fried Green Tomatoes* 111

Northwest Georgia
Retracing The Great Locomotive Chase 113
A Driving Tour Of The Great Locomotive Chase 121

Paulding County
Early Northwest Georgia Railroad Disasters 123

Polk County
All Aboard The Silver Comet Rail Trail 128
The Wreck Of The Royal Palm 135

Rabun County
Recollections Of An RPO Clerk On The Tallulah Falls Railroad 143
Searching For Clues To The Historic Blue Ridge Railroad. 152

Stephens County
Railroader David J. Fant And The Valley Of Death. 159

Walker County
The Pigeon Mountain Railroads 162

White County
The Gainesville – Northwestern Railroad in Helen, Georgia 166

Whitfield County
A Railroad Landmark Old Dalton Depot. 169
The Wreck Of The W & A Railroad At Willowdale 171

Subject Index 176
Full Name Index 183

The Battle of Allatoona Pass

Little known to many U.S. Civil War buffs, a strategic portion of the old Western & Atlantic Railroad at Allatoona Pass was the site of a bloody conflict during the autumn of 1864. Today, this battlefield from yesteryear offers a scenic hiking trail, as well as a unique site for visitation by travelers and locals alike.

On a warm summer afternoon - perhaps not too different from the "hazy drowsy Indian summer day" of October 5, 1864, when the Battle of Allatoona took place – I walked over the battlements which once made up Allatoona Pass. Diane (Mrs. Dennis) Mooney and her son, Lance, walked with me through the 100-foot-long dug-out pass where the Western & Atlantic Railroad once bisected the Allatoona Mountain Range. Today, the steel ribbons from this rail line are long gone. The once-important railroad through the pass is little more than a dirt trail today, bordered on each side by steep 65-foot embankments attesting to the depth to which the line's builders were forced to dig. The silence and peacefulness of this site belie the bloody history of the spot.

The Mooneys live in what is known today as the Clayton House, a two-story clapboard residence across Old Allatoona Road from the pass. John Clayton, one of the earlier Bartow County settlers, is believed to have been a wealthy miner.

Mr. Clayton built this home in the 1830s at a time when most local dwellers could afford little more than rustic log cabins. "He died one month after the battle," explained Mrs. Mooney, "partly from the shock of the incident."

Battle History

From May through October of 1864, the Clayton House served as a headquarters for the Union Army in this vicinity. During the battle, the house, at one time or another, served both sides as a hospital.

Mrs. Mooney, who inherited the structure from her parents, can readily point out bullet holes in the upstairs walls and a dark blotch on one floor that is believed to be blood from the many surgeries which took place in the home.

A white marble marker in the front yard commemorates the battle and the men who died here. With the help of a U.S. Army Corps Of Engineers archaeologist, the Mooneys located the graves of 21 unknown soldiers buried in their back yard. As of this writing, individual markers are scheduled to be placed upon the sites.

TALES OF THE RAILS IN GEORGIA

The Mooney family which owned the Clayton-Mooney home at Allatoona was photogaphed in front of the structure in 1994. This early home which was built approximately 75 yards from the W&A Railroad appears in several historic Civil War photos of the strategic Allatoona Pass through which the railroad traveled. The walls of the home still have bullet holes sustained from the battle which transpired there. (Photo by Olin Jackson)

This illustration which appeared in a book published a few years after the battle shows Major-General S.G. French who was the commander of the Confederate forces which attempted unsuccessfully to capture and destroy the railroad at Allatoona Pass in 1864. In a communique, French later painfully recalled the battle as "one of the most sanguinary of the war."

The Mooneys often host a living history and memorial service on their property in the springtime. "In addition to the regular re-enactors, we invite descendants of soldiers from both sides of the conflict to participate," Mrs. Mooney says.

In 1864, the road at this spot represented the main route from Kingston through Marietta to Atlanta. On his zig-zag march southward in early June of that year, Gen. William T. Sherman sought a depot where supplies could be safely stockpiled for the remainder of the Atlanta campaign. He selected Allatoona Pass and ordered that forts be built on either side of the pass.

Log stockades, abatis (obstacles formed of trees felled toward the enemy) thickly-laced with telegraph wire, and outer rows of trenches protected the forts.

In the fall of 1864, the village (named for nearby Allatoona Creek which the Indians had named in their days of occupation of the area) located at the south end of the cut, included eight merchant shops, eight homes, a railroad depot, and several large new warehouses (for the storage of large quantities of rations of hardtack stockpiled by Sherman).

Interestingly, 9,000 head of cattle grazed nearby beside the Etowah River near Emerson. Today, very little remains of the former community of Allatoona Pass.

The Battle Begins

In 1864, after Atlanta had fallen, federal soldiers returned to Allatoona Pass to retrieve the stores of hardtack which would be needed to feed the troops during the remainder of Sherman's *"March To The Sea."* To eliminate the railroad supply line, Confederate Lt. Gen. John G. Hood sent Maj. Gen. S.G. French with approximately 2,500 men to capture Allatoona Pass and *"to fill up the deep cut at Allatoona with logs, brush, dirt, and debris, etc."* Hood hoped to deny Sherman the use of this particular railroad since it was the main federal supply line.

In the midst of an autumn downpour, Gen. French and his men left Big Shanty and trudged up the railroad through Acworth and across Allatoona Creek. At 7:00 a.m., French's artillery commenced firing upon the federal guns which returned the fire.

French then sent in a courier with the following message for Gen. John M. Corse (who had recently hurried down from Rome with 1,054 men to reinforce the garrison at Allatoona Pass): "I have placed the forces under my command in such positions that you are surrounded, and to avoid a needless effusion of blood, I call on you to surrender your forces at once."

Corse, with approximately 1,000 fewer men than French, reportedly replied: "Your communication demanding surrender of my command I acknowledge receipt of, and respectfully reply that we are prepared for the 'needless effusion of blood' whenever it is agreeable with you."

French later claimed he never received the reply, and the fighting resumed. With bloodcurdling screams, Confederates leaped from the forest surrounding the fort and charged forward. Corse later wrote that "a solid mass of gray advanced from the woods and started up the hill, with artillery support from the rear."

Men were killed steadily in hand-to-hand combat, using bayonets and swords to stab and slash, and rifles and even rocks to club and crush. The federals fired their repeating rifles so rapidly that they became too hot to hold.

In the end, French realized he would be unable to accomplish his mission - that of interrupting and damaging the rail line at Allatoona Pass. Midway through the afternoon, he reluctantly ordered his troops to retire following considerable "needless effusion of blood."

In seven hours of fighting, 1,505 men - nearly one-third of the 5,000 engaged - were killed or wounded. French reportedly lost 700 men. Corse lost even more. Yet it seems it was French who was the most regretful.

"History will record the Battle of Allatoona Pass as one of the most sanguinary of the war," he wrote in a communique. In his postwar book, *Two Wars*, French bitterly recalled Allatoona as a mistake. "It was Hood's ignorance of the enemy's position that caused the battle; it should never have been made."

Relics From Civil War Days

Immediately south of the Clayton House stands an empty brick building which was once a general store. From its shelves and from within its bins, horseshoe nails, shoes, clothing, foodstuffs - the staples of life - were once sold to hearty country residents.

Acworth resident Don Armstrong - the grandson of one John Armstrong - maintains that his grandfather - who was a carpenter - came from North Carolina after the war and built the store in 1892.

Armstrong says his grandfather also built the small house beside the Clayton House, as well as the two-story "Steamboat Gothic" house south of the store.

It was through this same Allatoona Pass that James J. Andrews, a contraband merchant and spy, and his coterie of raiders sped on April 12, 1862, having just hijacked the General, Engine #3 from Big Shanty Station in Kennesaw.

"With a full head of steam, the locomotive, tender and three boxcars raced from Big Shanty, beginning what is often said to have been the most daring American railroad adventure ever attempted," wrote Joe F.

TALES OF THE RAILS IN GEORGIA

Gen. William T. Sherman needed the stores of hardtack in the railroad warehouses at Allatoona Pass to feed his men during the remainder of his infamous "March To The Sea." He sent Gen. John M. Corse and 1,054 men who successfully reinforced and defended the garrison at the Pass.

This artist's conception, illustrated in 1907, provides a glimpse of the Battle of Allatoona Pass. It was drawn from remembrances described by survivors of the engagement.

Head in the March, 1994 issue of the Etowah Valley Historical Society's newsletter.

Andrews' objective, ironically enough, was to burn bridges and destroy as much of the railroad as possible - but this time, it was being done so that Confederate troops wouldn't be able to use the line for supplies. The destruction would have more quickly enabled Union troops to advance upon Chattanooga, and would have prevented Confederate troops in Atlanta from moving northward to defend against the invading Yankees.

After speeding past Hugo - a wood and water stop in Bartow County - the train with Andrews and his raiders went past the Clayton House and hurtled onward into Allatoona Pass.

Not too far behind, William A. Fuller, conductor of the General, and fellow Confederates, pursued hotly. When the engine ran low on fuel in Ringgold near the Tennessee state line, Andrews abandoned it, and he and most of his men were captured shortly thereafter.

Unknown Soldier's Grave

About half a mile south of the entrance to Allatoona Pass, the body of an unknown soldier was buried shortly after the battle in quiet repose beside the railroad bed. One story maintains the remains in this grave are those of a young man whose lifeless body was being shipped home by rail in a box labeled simply as "Allatoona, Georgia." Supposedly, no mark showed the origin of the body. It reportedly reached its destination days after a battle, and had understandably reached a high state of decay.

Six young women - as the story goes - took over a job normally reserved for the men. In what could only be interpreted as an attempt to ascertain identity, they bravely pried off the lid of the box with a crowbar.

The Battle Of Allatoona Pass — Bartow County

Inside, they reportedly found only a young man dressed in Confederate grey. With him lay a rolled-up, broad-brimmed black hat.

The women dug a grave and placed a crude marker at the spot to mark it for posterity. In 1980, a group of surveyors erected a gravestone at the site.

In the 1940s, when Allatoona Dam was being constructed, the gravesite would have been buried beneath the waters of the lake rising behind the dam. As a result, the body was exhumed and then reburied a short distance from the original site, reportedly so that the gravesite could be maintained by the railroad's maintenance crew. Today, the lonely grave lies in an abandoned field, since the railroad line was also relocated sometime later to accommodate the lake construction.

Some people today - including Don Armstrong - disagree with the above story of the origin of the body in the solider grave. Armstrong says he grew up listening to old soldiers talking around a pot-bellied stove in the old store. From their comments, he believes that a more accurate explanation would be that train crewmen found the body of a soldier along the tracks and simply buried it.

Yet another explanation for the identity of the body in the gravesite has been offered by Robert White, former stationmaster of the Cartersville, Georgia Depot, and the late Colonel Thomas Spencer, a journalist and historian. According to these two man, there are two unknown soldier graves at Allatoona Pass, not merely one, and the bodies were originally buried on opposite sides of the former track bed.

According to Etowah Valley Historical Society member Joe Head who researched the information from these two gentlemen, "a lesser-known grave site lies within the pass on the east side of the original track

Photographed shortly after the battle, the community of Allatoona shows the Clayton-Mooney home (far left center), the only structure from this photo still standing as of this writing today. The stores of hardtack protected by the federals were housed in warehouses in this vicinity. The garrison protecting the site was located on the prominences on both sides of the Pass here. Today, this garrison is a protected historic site.

bed and has no marker. It is assumed that this Confederate soldier was buried a few days after the battle (quite possibly the same burial as the one associated above with the women of Allatoona)."

The Abernathy family (relatives of Head) of Cartersville is credited by Head with this lesser-known burial. Unfortunately, the location of this grave is virtually unknown today, because it has not been maintained by the railroad and the vicinity of the grave has been repeatedly disturbed by relic hunters.

Head says the second and more visible grave (near the northern entrance of the pass and a few feet west of the tracks) was dug for another soldier who died in the battle.

"Local historians believe this is the grave site of Private Andrew Jackson Houston of the 135th Mississippi Regiment who fell during the Battle of Allatoona," he recorded. "In 1950, the railroad relocated and marked this grave approximately one-half mile south of the pass and a few yards west of the existing tracks." This grave is maintained today by area residents, and is the best known of a number of unknown solder graves in the area.

Finally, in his publication entitled *The Western & Atlantic Railroad / Marietta: The Gem City Of Georgia*, former Georgia Governor Joseph M. Brown, an ardent student of history - and in particular the history of the Western & Atlantic Railroad - wrote a description of this soldier's gravesite in 1887.

"The most characteristic memorial of this bloody and famous struggle which now salutes the eye of the tourist, as the train darts through the deep, fern-lined (Allatoona) pass, is a lone grave at its northwestern end, immediately by the track, on the west side. This is the resting-place of a Confederate soldier, who was buried on the spot where he fell. For years past, the trackhands of the Western & Atlantic Railroad have held this grave under their special charge. . . A neat marble headstone has been placed there on which is the following inscription: *An Unknown Hero. He Died For The Cause He Thought Was Right.*"

To Reach Allatoona Pass

Allatoona Pass is one hour north of Atlanta off Interstate 75. Just before reaching the Cartersville, Georgia exit, take the Emerson-Allatoona Road exit and head east, continuing for one and one-half miles. Signs direct visitors to the pass which is bordered by Lake Allatoona. The Etowah Valley Historical Society in Bartow County has formally requested the U.S. Army Corps of Engineers reopen the pass as a historical hiking trail, with paths, parking and signage. Only time will tell to what degree this historic site will be preserved for future generations.

ENDNOTES

1/ *Southern Recorder*, 16 May, 1871.
2/ *Southern Recorder*, 16 May, 1871.
3/ *Southern Recorder*, 11 July, 1871.
4/ *Southern Recorder*, 11 July, 1871.
5/ A carbine is a short, lightweight rifle.
6/ *Southern Recorder*, 11 July, 1871, and *Macon Telegraph & Messenger*, 9 July, 1871.
7/ *Southern Recorder*, 11 July, 1871.
8/ *Southern Recorder*, 23 April, 1872.
9/ Correspondence from relative, Edward L. Strother, to the authors dated 20 February, 2002.
10/ *Federal Union*, 7 June, 1870 and *Register*, Alvaretta Kenan, The Kenan Family (self-published, 1967) p. 99.
11/ Henderson, Lillian, *Roster of Confederate Soldiers of Georgia*, 1861-1865 (Hapeville, GA, Longina & Porter, 1964.)
12/ *Federal Union*, 12 July, 1871.
13/ *American Union*, 27 July, 1871, *Union Recorder*, 6 December, 1870, and *Union Recorder*, 24 April, 1866.
14/ *Southern Recorder*, 5 June, 1866.
15/ *Southern Recorder*, 10 April, 1866.
16/ *Southern Recorder*, 6 June, 1866.
17/ *Southern Recorder*, 21 December, 1869.
18/ *American Union*, 6 July, 1871.
19/ *American Union*, 27 July, 1871.
20/ *American Union*, 27 July, 1871 and Bonner, James C., Milledgeville, *Georgia's Antebellum Capital*. (Athens: UGA Press, 1978) pp 211-212.
21/ Bertram Wyatt-Brown. *Honor and Violence In The Old South* (New York: Oxford University Press, 1986): 149-153.
22/ Seawright, "Ghost Fry."
23/ *American Union*, 27 July, 1871.
24/ The Kenan Family
25/ Harrington, Hugh T., editor, Methodist Church Record Books, Milledgeville, Georgia, 1811-1876, Milledgeville, Boyd Publishing, 1997, p. 158.
26/ *Federal Union*, 12 July, 1871.
27/ *Federal Union*, 12 July, 1871.
28/ *Federal Union*, 12 July, 1871.
29/ Harrington, Hugh T. and Susan J. Harrington, ed. *The Dead Book: Burials In The City Cemetery, Milledgeville, Georgia, 1869-1904*, (Milledgeville, GA, Boyd Publishing Co, 1998) p 90.
30/ *Union Recorder*, 25 December, 1888.

Kingston, GA: The Early Years

It began as a stagecoach stop. Later, as an important depot on the new Western & Atlantic Railroad, it blossomed as a summer resort, a thriving mercantile center, and finally, as a pivotal organizing point for both Confederate and Union forces during the U.S. Civil War. Today, it is little more than a ghost town.

Located in western Bartow County at an important stop on the railroad between Atlanta and Chattanooga, Kingston was once a prosperous town of at least 40 businesses and four hotels. However, as was the case with many early communities, Kingston's lifeblood was the railroad. As the flow of passenger trains diminished, so also did Kingston's prosperity.

Today, trees literally grow through the deteriorating roofs that once sheltered businesses in the old downtown area. The brick walls of some of the buildings are crumbling, and the only things that now thrive there are the honeysuckle and morning glories.

Mrs. Mary Lee Harper witnessed the tide turning. In 1930, she came to Kingston from Rome as a bride when she "married a Kingston boy."

"I remember when Kingston was hot - people coming and going all the time," she explained in an interview in 1992, with sadness in her voice. "It's dead now though - pitiful really.

"Used to be we'd come to town about every day to see the trains and to be seen," she smiled. "Things changed, rather gradually, and now there's no reason even to go downtown."

Indeed, Railroad Street in the sparsely-populated community appears abandoned as of this writing. There are

As the flow

of passenger trains

diminished, so also did

Kingston's prosperity.

7

TALES OF THE RAILS IN GEORGIA

Both Confederate and Union forces controlled Kingston at different times during the U.S. Civil War. The community was considered a strategic site on the Western & Atlantic Railroad. This sketch of Kingston appeared in *Harper's Weekly* magazine on July 2, 1864.

Just as did a number of other communities, Kingston evolved and grew due to its location on the Western & Atlantic Railroad. As railroad passenger service diminished, so also did the commerce of this town. Today, it includes some 18 buildings and sites listed on the *National Register of Historic Places*.

Railroad Street (1900) - The Kingston Inn (far left) which burned in March of 1911, stood on the site occupied today by the Ranson Mercantile building.

no people milling about - waiting on the next train, or a turn in the barber's chair, dining or checking into the hotel, depositing money or reading a local paper.

Preserving The Past

There would probably be nothing left of the old downtown district at all were it not for the efforts of a few individuals such as Vernon Ayers, an antique dealer and collector, and long-time resident of Kingston. As of this writing, Mr. Ayers lives in the century-old Desoto Hotel, one of the few original downtown businesses still somewhat intact, though far from the showplace it once was. Mr. Ayers was successful in steering through the listing of the Desoto in the *National Register of Historic Places*. When he was mayor of Kingston in the early 1980s, he designated Railroad Street as a historic district.

Ayers is a railroad and history enthusiast, and says the Desoto was built in 1890. It survived a disastrous town fire in 1911, and was well-known for its food in the early part of the century before it was closed in 1947.

Mrs. Harper remembers dining at the Desoto with her family. "They had good food, and they fed lots of people - locals as well as folks waiting to switch trains," she continued.

"The hotel currently serves a dual purpose for me," Mr. Ayers explained in an interview in the early 1990s. "It is both my residence and my antique shop."

Mr. Ayers' pride and joy is his extensive collection of 17th, 18th, and 19th century antiques. "As many of my visitors say," he smiles, "it is one of Georgia's best-kept secrets."

The abandoned downtown suggests that Kingston is home to many secrets, and no doubt many untold stories. Twelve historic markers are scattered over the town, a testament to the outstanding moments which have transcended the history of this north Georgia community, and no doubt helped shape the future of a nation. Some 18 buildings and sites in the town are listed in the *National Register of Historic Places* today.

"Per capita, that's more listings than any other city in Georgia," Mr. Ayers beamed proudly.

The Early Days

The historic markers reveal much of Kingston's rich past. It was established in 1832 and named in honor of John Pendleton King, president and financier of the Western and Atlantic (W&A) Railroad. King was a lawyer, and served in the Georgia State Legislature and later in the U.S. Congress.

Even before the state of Georgia authorized the building of the W&A Railroad in 1836, businessmen and travelers journeyed by horseback and stagecoach to Kingston to trade at the town's cotton markets, drink from its springs and escape the heat and mosquitoes of the state's southern plains.

Ironically, Kingston's fate was sealed on the day its real growth began - a date in November of 1849, when the W&A Railroad was completed in Georgia, hailing the state's entrance into the national railroad transportation system connecting the Mississippi River with the Atlantic Ocean.

The celebration of the completion of the railroad on this day also set the stage for a major role Kingston was destined to play in the U.S. Civil War. The Chattanooga-Atlanta trains often stopped in Kingston to take on water, fuel and passengers. With the completion of the Memphis branch railroad from Kingston to Rome in 1850, Kingston became an important distribution point on the W&A, connecting it with the riverboat transportation on the Coosa River.

Railroad Street (1991) - The corner of the old Masonic Hall is visible (far left). The Desoto Hotel apears prominently (center). The structure in the distance with the corner entranceway is the former Ranson Mercantile building. Due to thriving railroad freight and passenger services, this street was regularly filled with pedestrians, businessmen and mercantile traffic in the late 1800s and early 1900s, but has been reduced to a ghostly relic of its former glory in this photo.

The Desoto Hotel was photographed here circa 1918. In an effort to freshen up the image of the facility following World War I, it was renamed the New Kingston Hotel. Then-owner Tom Bryant stands in front. The Desoto/Kingston was built (and ultimately died) in relation to the vitality of the railroad.

The antebellum Benjamin Reynolds home in Kingston was built in 1846 and still stands as of this writing.

Hallowed graves are honored and decorated each year in Kingston as Confederate Memorial Day is observed. Because of its strategic location on the W&A Railroad, Kingston became a busy hospital center during the U.S. Civil War. This substantial graveyard speaks of the tragedies of this war.

The Civil War

Because of this strategic location on the railroad, Kingston became a busy supply and hospital center during the war. In the fall of 1861, so many soldiers in need of care were coming through the town on the railroad that the women of the town established temporary quarters for them in churches, vacant stores and private homes. Several of these homes still exist in good condition today, most notably the Reynolds House, built in 1846 by Benjamin Reynolds, and the home built in 1854 by the author and inventor of the sewing machine - Dr. Francis Robert Goulding.

On two occasions, Kingston took center stage in the unfolding drama of the war, both times sharing the spotlight with famous Civil War generals.

In April of 1862, a group of Union raiders led by James J. Andrews seized the locomotive *General* at Big Shanty (present-day Kennesaw, Georgia) with the intention of taking it to Chattanooga and destroying all the bridges on the route, thus crippling the W&A and the Confederate Army's ability to move soldiers, ammunition and supplies. Andrews' raiders – actually spies - however, suffered a set-back when they rolled into the busy hub of Kingston on the *General*.

According to James C. Bogle, a leading authority on the "Great Locomotive Chase" as historians have dubbed it, Andrews and his men spent a very long and frustrating hour and five minutes in Kingston before they were able to pull out. As explained, the community by this time was a busy commercial center, and delays in access to switch-tracks and supplies were commonplace. It is the consensus of historians that the delay in Kingston caused the raiders' mission to fail.

Another famous general in the Civil War, William T. Sherman of the Union Army, is also forever linked with Kingston. Sherman was headquartered at the Thomas Van Buren Hargis home in Kingston May 19-23, 1864, and returned in November to plan his "March To The Sea." There were eight separate skirmishes in Kingston during this time, and it was here that Sherman received permission from General Ulysses S. Grant to carry out his fateful destructive march through Atlanta and onward to Savannah.

Kingston, GA: The Early Years

According to Mr. Ayers, the Hargis home burned in 1947, but the field desk that Sherman used while in Kingston has survived and is today owned by Ayers. "I had known of its existence for many years, and when the opportunity came to acquire it, I couldn't resist," he says.

Sherman's troops destroyed much of Kingston. The only church remaining after he departed was the Kingston Methodist Church. It opened its doors to all denominations and was also used as a schoolhouse.

When the war ended in 1865, the last remnant of the Confederate Army east of the Mississippi was paroled in Kingston. Brig. Gen. William T. Wofford arranged with Brig. Gen. Henry M. Judah, U.S.A. for the surrender of some 3,000 to 4,000 Confederate soldiers, mostly Georgians not paroled in Virginia, North Carolina and elsewhere.

While the Federals and Confederates gathered in Kingston for the surrender, the people of Kingston observed the first Confederate Memorial Day in the nation.

The Ladies Of Kingston

Local folklore maintains that in the spring of 1865, the ladies of the town wanted to use the "profusion of spring flowers" to decorate the soldiers' graves. To do this they needed the consent of the military. The ladies approached the commanding officer with their request. He gave his consent with one stipulation - that they decorate all graves, Southern and Federal alike.

Local folklore maintains that in the spring of 1865, the ladies of the town wanted to use the "profusion of spring flowers" to decorate the soldiers' graves.

At that time, there were more than 275 Confederates and many Federals buried in the Kingston cemetery, but some have since been removed. Today, there are 249 unknown Confederate graves, one known Confederate, and two unknown Federals buried at the spot.

The tradition of honoring the men who died in and around Kingston during the Civil War continues today. Each spring, Kingston residents staunchly observe Confederate Memorial Day, due largely to the Woman's History Club there.

Founded in 1900 the club began as a monthly afternoon tea, designed primarily for the entertainment of members. They, however, have become almost as much a part of the history of Kingston as the history they set out to document and preserve.

According to Mrs. Harper, one of the elder members of the organization, the club has provided many services to the town and the state of Georgia over the years, including the maintenance and observance of the Memorial Day celebrations each year without a single lapse. "I've participated in many of the Memorial Day services," Mrs. Harper stated. "I enjoy the speakers and the good feeling it gives you."

The Woman's History Club is also responsible for establishing and maintaining the Confederate Memorial Museum of Kingston. Opened in 1971, the museum houses a collection of Confederate artifacts, including swords, bayonets, cannon balls and civil war script money, and is open to the pub-

TALES OF THE RAILS IN GEORGIA

lic on special occasions. Other items in the museum include a case of Indian artifacts; the bulletin board, a desk and bench from the Kingston Depot; exhibits on cotton and saltpeter mines; and various other natural resources found in Bartow County.

Remnants Of The Past

Scrap books and photographs attesting to Kingston's prosperity at the turn of the century are also on display. Pages from the *Kingston Times*, a newspaper circulated around 1915, reveal a prospering community with 40 businesses, several banks and hotels. There are stories about the massive fire of 1911, and the subsequent rebuilding of the downtown area.

Mrs. Harper said there was always something going on back in those days when the passenger trains were running. "Lots of folks would come in on the trains from Rome and wait for one of the north-south trains going to Chattanooga or Atlanta," she explained.

The *Kingston Times*, however, didn't last, nor did Kingston's good times. The community lived by the railroad and died by it, stranded and strangled as the flow of passenger traffic dwindled and died.

It is almost ironic that while photographs of the old downtown Railroad Street have been meticulously preserved in the museum, the actual downtown buildings themselves, many of which still stand, have been largely neglected. By the 1950s they were on the decline, headed toward abandonment, and an era had ended.

In the 40 years since, little has changed in Kingston. Attempts to attract industry have failed. Dissension among the community's leaders stymied efforts for progress. There are a couple of gas stations and a store or two, but Mr. Ayers and Mrs. Harper say that most of the 800 or so residents work and shop in nearby Rome or Cartersville.

Interstate 75 to the east and U.S. Highway 411 to the south have bypassed Kingston. Freight trains still come, but they too pass by without stopping.

Kingston's future is uncertain at best. The town's fate has been so closely linked with the railroad, it is doubtful it will prosper again without the revival of passenger train service.

As for Vernon Ayers, who grew up in another railroad town - nearby Blue Ridge - which has also lived and died by the railroad, he says he isn't waiting for the resurrection of passenger rail service.

"This old hotel has marvelous possibilities as a bed-and-breakfast inn because of the close proximity to Atlanta, Chattanooga and Alabama," he explains. "Not a week goes by that somebody doesn't come to photograph Railroad Street," he adds. "With the restoration of Barnsley Gardens only five miles away, and the completion of the new Anheuser-Busch Brewery east of the city, Kingston is destined to be rediscovered and revitalized."

Whatever the destiny of Kingston, its success or failure may hinge once again upon the railroad, especially if a rapid rail system extending into the outlying areas of metropolitan Atlanta is even completed.

> *The town's fate has been so closely linked with the railroad, it is doubtful it will prosper again without the revival of passenger train service.*

The Story Of A Community Called Etowah

The Remnants Of A Pre-Civil War Industrial Community Which Was A Stunning Achievement In Its Day, Lie Wasted And Forgotten In The Mud Of Lake Allatoona.

The waters of Lake Allatoona near the dam at Georgia Highway 294 North are relatively calm today, as are the forests and woods nearby. There was a time, however - prior to the construction of the lake when this spot was occupied by a unique achievement in Georgia history. . . .

Resting on the lake bottom are the ruins of a town that, for a brief span of time, was responsible for a remarkable accomplishment in industrial development, particularly for this area of Georgia in the two decades prior to the U.S. Civil War. The town was called "Etowah," an aboriginal place-name of the region.

At its peak, Etowah was a small town of 2,000 to 4,000 inhabitants. It was an astounding production center for iron, flour, lumber and iron goods, all in a self-contained town that even had its own railroad. No other such town had existed in Georgia prior to the Civil War. Today, this community has been virtually forgotten by historians.

The story of Etowah is especially unusual because the town was not the product of some far-fetched manufacturing tycoon. The opportunities for mining and manufacturing in this area prior to Etowah's development had been well-known, even before the native Indians were forced from their north Georgia homeland. However, the state of

The story of Etowah is especially unusual because the town was not the product of some far-fetched manufacturing tycoon.

Mark A. Cooper, a developer of the mills and community called Etowah, was photographed here at the age of 70. He sold out his holdings in Etowah for a handsome fee - enough upon which to retire. However, after the sale, he invested heavily in the Confederacy, and at war's end, he was destitute.

Georgia, coasting along on an agrarian economic system, did little to develop the region's resources of waterpower, iron, gold, copper, talc, coal marble and slate, choosing instead to leave such ventures to more daring private investors.

One such gambler was Jacob Stroup, (1771-1846) who had built iron furnaces in the Carolinas prior to starting another in Habersham County, Georgia, in 1832. Four years later, he built the first furnace in what today is Bartow County, Georgia. This small furnace for purifying local iron ore into the pig iron used in manufacturing, was adjoined by a sawmill, gristmill, and 1,300 acres of timber and mineral-rich land, and formed the nucleus for the thriving township known as Etowah.

In 1842, Stroup sold out to his son Moses, who that same year, sold a half interest in the property to one Mark Anthony Cooper (1800-1885) who would shortly prove to be the brain trust behind the eventual development of Etowah.

Cooper had lived through a succession of successful careers, only to be thwarted each time from reaping the true rewards of his hard work. He built one of Georgia's early cotton factories and had been a banker in Columbus, Georgia; a major in the Seminole War of 1836; and a Georgia congressman. After a narrow defeat in a race for the Georgia governorship in 1843, he retired to a Murray County, Georgia farm.

While campaigning for the gubernatorial race in north Georgia however, Cooper met the Stroups, and took a fancy to the production of iron. Unable to resist the lure of yet another business opportunity, he decided to give his professional talents another chance, and entered into a partnership with Stroup.

Almost immediately, Cooper realized his new-found endeavor faced some serious problems. The iron they were producing cost too much to compete in distant markets, and in agricultural Georgia, there was little demand for the product.

Cooper and Stroup soon began developing new uses for the materials and water power at Etowah. In 1844, they abandoned their old furnace entirely, and erected a larger more efficient one capable of making hollowware such as skillets (which could be sold locally). Two years later, they began a rolling mill with which to make railroad tracks and bar iron. It was in operation by 1849, as was their large flour mill which was able to produce up to 300 barrels of flour a day.

The Story Of A Community Called Etowah — Bartow County

The township of Etowah grew into a vibrant little village by the mid-1800s. As a result, a number of businesses existed in the town. Among them were a bank, a hotel, a four-story flour mill, and a brewery. This picture-postcard from the early 1900s shows the ruins of the bank at Etowah.

By 1859, Etowah also had carpentry shops, a nail and spike factory, a barrel factory, a corn mill, gold and copper mines and 12,000 acres of land in four counties. In that day and time, it was one of the most unlikely enterprises ever undertaken in the north Georgia backwoods, and it grew in spite of its logistical drawbacks.

The number of people needed to run these operations grew proportionately. At its peak, the community at Etowah had an international work-force of between 500 and 600 laborers, including some 100 blacks. The employees included miners, furnace workers, mill operators, carpenters, timber cutters, charcoal manufacturers and others.

The thriving little town had a combination school and church; a boarding house, a bordello, a bank, a post office, a brewery, a company store and log houses for the workers and their families. However, despite the fact that it was productive and growing, Etowah still was not a success financially.

Cooper would later claim that the flour mill was profitable, driving all but Georgia-produced flour from the state, but critics claimed he undercut his local competition by selling flour at cost. Cooper's iron sales were described as: "most disastrous, owing to the depression in the trade." By most all accounts, the town's industries were steadily losing money.

To finance continued expansion and stave off economic collapse, Cooper and Stroup added a Mr. L. M. Wiley as a partner in the operation. Cooper eventually loaned Stroup money for his share of the extra funds needed for additional expansion, and when Sroup was unable to repay the loan, Cooper assumed Stroup's share of

The immense stone piers which once supported the tracks of the Western & Atlantic Railroad (photographed here in 1999) still stand in the riverbed of the Etowah River a short distance from the ruins of the former factories of Etowah. This strategic 620-foot-long span, destroyed by the retreating Confederates in May of 1864, was rebuilt by Union Army engineers in just six days, and then, after its usefulness had expired, was destroyed once again - this time by Union troops - after Sherman departed Atlanta for Savannah on his infamous "March To The Sea." In 1858-'59, Mark Cooper financed a spur line from Etowah to the Western & Atlantic Railroad. His locomotive - "Yonah" - was involved in the "Great Locomotive Chase" on the W&A Railroad during the Civil War. Cooper also heavily used the W&A for transport of coal from his mines in Dade County to the mills in Etowah. (Photo by Dan Roper)

the business and the debt.

In 1852, the company's creditors forced the sale of Etowah. The two remaining partners ultimately bought back the company, but by 1857, Wiley wanted out, and insisted that Cooper buy him out. With money borrowed from friends, Cooper did just that. This apparently (and understandably) represented a low point in Cooper's life, for when he was able to repay his friends for the loan, he erected a monument in front of his bank to honor the friends who had supported him.

In 1856, Cooper had formally incorporated the Etowah Manufacturing and Mining company, and after publishing a map and an illustrated prospectus of the company, he took on another partner by the name of A. Hicks. The operations at Etowah apparently fared no better however, and Cooper would later claim in his memoirs that the enterprise failed and recovered on three separate occasions.

The new owners of Etowah however, stridently sought an answer to their financial woes through stringent cost-cutting procedures. Cooper acquired coal mines in nearby Dade County, Georgia, to fuel his iron furnaces. As a politician, he had been instrumental in the creation of the state-owned Western & Atlantic Railroad that passed within a few miles of Etowah. He hoped to cut transportation costs at his iron works by bringing the railroad to it, yet, in 1857 the state legislature rejected his offer of railroad iron made at Etowah's rolling mill in exchange for the state financing of a spur track to Etowah.

Undeterred, Cooper financed his own railroad in 1858-1859, a short line which led directly to the Western & Atlantic. He had already incorporated his own railroad company in 1847 (Cooper's locomotive - "Yonah" - was later involved in the "Great Locomotive Chase" during the Civil War).

Despite all his best efforts however, the nationwide "Panic of 1857" severely hurt Cooper's markets, and by 1860, Etowah was clearly in decline. At that time, Cooper published a new pamphlet about his Etowah property, probably hoping to sell out.

The U. S. Civil War soon brought buyers to his doorstep. In 1862, William T. Quinby and William A. Robinson bought Etowah for $450,000, which was a tremendous sum at that time. Quinby and Robinson had been major arms manufacturers before Union forces captured Memphis, Tennessee, taking over their plant there. Etowah was their ticket back into war products production.

After paying his debts, Cooper still had $200,000, which was more than enough to make him wealthy for the rest of his life. As in his other endeavors, however, "Lady Luck" eluded him once again. He invested heavily in the Confederacy, and by the war's end, he had lost his entire fortune.

The Etowah mills, town, and furnaces were destroyed by Union forces in 1864, after the machinery and slaves had been removed by Robinson. After the Civil War, the remains of the community were forgotten. Except for one furnace, the entire site which once represented the town of Etowah now rests undisturbed beneath the murky waters of Lake Allatoona,

Mark Anthony Cooper took credit in his memoirs for a number of firsts in north Georgia, but he apparently never understood the true scope of his achievements at Etowah. Not only did he pioneer industrialization in a state dominated by agriculture ("King Cotton"), he created an interrelated system of mining, manufacturing and transportation unique in Georgia history.

Cooper's Georgia coal mines provided fuel which was transported on the Western & Atlantic Railroad (which he had helped create) to his own railroad for shipment to Etowah. At Etowah, iron was produced from the coal, charcoal, and local iron ore at his water-powered rolling mill, and then shipped to the Atlanta Rolling Mill, for use in the refurbishing of the worn rails of the Western & Atlantic Railroad.

Mark Anthony Cooper was also a founder of the South Central Agricultural Society, which encouraged the Georgia manufacture of products for farmers. He joined the state's other leading manufacturers as a trustee for the state's first proposed school of mechanical engineering. He was also a trustee for Mercer University and the University of Georgia.

The career of Mark Anthony Cooper, his industrial community of Etowah, and his acclaim as Georgia's most important early industrialist are all the more fascinating considering the almost happenstance development of his industrial community in Bartow County. As with his other careers in banking, the military and politics, Cooper seemed to just "try on" each new profession, to "see if it fit him," accomplished a great deal in the process, and then quietly moved on.

[Author's Note: For biographical data on Cooper, see the sketch by James Dorsey in Dictionary Of Georgia Biography, (1983). Published sources on Etowah and its people include Gregory Jeane's An Archival and Field Survey . . . Allatoona Lake, Georgia (1986), and Lucy J. Cunyus' The History of Bartow County (1933).]

> *The Etowah mills, town, and furnaces were destroyed by Union forces in 1864, after the machinery and slaves had been removed by Robinson.*

The Marker That Missed Its Mark

In the shadow of historic Holly Springs Depot, a lonely marker conceals an unusual story.

For over three-quarters of a century, a forlorn granite marker which resembles a tombstone has existed behind the railroad depot in Holly Springs in Georgia's Cherokee County. The marker, surprisingly enough, was not intended as a burial site marker, but as an identification of the birthplace of one Julian M. Hughes. Making this situation even more unusual, is the fact that the marker never made it to it's intended destination.

The inscription on the marker reads: *Birthplace of Julian M. Hughes Feby. 3, 1860 Here* *early one morn I was born among the hills and midst the charms of lovely Cherokee in dear old Georgia so sweet to me.*

Hughes was born near Holly Springs. His grandfather and grandmother – George and Margaret Hughes – came to Cherokee County from Pickens County, South Carolina, between 1843 and 1845. George died in 1847, and is buried at Enon Cemetery near Woodstock. Margaret was left to rear the young ones in this large family of at least twelve children by herself.

One of these twelve children was James Louis Hughes,

> *The marker, surprisingly enough, was not intended as a burial site marker, but as an identification of the birthplace of one Julian M. Hughes.*

who was the father of Julian M. Hughes. Family recollections maintain that Julian's mother was Jane McCollum, however, no marriage record has been found to confirm her surname.

Julian was the oldest of James Louis' and Jane's five children. Other children were Benjamin Furlough who lived in Kennesaw in Cobb County; James Tyrie who moved to Somerset, Pulaski County, Kentucky; George M. who died in 1888 at age 18; and Bunnie Levingston "Levy" Hughes Denton Dillard who lived in Cobb County.

James Louis Hughes moved his family to Kennesaw between 1872 and 1874 where, according to his great granddaughter – Joyce Denton Lathem - he was a telegrapher for the Western & Atlantic Railroad.

Julian's mother – Jane Hughes – died in 1884, and is buried in Kennesaw. James Louis married again and had two more children – Ethel Hughes Owen and Dewey Hughes.

To date, no records have been found which indicate when Julian M. Hughes permanently departed Georgia. He was evidently still making his home here when he left in February of 1891 on a six-month tour of Europe.

It is assumed that Julian made his home in Cincinnati, Ohio, for a short period after his return, because his obituary states that he moved to Peru, Indiana, from Cincinnati 45 years prior to his death in 1937.

At the time of his retirement and several years prior to his death, Julian Hughes had served for a number of years as chief clerk in the Wabash

Photographed in 1990, a curious youngster, Burke Jackson, examines Julian M. Hughes' marker behind the Holly Springs Depot in Cherokee County. (Photo by Olin Jackson)

Railroad's Division Superintendent's office in Peru, Indiana. He apparently was well-established in his community, holding membership in the Baptist Church, the Baptist Fellowship Forum, the Masonic Lodge, and the Peru Reading Club.

Despite his departure from his native state, Mr. Hughes apparently felt compelled to leave a permanent reminder of his Georgia and Cherokee County heritage. In 1908, he purchased from Luther F. Clayton for $1.00, a three-foot-by-six-foot portion of Land Lot Number 270 in the 15th District and 2nd Section of Cherokee County. The deed reads "at a place on said lot of land, known and located as the BIRTHPLACE of said JULIAN M. HUGHES, on which space to erect a BIRTHPLACE MONUMENT, and I hereby grant to him, his heirs and assigns

He was evidently still making his home here when he left in February of 1891 on a six-month tour of Europe.

the right and privilege of passing over other land in lot number two hundred and seventy to visit the Monument, and to others who may be required to go to and from the spot for the purpose of erecting the Monument and for the purpose of repairing it or to see it."

This deed was so unusual that *The Cherokee Advance*, a local newspaper at the time, carried the following item in the Friday, March 20, 1908 edition: "Clerk of Court Olin Fincher received a deed for a small piece of land, about 3 feet square, to be recorded last week. Julian M. Hughes bought the property and will erect a marble shaft to mark his birth place. Mr. Hughes was born and reared in this county near Woodstock, and is now living in Peru, Indiana, where he has a lucrative position as Superintendent of the Wabash Railroad Company with headquarters in that place. Many of our citizens remember Mr. Hughes and will be glad to learn that he is doing well."

The stone marker arrived by train a short time later. According to Mr. Frank Barrett, a native of Holly Springs, folklore maintains that the marker was off-loaded onto a wagon from the train. It was then to be hauled a short distance away and placed in the spot selected and purchased by Julian Hughes. Fate, however, intervened, and the wagon collapsed beneath the weight of the heavy monument. For reasons unexplained, the marker, to this day, has never been moved from that spot.

A study of the land lots in this area lends credence to this story. Land Lot 270 is a full forty-acre land lot away from where the Holly Springs Depot exists. Interestingly, as late as 1971, deeds for Land Lot 270 still bore a description of the setting aside of this three-foot-by-six-foot strip of land and right-of-access to it even though the monument never reached its final destination.

At the very least, Julian would probably be glad to know that his misplaced marker is being carefully maintained today. According to Frank Barrett, vibrations from passing trains over the years had caused some shifting in the monument, but the City of Holly Springs, which, as of this writing, uses the old railroad depot as a City Hall, has had the stone reset.

This however, is not the end of the story. Julian M. Hughes died of pneumonia in the early morning hours of March 13, 1937, in the Wabash Railroad Hospital in Peru, Indiana. He was interred at Mount Hope Cemetery in Peru.

In the cemetery at Kennesaw, Georgia, there is a large red granite monument bearing the name of JULIAN M. HUGHES, 1860-1937. On the reverse side of this monument under the heading HUGHES FAMILY are listed members of the family buried in plots at this site. Julian M. Hughes, however, is not one of those interred here.

It can only be considered ironic that this native Georgian, who so loved his home and wished to leave permanent and lasting signs of his passing in the red clay hills of Cherokee County, Georgia, in fact, has left not one, but two markers which identify neither the actual spot of his birth nor his burial.

For reasons unexplained, the marker, to this day, has never been moved from that spot.

Camp McDonald And The Great Locomotive Chase

On a miserably rainy morning in April of 1862, twenty Federal saboteurs set out on a secret mission of espionage and intrigue into Confederate Georgia during the U.S. Civil War. Their objective was to capture a locomotive parked in front of a military training camp at which thousands of Confederate troops were stationed.

The parade grounds and tent city which once composed a Confederate army training site known as Camp McDonald are long gone today. Commercial buildings and the city streets of the town of Kennesaw, Georgia, have replaced the tents, pickets, horses, military equipment and temporary structures which formerly occupied this historic ground, but Camp McDonald is anything but forgotten. Who could forget a military facility composed of thousands of Confederate soldiers who allowed twenty Federal saboteurs to steal a Confederate locomotive and three boxcars parked inside the guarded camp?

The line once known as the Western & Atlantic Railroad still exists today at this site in downtown Kennesaw, but it is used by modern freight trains today. Nearby, in a museum on the east side of the railroad tracks is the fabled "General," the locomotive stolen by the Yankee saboteurs who came to be known as "Andrews' Raiders."

On April 12, 1862, during a twenty minute breakfast stop at the Lacy Hotel within Camp McDonald's perimeter, Andrews and his men simply moved forward to the cab of the General, pulled the throttle, and steamed away to the north toward Chattanooga.

Although most historians today agree that the seizure of the train was accomplished with extraordinary daring, they are divided on the actual role played by Governor Joseph E. Brown in the creation of a vulnerable defense posture at Camp McDonald. As the commander in chief of the Georgia military, Brown was responsible for the local defense of Georgia. Evidence suggests that his actions and orders as commander caused Camp McDonald and the Western & Atlantic Railroad to be exceedingly vulnerable to Federal espionage agents.

A Weak Defense

In February of 1862, in response to increasing Northern pressure on the deep South, the Confederate War Department sent all governors a call for more troops. Georgia was asked for twelve regiments. They would be armed and supplied by the Confederacy, and each soldier would receive a $50 bounty for enlisting.

As a result of this action, Governor Brown ordered that Camp McDonald be reopened in March of 1862. He had first opened the camp in June of 1861 to organize and train the 4th Brigade of Georgia Volunteers, and had closed it in July of that same year after the regiments of the brigade were sent to the front in Virginia.[1]

As Sarah Temple reported in her excellent history of Cobb County, Camp McDonald was the largest of Georgia's instructional camps. The tent city and parade grounds of the facility were located west of the railroad tracks at the train stop known as "Big Shanty." An eating establishment - the Lacy Hotel - set up for passengers on the train was located on the east side of the tracks.

As William Smedlund described in his book on Georgia's camps, there were no fortifications or walls of any kind around Camp McDonald since it was located in the "rear area" which was considered inviolable from attack by Northern invaders. The large rolling fields made ideal camping areas and drill fields, and fresh-water springs in the vicinity provided ample water for all. Sentries were posted about the camp - but for guard training purposes only - since there was no concern for an enemy attack at this site.[2]

There is evidence that Governor Brown was more a student of the warfare of antiquity than that of a military strategist. He launched at least one arms manufacturing enterprise which was truly bizarre. With considerable military aplomb, he had earlier promised Georgians that each enemy thrust on land must be driven back "by the use of cold steel at close quarters."[3] To emphasize and underline this statement, he introduced his dream weapon – the "Georgia Pike." He assured fellow Georgians that by using his pike, any Northern invader would be driven "from our genial territory back to his frozen home."[4]

Brown appealed to the mechanics of Georgia to put aside all unnecessary work and make ten thousand pikes. As an earnest advocate of the pike, he argued that "if the defenders at Fort Donelson had been armed with pikes, the outcome of that battle would have been quite different." He further asserted that "the long-range gun might fail to fire or miss its mark, thus wasting ammunition, but the short-range pike and terrible knife. . . . wielded by a stalwart patriot's arm, never fails to fire, and never wastes a single load."[5]

For each pike accepted by the Confederate Arsenal, Brown instructed the government to pay $5. For each side knife with tipped scabbard, belt, and clasp, the government paid $4.60. In all, 7,099 pikes and 4,908 side knives were received into the arsenal at Milledgeville.[6]

Rodney Brown, in his *American Polearms* reported that new recruits at camps of instruction such as Camp McDonald in Georgia were issued pikes which were used for training drills and as primary infantry weapons in sham battles. The ancient devices were also used by sentries on guard duty in rear areas, as was the case at Camp McDonald in 1862.

The pikes and knives were also issued to some coastal defense units as their primary weapon in lieu of a musket. On 12 February, 1862, the *Southern Banner* newspaper of Athens, Georgia, reported that "a perfect novelty, a company of volunteers from the hills of Habersham County, Georgia, and armed with pikes, passed through town on their way to defend the coast.'"[7]

According to accounts of that day, not

There is evidence that Governor Brown was more a student of the warfare of antiquity than that of a military strategist.

all soldiers were thrilled to be issued the archaic pikes. According to Rodney Brown, some recruits simply laughed at the idea of using a sharp pointed stick against an enemy who was armed with large caliber muskets and repeating riffles. With great hilarity, the Confederate trainees chased each other around the camp brandishing their medieval-looking weapons.

I.G. Bradwell wrote, in the *Confederate Veteran*, that when he enlisted, his regiment was promised they would be issued new Enfield rifles. However, when, instead, wagon loads of pikes arrived for issue, there was a near riot among the soldiers until the pikes were laid aside and the men were issued not the coveted Enfield rifles, but old smooth-bore muskets. In the end, the soldiers treated the whole idea of using pikes in battle against an enemy with firearms as a cruel joke.[8]

Biographer Joseph E. Parks pointed out that Gov. Brown was particularly eager to issue his pikes and accompanying side knives to his troops because he was being ridiculed by members of the Georgia General Assembly for his wastefulness of scarce defense dollars on outdated and impractical weapons. As a result of this embarrassing predicament, only pikes were issued to recruits at rear area installations such as Camp McDonald, and even guard duty was performed by sentries armed with what were, by that time, being mockingly referred to as "Joe Brown Pikes."[9]

Camp McDonald

Smedlund wrote that the regiments at Camp McDonald were scattered for a great distance southward along the west side of the railroad. A special row of tents on the high ground to the northwest end of the camp housed the camp commander and the commander-in-chief of the Georgia Army, Governor Brown.

Brown, who lived a short distance away near what today is Canton, Georgia, reportedly spent a great deal of time at Camp McDonald. He thought camp life might

In 1862 Georgia Governor Joseph E. Brown ordered 10,000 pikes be manufactured for use in arming his troops when no firearms were available.

This present-day photo was taken looking south from the Camp McDonald or west side of the railroad tracks at Big Shanty (present-day Kennesaw). In the foreground are three stone markers. The one on the left remembers William A. Fuller, conductor of the stolen train who gained fame for his tenacious pursuit of the raiders. The small marker in the middle honors Colonel William Phillips, commander of the 4th Georgia Volunteer Brigade, who trained his men at Camp McDonald in June of 1861. The stone marker on the right marks the spot at which the locomotive "General" was seized by Federal raiders on April 12, 1862. Across the railroad tracks on the east side (in the background) is the present-day depot which did not exist in 1862. Just south of this depot, the Lacy Hotel (which burned in 1864) once stood. It was at the Lacy that the train crew was having breakfast when their train was stolen. (Photo by Joe Griffith)

This modern photograph looking southward, was taken from the approximate spot where James J. Andrews, leader of a band of 20 Federal raiders, climbed aboard the locomotive "General" and seized the train on April 12, 1862. A sentry at Camp McDonald, armed with a "Joe Brown Pike," stood near the locomotive at this spot. (Photo by Joe Griffith)

After being seized by James J. Andrews and his men, the General with its three boxcars quickly gained momentum and steamed around this bend out of sight. Sprawling Camp McDonald, located to the left of these tracks and caught completely off-guard, offered no resistance to the raiders. (Photo by Joe Griffith)

improve his health. The dispatches he issued from there were signed "commander-in-chief."

Nearby were the tents of the cadets from Georgia Military Institute in Marietta. They served as drillmasters and instructors for the recruits. In early April of 1862, there were at least five regiments and a separate battalion of infantry consisting of the 39th, 40th, 41st, 42nd, 43rd, and 52nd Georgia Volunteer Infantry Regiments and the 9th Battalion Georgia Volunteer Infantry undergoing training at the camp. As a result, the camp was more crowded in 1862 than when it first opened in the summer of 1861.[10]

On 13 March of 1862, Captain Augustus F. Boyd of Company B, 52nd Georgia Volunteer Regiment, wrote in a letter to his wife, Sarah, about the crowded conditions he had encountered when he "arrived at Camp McDonald on Thursday last, amid great storms of rain and the authority had no tents for us and we with several other companies from our region stopped east of Camp McDonald some two miles."

Captain Boyd also wrote that "a measles epidemic was rampant at Camp McDonald. . . Most of the soldiers of the Georgia 52nd became ill in March, April, and May, and many died."[11]

It had only been one year since Fort Sumter, and war fever was still running high among the citizens in the countryside near the camp. The word from the front in Virginia was that the war was going well for the Confederacy and it would be over in another six weeks, with a complete victory for the South. The prevailing optimism in the Peach State was that the Federals were no match for their gallant Confederate soldiers.

The famous Georgia poet, Sidney Lanier, who was a Confederate soldier, attributed his countrymen's passion for war to the conceit of the Southern people. In fact, Lanier, himself, admitted to being a Southern zealot, and early in the war had no doubt that he could whip more than his share of Yankees. "Boys rushed into the ranks," shouted the Atlanta *Southern Confederacy* newspaper on February 12, 1862.[12]

Mattie Harris Lyon, who lived in the countryside on a plantation seven miles from Marietta in 1862, in her little book *My Memories Of The War Between The States* recalled that relatives and friends of soldiers and the idle curious traveled from Marietta and Atlanta by train and laid over to visit the camp to see the men drill and maneuver prior to being sent north to the front in

Virginia. Especially popular with the visitors were the drills, sham battles, and the parades with bands playing and flags streaming.

As a result of his mistrust of the Confederate government's ability to provide an adequate local defense during this dramatic first year of the war, Governor Brown took it upon himself to raise two state local defense armies. During early June of 1861, acting under his powers as commander-in-chief as authorized by the Georgia State Legislature, he organized his first army of state troops at Camp McDonald. It was a reinforced unit - the 4th Brigade of Georgia Volunteers - commanded by Colonel William Phillips, and consisted of four regiments of infantry, a squadron of cavalry, and two batteries of artillery.[13]

A Band Of Raiders

Meanwhile, General Don Carlos Buell commanded the Union Army in middle Tennessee in the spring of 1862. A spy named James J. Andrews was normally in the employ of Gen. Buell. Andrews had provided valuable information to the Union Army in the first year of the war, and was about to attempt an even more daring escapade into Confederate Georgia.

In March of 1862, Buell had sent Andrews and a party of eight men on a secret mission to burn the bridges west of Chattanooga, but the raid had failed due to a lack of expected cooperation from local townspeople. After that defeat, Andrews had visited the Atlanta area posing as a blockade runner. He inspected all of the Confederate rail lines in that vicinity and northward to Chattanooga. He then returned to Buell with a plan for a second attempt to destroy the bridges.[14]

On the eve of his march from Shelbyville, Tennessee to Huntsville, Alabama, Buell sent Andrews to Union Brigadier General Ormsby Mitchell who commanded a division of Buell's troops. Andrews and Mitchell discussed the details of the proposed raid.

James J. Andrews as he appeared at the time of the daring raid at Big Shanty, Georgia.

Captain William A. Fuller, conductor of the stolen train, was photographed in March of 1904, some 42 years after the raid.

This wartime illustration from *Harper's Pictorial History Of The Great Rebellion*, shows Chattanooga, Tennessee on the north bank of the Tennessee River. The objective of Andrews' Raid was to cut off Chattanooga from support from the south.

Mitchell ultimately approved the plan and authorized Andrews to lead a party of twenty-four men into enemy territory to capture a train, then proceed back northward on a railroad sabotage mission, burning bridges along the northern portion of the Georgia State Railroad and on the East Tennessee Railroad where it approached the Georgia border.

The destructive mission was intended to block any reinforcement from the south and thereby isolate Chattanooga. When the blocking mission was completed, Mitchell could then move into a virtually undefended Chattanooga with ease, and without further concern for a rapid enemy response by rail from Georgia. It was a bold - and perhaps foolhardy - plan.[15]

For the proposed raid, 23 soldiers from three Ohio regiments were selected for their courage and combat experience. In addition to Andrews, there was one other civilian – William Campbell of Salineville, Ohio. He happened to be visiting a friend in the camp at the time Andrews was seeking men.

All of the 24 men selected were told the mission would be secret, very dangerous, and behind enemy lines. According to William Pittenger, who was one of the soldiers, "not a man chosen declined the perilous honor." The men were also told they would not be in uniform and would wear ordinary civilian dress. Each man would be provided with clothing, Confederate money, and a small caliber revolver to be carried in a holster on the rear of his belt hidden from view under his coat.

Andrews dressed as a businessman. He wore a top hat and frock coat, and carried saddle bags on his left arm to set him apart as a man of authority. Also, he was tall and bearded, which added to the effectiveness of his Southern upper crust disguise.[16]

As the men traveled southward, they passed Big Shanty - where the train was to be seized the following morning - about eight miles north of Marietta. Upon reaching Big Shanty, the men discovered to their dismay that a large sprawling Confederate camp – humming with thousands of troops – surrounded the train.

Looking out of his train window at the busy military camp, Pittenger recalled his thoughts at the time. He wrote:

"To succeed in our enterprise, it would be necessary first to capture the engine in a guarded camp with soldiers standing around as spectators, and then to run it from one to two-hundred miles through the enemy's country, and to deceive or overpower all trains that should be met – a large contract for twenty men."[17]

By Friday night of April 11, 1862, Pittenger confirmed that Andrews and twenty-one of his raiders were staying at two different hotels in Marietta, Georgia. Most took rooms at what is known today as the Kennesaw House alongside the railroad depot. The remainder took quarters at the nearby Marietta House on the town square.

Along the way, the raiders' numbers had been reduced from 25 to 22 (counting Andrews). One man did not show up at all. Two others came under suspicion near Chattanooga on the way down and were forced to join the Confederate Army near Jasper, Tennessee – just as they had said they wanted to do when questioned by authorities.[18]

A Determined Leader

Pittenger wrote that the men were aroused shortly before daybreak at about 4:00 a.m. on Saturday morning of April 12. While they dressed, Andrews went from room to room going over the details of each man's role in the raid. They spoke in whispers so as not to be overheard through the thin walls of the hotel rooms. According to Pittenger, Andrews quietly instructed each man thusly:

"When the train stops at Big Shanty for breakfast, keep your places till I tell you to go. Get seats near each other in the same car, and say nothing about the matter on the way up. If anything unexpected occurs, look to me for the word. You, you, and you [designating the men] will go with me on the engine; the rest of you will go on the left of the train forward of where it is uncoupled, and climb on the cars in the best places you can, when the order is given. If anybody interferes, shoot him, but don't fire until it is necessary."[19]

In his writings, Pittenger also explained that one of the men – Sergeant Major Ross – was against continuing the raid and protested that "the circumstances have changed since we set out and . . . that many more troops were at Big Shanty than formerly; that we had noticed the crowded state of the road as we came down, and that Mitchell's movements would make it worse." Therefore, Ross respectfully asked Andrews to either postpone or abort the raid.

Andrews, in response, quietly admitted to Ross that everything he said was true, but countered by pointing out the opportunities inherent in the situation:

"The military excitement and commotion, and the number of trains on the road will make our train the less likely to be suspected," Andrews said. "And as to the troops at Big Shanty, if we do our work promptly, they will have no chance to interfere. Capturing the train in the camp will be easier than anywhere else, because no one would believe it possible, and there will therefore be no guard."[20]

Pittenger reported that in spite of Andrews' explanation, several other raiders joined in the respectful protest against going on with the raid. Andrews reportedly listened to their complaints and then closed the meeting by saying: "Boys, I tried this once before and failed; Now, I will succeed or leave my bones in Dixie." Then, according to Pittenger, Andrews grasped the hands of each of the raiders and they left the room to go next door to the depot to catch the morning train to Big Shanty as a misty rain descended upon them.[21]

According to Pittenger, the raiders purchased tickets at the depot before 5:00 a.m. Their destinations were different towns up

Chattanooga, Tennessee, was photographed here in 1863 during the war. Lookout Mountain is faintly visible in the distance. The objective of the raid being conducted by James J. Andrews was to cut off supply lines and the support of Chattanooga from the south. (Photo courtesy of National Archives)

The Kennesaw House, at which James J. Andrews and his men overnighted prior to beginning their famous episode in history, still stands in downtown Marietta beside the railroad tracks.

the line so they would not attract suspicion by all going from Marietta to Big Shanty. At boarding time, two of the raiders who were staying at the Marietta House failed to appear, having overslept, thus reducing the number of raiders to 20 as the train pulled out at 5:15 a.m.

The conductor of the train, William A. Fuller, entered the car and began to take tickets. Fuller had been warned by military

TALES OF THE RAILS IN GEORGIA

The historic locomotive "General" was photographed here (date unknown) with its tender still bearing the inscription "W&A R.R."

authorities to keep an eye out for deserters, but was not suspicious of the raiders even though they had all boarded the train at Marietta. He recognized Andrews in his guise as a traveling businessman who had previously ridden his train, but he did not know him by name.[23]

Subterfuge At The Camp

Pittenger observed that after about a 45-minute trip at 6:00 a.m., the train approached Big Shanty and Camp McDonald. The white tents of the enemy soldiers could be seen with the sentries walking their posts. Pittenger described it thusly:

"Big Shanty had been selected for the seizure because it was a breakfast station, and because it had no telegraph office. When Andrews had been here on the previous expedition, few troops were seen, but the number was now greatly increased. It is difficult to tell just how many were actually here, for they were constantly coming and going; but there seems to have been three or four regiments, numbering not far from a thousand men each. They were encamped almost entirely on the west side of the road, but their camp guard included the railroad depot."[24]

Pittenger continued by explaining that when the train rolled to a stop, the entire crew – including the engineer, fireman, and conductor, and most of the passengers – got off and went quickly into the Lacy Hotel for breakfast. They all apparently relished the meal at the Lacy, and no guard was left on the train!

The raiders kept their seats, awaiting a signal from Andrews. As the last passengers going to breakfast cleared the front door of the coach, Andrews and Knight fell in behind them, but instead of going off on the right side of the train, they got off on the left side next to the camp. As a result, they were hidden from the view of anyone in the Lacy Hotel as they went about their espionage.

The men walked confidently forward together to see if the tracks ahead were clear. When they had confirmed that no train obstructed their departure, they walked back to the rear of the third empty boxcar where Andrews told Knight to uncouple the remaining cars and wait for him there. Then, Andrews walked back to the passenger car where the remaining raiders were waiting and, in a calm voice, said: "Come on boys; it's time to go."[25]

Pittenger explained that the raiders left the coach car quietly so that the remaining passengers – who had not gone up to the Lacy for breakfast – would not be alarmed. Andrews immediately went forward and Knight, seeing him coming, also hurried forward and climbed aboard the engine.

At this point, Knight cut the bell rope that was tied to the Big Shanty loading dock; put his hand on the throttle, and stood ready, his eyes fixed on Andrews awaiting a signal to depart.[26] Andrews stood on the lower step of the engine, leaning back to see his men running forward and scrambling aboard the empty boxcars. An extra engineer and a firemen among the raiders ran forward to the engine to their posts beside Knight in the cab.[27]

Meanwhile, as Pittenger pointed out in his recounting of the incident: "All this time a sentry was standing not a dozen feet from the engine quietly watching, as if this was the most ordinary proceeding, and a number of other soldiers were idling but a short distance away."[28]

The late Wilbur G. Kurtz, Sr., an Atlanta artist and historian and the son-in-law of conductor William Fuller, interviewed many of those involved in the raid. In the postscript to the MacLennan Roberts book, *The Great Locomotive Chase*, he wrote that recruits at Camp McDonald were armed with "Joe Brown Pikes" because of a shortage of firearms. Kurtz interviewed Henry Whitley of Company F, 56th Georgia Regiment, who was the sentry who stood and watched the raiders steal the train that day. Whitley told him that he also was armed with nothing more than a pike.[29]

Pittenger added that when everything was ready and the last raider was pulled into a boxcar, Andrews climbed aboard the engine, nodded to Knight, and the engine spun its wheels, then took hold, and quickly gained momentum toward the curve in the rail line, leaving Camp McDonald in its wake and taking the 20 men to a date with destiny.

All of this happened so quickly that none of the camp's soldiers raised their weapons, sounded an alarm, or even showed a sign that they suspected anything was wrong as the engine – with only three boxcars attached – pulled away. The theft of a train at Camp McDonald in the midst of thousands of enemy soldiers had been done by twenty raiders "without firing a shot or an angry gesture."[30]

Flight To Eternity

The remainder of this daring incident from the U.S. Civil War is a matter of history today. Though he was imminently successful in his theft of the locomotive called General, James J. Andrews and his men ultimately failed in their mission. After a dramatic flight northward up the railroad, the raiders eventually abandoned the train two miles north of Ringgold, Georgia, having completed only moderate damage to the railroad and failing to destroy any bridges. The saboteurs were all captured as they fled on foot into the north Georgia countryside. Several were later executed in Atlanta, and several managed to successfully escape, fleeing back to the North where they later were awarded the Medal of Honor.

Meanwhile, back at Camp McDonald, an enraged cadre was trying to put the best face on a very embarrassing incident. The railroad raid at the camp was an extraordinary feat of daring, but as Andrews had predicted at Marietta on the morning of the event, their success in capturing the train was enabled by the lack of a local defense preparedness by both the railroad and camp authorities. This lack of preparedness ultimately fell upon the shoulders of the lone governor of the state, Joseph Emerson Brown.

Endnotes

1/ Allen D. Candler, ed., *The Confederate Records of the State of Georgia*, 5 vols. (Atlanta, GA: Charles P. Byrd, State Printer, 1909), vol. 2, p. 187-195 (hereafter referred to as CR, 2:187-195); Joseph H. Parks, Joseph E. Brown of Georgia (Baton

Rouge, LA: Louisiana State University Press, 1977), 182-83; William S. Smedlund, *Camp Fires of Georgia's Troops, 1861-1865* (Lithonia, GA: Kennesaw Mountain Press, 1994), 201-205; *War of the Rebellion: Official Records of the Union and Confederate Armies*, 70 vols, in 128 pts. (Washington, DC: Government Printing Office, 1880-1901), ser. 4, vol.1:902 (hereafter referred to as OR).

2/ CR, 2:89-91; Smedlund, 201-205; Sarah Blackwell Gober Temple, *The First Hundred Years: A Short History of Cobb County in Georgia* (Atlanta, GA: Walter W. Brown Publishing Company, 1935; reprint, Athens, GA: Agee Publishers, Inc., 1989), 238-241.

3/ CR, 2:194-198; OR ser. 4, vol. 1:917.

4/ Rodney Hilton Brown, *American Pole Arms 1526-1865* (New Milford, CN: N. Letterman & Company, 1967), 118-135; CR 2:199; Parks, 184. The "Georgia Pike" was a pole arm that had a long double-edged blade secured to its six foot wooden shaft by a ferrule made out of brass or iron and two long wrought iron side straps. The butt end usually had a cap or long cast iron shoe to prevent splintering. The Georgia pattern pikes were normally produced at the Confederate armories. The principal pike manufactured in Georgia and known as the "Joe Brown Pike" was of the "clover-leaf" design which means it had the usual ten inch double-edged blade and two additional side "bridle-cutter" blades which gave it the clover-leaf or cross appearance. The side blades were used as bridle cutters to engage cavalrymen and cut the reins of their horses, thus rendering them out of control and making the rider vulnerable to a thrust from the pike's main blade.

5/ CR, 2:199-200; Louise Biles Hill, *Joseph E. Brown and the Confederacy* (Chapel Hill, NC: University of North Carolina Press, 1939), 249.

6/ CR 2:349-353.

7/ "A Perfect Novelty," *Athens Southern Banner*, 12 February 1862; Rodney Brown, 134; Kenneth Coleman, *Confederate Athens* (Athens, GA: University of Georgia Press, 1968), 43.

8/ I.G. Bradwell, "Soldier Life in the Confederate Army," *Confederate Veteran* 24, no. 1 (1916): 21; Rodney Brown, 134.

9/ Henry H. Kurtz, Jr., "Hijack of a Locomotive: The Andrews Raid Revisited," *Atlanta History: A Journal of Georgia and the South* 34, no. 3 (1990): 2; MacClennan Roberts, *The Great Locomotive Chase* (New York: Dell Publishing Company, 1956), postscript by Wilbur G. Kurtz, Sr., 155; Parks, 242.

10/ Parks, 151-154; Smedlund, 11-12.

11/ Gary Ray Goodson, ed., *The American Civil War 1861-1865, The Georgia Confederate 7,000*, Part II: Letters and Diaries (Shawnee, CO: Goodson Enterprises, Inc., 1997), 19.

12/ "Boys Rushed Into The Ranks," *Atlanta Southern Confederacy*, 12 February 1862; Edwin Mims, *Sidney Lanier* (Boston: Houghton Mifflin, 1905), 44-47; Temple, 244, 251-253.

13/ Joseph Tyrone Derry, "Georgia," Vol. 7, in Clement A. Evans, ed., *Confederate Military History*, 17 vols (Wilmington, NC: Broadfoot Press, 1987), 53-54; Hill, 62-63; Parks, 55.

14/ William Pittenger, "Locomotive Chase in Georgia," *The Century Magazine*. 36, No. 1 (1888): 141-142; Wilbur G. Kurtz, Sr., "The Andrews Raid," *Atlanta Historical Bulletin* 13, no. 4 (1968): 12.

15/ William Pittenger, *Daring and Suffering: A History of the Great Railroad Adventure Into Georgia In 1862* (New York: The War Publishing Company, 1887), 97; Derry, 95-96; John A Wilson, *Adventures of Alf. Wilson: A Thrilling Episode of the Dark Days of the Rebellion* (Marietta, GA: Continental Book Company, 1972), 17.

16/ Pittenger, *Locomotive Chase in Georgia*, 142; Wilbur G. Kurtz, Sr., "The Andrews Railroad Raid," *Civil War Times Illustrated* 5, no. 1 (1966): 8-13; Wilson, 15-18.

17/ Pittenger, *Locomotive Chase In Georgia*, 143; Wilson, 18-25.

18/ Pittenger, *Daring and Suffering*, 98-99; Daniel O. Cox, Telephone interview with the author, 20 February, 2002; Wilson, 26.

19/ Pittenger, *Daring and Suffering*, 99-100; Charles Kendell O'Neill, *Wild Train: The Story Of Andrews Raiders* (New York: Random House, 1956), 129.

20/ Pittenger, *Daring and Suffering*, 100-101.

21/ Ibid, 101.

22/ Fuller, 10, 21; Kurtz, Sr., "The Andrews Raid," 17; O'Neill, 131-32.

23/ Pittenger, *Daring and Suffering*, 102.

24/ Pittenger, *Daring and Suffering*, 102-103; O'Neill, 132-133; Wilson, 28.

25/ Pittenger, *Daring and Suffering*, 102-103; Fuller, 30; O'Neill, 135-36; Wilson, 29.

26/ Pittenger, *Daring and Suffering*, 103; Wilson, 29.

27/ Pittenger, *Daring and Suffering*, 104-105.

28/ Ibid, 105.

29/ Pittenger, *Daring and Suffering*, 105; Lillian Henderson, ed., *The Rosters of Confederate Soldiers of Georgia*, vol. 5 (Spartanburg, SC: The Reprint Company, 1982), 883; Kurtz, Jr., 6; O'Neill, 137; Roberts, 155; Wilson, 28-29.

30/ Pittenger, *Daring and Suffering*, 105; O'Neill, 137; Wilson, 29.

The Place Where Andrews' Raiders Slept

As soon as the big brick building is seen, it conjures up images of historic events in the mind of the beholder. And sure enough, if you do some checking, you'll find out that a group of famous espionage agents known in U.S. Civil War history as "Andrews' Raiders, once slept in this structure.

"Few buildings anywhere in Georgia have a history as interesting as that of the Kennesaw House in Marietta. It pre-dates the Civil War and provided accommodations for a group known as 'Andrews' Raiders' on a night in 1862 before they hijacked a Confederate train pulled by the locomotive 'General.'" So wrote Joe Kirby in an article in the *Marietta Daily Journal* newspaper.

Today, this captivating structure just off the square in Marietta houses the Marietta Historical Museum, a non-profit endeavor offering a wide variety of historic area memorabilia for public viewing.

Strange Occurrences

Prior to the war, the Kennesaw House was a summer resort for the wealthy. Many of these visitors came to partake of the waters of a unique spring in the vicinity.

Historical Museum founder Dan Cox recently rediscovered that spring behind present-day Kennestone Hospital. He maintains there is a lot of interesting history involving his community that is not well-known, and that

Prior to the war, the Kennesaw House was a summer resort for the wealthy.

31

The Kennesaw House, which still stands as of this writing, provided accommodations for Andrews' Raiders on a night in 1862 before the men hijacked a train pulled by the Confederate locomotive "General."

Andrews' Raiders decided to overnight at The Kennesaw House due to the hotel's close proximity to the Marietta Depot, photographed here in 1995. The Kennesaw House is only a few steps away.

includes a "ghost" in the Kennesaw House.

Mr. Cox emphasizes that he doesn't believe in ghosts, "but I think I've seen one as I've worked here," he adds with a smile. The image Cox says he 'saw' stood about 5'6" tall and wore a flat hat with a brim, a cream-colored coat that hung three-fourths of the way down the thigh, and boots that came to mid-calf.

Cobb County Police Lieutenant Henry Higgins, a volunteer at the museum, supports Mr. Cox's contention. "I've seen the 'ghost' three times," he said. "We've attributed it to a lot of things up here - headlights reflecting on the windows, passing trains, and so forth. Just about the time you see him, he's gone."

Cox acknowledges that in this historic building, imaginations tend to run wild. "Doors swing for no reason (probably due to the air from a heating system vent), and boards creak." Regardless of the "spirits," the developers of the museum in the historic structure seem to be having a good time with their project and have discovered a number of historic items which are now on display.

History is not clear as to whether Dix Fletcher or John Heyward Glover (Marietta's first mayor) built the old hotel in the 1850s. However, it is a matter of record that it was known as Fletcher House, and ultimately was later renamed the Kennesaw House.

Mr. Cox may be the first individual to have put a name to the specter thought to roam the Kennesaw House. He thinks it is Dr. Daniel Wilder, a Union Army physician and the nephew of Dix and Louisa Fletcher, Union sympathizers who owned the property.

"When Union troops looted and pillaged Marietta during General William Sherman's occupation, Wilder prevented them from absconding with the Fletcher family's belongings, including a blind horse, flour and pots," says Connie (Mrs. Dan) Cox, who, with Henry E. Higgins, edited Mrs. Fletcher's diary for publication, renaming it *Journal Of A Landlady*.

The aged chronicle covered the years 1857 to 1883 in Marietta. It ultimately revealed a number of interesting facts about Marietta and the Kennesaw House.

Early History

Aside from its other early uses, the

The Place Where Andrews' Raiders Slept   Cobb County

Marietta has long been a busy commercial center, and the Kennesaw House provided accommodations for many travelers. This photograph was taken in 1890.

Kennesaw House also was used as a Confederate hospital where wounded soldiers were fed and treated following a number of area battles.

As enthusiastic as he is, Mr. Cox says he didn't always espouse his current love for history that has led him to develop the museum on the second floor of the Kennesaw House. "I didn't like it until my son, Carey, had an elementary school project on researching our family history."

The research revealed that their Cox ancestors could be traced back some 156 years in the Marietta area. In 1840, Dr. Carey Cox built the first hospital in the city, and specialized in homeopathic cures, particularly one using the waters from the spring behind present-day Kennestone Hospital.

According to accounts, patients would drink the water in small quantities and many reportedly experienced more healthful conditions thereafter. Mr. Cox says an analysis of the water revealed a high iron content. "My theory is that anemic people benefited from drinking the water," he explains.

The locomotive "Texas" photographed here circa 1890s, was used by Capt. William A. Fuller in the pursuit and capture of Andrews' Raiders on the engine "General."

Opening A Museum

As a result of the research into his fam-

33

TALES OF THE RAILS IN GEORGIA

The General, preserved permanently today in a museum in Kennesaw, Georgia, is available for public viewing.

ily genealogy, Mr. Cox says his work eventually fueled an almost overwhelming interest in the history of the area, ultimately expanding to include the preservation of historic real estate.

While driving by the Kennesaw House one day, Cox's wife asked "Why doesn't the city buy the building and develop a museum?"

Dan almost immediately seized upon the idea. He got a city council member to set up an appointment with Joe Mack Wilson (then mayor and now deceased) in November of 1992. "I thought the process would take perhaps a year," he mused, "but three weeks later, Wilson had gotten the Downtown Marietta Development Authority to buy the building for $525,000 to ensure its preservation.

"And because it was my idea," Cox continued, "I got the job of Executive Director of the project. Most of the work, however, has been done by volunteers."

The "Marietta Museum of History opened in 1995 starting with donated displays. "We've been lucky in the participation of people who have been members of the community for generations. That's meant a lot of donated items and volunteer help," Cox said.

Several Union spies spent the night in the corner front room prior to hijacking the locomotive General from nearby Kennesaw (at a site called Big Shanty) the following morning and speeding northward in the fabled chase. After his arrest, Marion Ross (one of the spies) wrote Eliza Fletcher (a dyed-in-the-wool rebel in contrast to her parents) for help. She refused him. Ross ultimately was hanged.

Information on Henry Green Cole, a Marietta businessman who married one of the Fletcher daughters, has also been exhibited in the museum. Cole owned a hotel (burned by Confederates) on the south side of the city's public square. He was an admitted Yankee spy, but reportedly did much to help rebuild the community after the war.

Other items in the museum include historic memorabilia of old Marietta, period photographs, old furnishings, and one of "Sherman's hairpins" (a twisted piece of rail from the railroad). Union soldiers had a habit of heating the rails until they were red-hot, so they could then be twisted around a tree or some other object, rendering them useless to the Confederates.

Several Union spies spent the night in the corner front room prior to hijacking the locomotive General from nearby Kennesaw (at a site called Big Shanty) the following morning and speeding northward in the fabled chase.

Riding The Rails On The SAM Shortline

A historic rail line, built in the 1880s during the days when Doc Holliday and Wyatt Earp were in their prime, has been put back into use. Today, an excursion train travels the route once again, taking sightseers to a collection of unique destinations in the southwestern corner of the state.

Southwest Georgia is an area rich in history and nostalgia. It is full of small towns where life moves slowly, and historic sites that have helped to shape our state's history. A new attraction – the SAM Shortline railroad – is taking advantage of the tourism opportunities offered by these towns.

SAM, short for the Savannah, Americus and Montgomery Railroad Company which once operated on the same tracks in the 1880s, is a state-sponsored excursion train which began operations in southwest Georgia this past October. Referred to by some as "Georgia's Rolling State Park," the SAM Shortline passes through two counties and five towns.

The train ride takes passengers through some of the most beautiful scenery in southwestern Georgia: fields white with cotton and orchards thick with pecan trees loaded with nuts; past aged country homes with green roofs and wrap-around porches, and across a trestle over picturesque Lake Blackshear.

The shortline train – which is quickly becoming a popular weekend getaway opportunity – consists of three vintage passenger cars, a commissary car which includes a gift shop and a snack bar, and the Samuel H. Hawkins dining car, which is named for the founder of the Savannah, Americus and Montgomery Railway.

Just a scant 40 miles or so down the

Referred to by some as "Georgia's Rolling State Park," the SAM Shortline passes through two counties and five towns.

TALES OF THE RAILS IN GEORGIA

Engine #1209 leads the SAM Shortline train. (Photo by Alline Kent)

The Samuel H. Hawkins dining car is an integral portion of the SAM Shortline. Riders may dine in this conveyance which was named for the original railroad's founder. (Photo by Alline Kent)

Georgia Department of Natural Resources (DNR) under the guidance of the Southwest Georgia Railway Excursion Authority. The engine which pulls the SAM train is owned and operated by the Heart of Georgia Railroad Company, which runs freight on the same lines Monday through Thursday.

SAM Shortline also has a prominent native son who is providing support and promotion for the endeavor. Former U.S. President Jimmy Carter – Sumter County's own – has been heavily involved in the development of the shortline since its conception.

Local officials hope that the SAM Shortline will bring economic development and stimulate tourism in the area. Besides the regular tourists who are interested in seeing beautiful and historic southwest Georgia, it is hoped the SAM Shortline will appeal to motor coach tours and school field trips as well. Participants can be dropped off by bus at any one of the train stops along the route and then picked up miles down the road at another stop.

On its regular excursions, SAM departs from Cordele and travels west with stops at the Georgia State Veteran's State Park and the towns of Leslie, Americus, Plains and Archery. Each stop offers a number of historic attractions and shopping opportunities. Passengers may board the train at any of the stops and return the same day. Depending on the train's schedule, passengers may also spend the night in a town and catch the train back to their point of origin the next day.

The SAM Railroad Company brought growth to southwest Georgia in the 1880s, allowing local farmers an opportunity to ship their products all over the country. Many of the towns that are still along the line today originated from this burst of commerce over 100 years ago.

Another big market the modern-day version of the railroad expects to "farm" is

road at Valdosta is the boyhood home of John Henry "Doc" Holliday, one of the heroes of the Old West gunfight at O.K. Corral in 1881. There are many other historic sites and scenic attractions in the vicinity of Cordele (where the SAM Shortline begins) too, so if a vacationer wanted to make this a week-long getaway, there are plenty of things to see and do.

The SAM Shortline is operated by the

the under 40ish crowd – those raised after the days when passenger trains were the main mode of transportation. For those people, the SAM Shortline will be a great way to enjoy the experience of a passenger train ride and the excitement it offers.

"All Aboard In Cordele"

The official starting point of the SAM Shortline is Cordele, Georgia, conveniently located right off of Interstate 75. Home to the Georgia state farmers market and billed as the "Watermelon Capital Of The World," Cordele has twelve hotels where out-of-towners can spend the night before catching the train. Nearby, Lake Blackshear offers fishing, boating and camping.

State Representative Johnny Floyd (D-Cordele), has been involved in the formation of the shortline from the beginning. He explained that the idea for SAM was a collaborative effort on the part of people from Cordele, Plains, Americus and Leslie, to enhance tourism along the Jimmy Carter Historic Trail.

"We think it's a great idea," Floyd said. "Interstate 75 runs right through Cordele and if we can draw people off the interstate, the sales tax dollars will mean a lot to us. So the shortline is important to us on two levels: economically and as a means of preserving the history of the area."

Georgia Veterans State Park

The first stop on the shortline – the Georgia Veteran's Memorial State Park – is barely 15 miles from the starting point in Cordele, but it could be the last stop for many passengers. Situated on Lake Blackshear, the 1,322-acre park offers an 18-hole golf course, a swimming pool and beach, nature trails and fishing.

Cottages, tents, and recreational vehicle sites are available. For those with more comfort in mind, The Retreat At Lake Blackshear opened this past autumn. With 88 rooms, a restaurant, a marina, conference

A M-3 Stuart light tank is just one of many armored vehicles among the U.S. military memorabilia on display at the Georgia Veterans Memorial Park a short distance from Cordele on the SAM Shortline. (Photo by Alline Kent)

A U.S. Army cavalry wagon at the Georgia Veterans Memorial Park was used during the Indian wars in the old West circa 1870s. This particular wagon was used more recently as a movie prop in the major motion picture "Fort Apache," filmed in the 1950s and starring John Wayne and Henry Fonda. (Photo by Alline Kent)

facilities and more, The Retreat offers accommodations for groups up to 450.

Established first and foremost as a memorial to U.S. veterans, the Georgia Veteran's Memorial Park features a museum inside the welcome center which highlights America's involvement from the Revolutionary War through the Gulf War. Uniforms, guns, and other items are displayed.

An additional room to celebrate the contributions of Cordele native Mac Hyman, author of the best-selling novel *No Time For Sergeants*, is under construction. Based upon Hyman's own experiences in the military, *No Time For Sergeants* was turned into an award-winning Broadway play. The movie version, filmed in 1958, is considered the vehicle that launched the career of television star Andy Griffith.

Outside the museum are many other exhibits which include tanks, bombers and helicopters from World War I through the Vietnam War. A Boeing B-29 – the only one still in existence – is also located at this site.

At Lovely Leslie

Leslie, a charming community of about 455 citizens, defines small-town perfection. This little slice of Southern Americana is located half-way between Americus and Albany. "For Sale" signs on the homes in this town usually don't last very long at all. Young couples usually snap up the homes here that are close to their jobs, yet "out in the country" enough to allow a "Mayberry" sort of existence.

It might well be that any economic boom the shortline brings to southwest Georgia will be heard the loudest in Leslie. Already, shops within walking distance of the train depot are being refurbished. A new antiques shop has opened; a welcome center and a park are planned, as is a new restaurant.

Bobby Hines – who has lived in Leslie since he was six years old – is the owner of Callie's Collectibles, an antiques store that has been in downtown Leslie for over 11 years. Hines says he plans to meet each and every train that stops in his town. His store occupies space that once was the Leslie Drug Company.

Hines is just one of many people who have expressed pleasure at the thought of a train stopping in town again. He says he remembers when a passenger train stopped there regularly, although that was many years ago.

Leslie is also home to the Georgia Rural Telephone Museum, housed in a renovated 1920s cotton warehouse. Contained in the museum is one of the largest collections of antique telephones and telephone memorabilia in the world. Some of the pieces date back to 1876.

Admiring Americus

In Americus, the train will stop directly across from the Habitat for Humanity's Global Village and Discovery Center, a six-acre complex. When completed, the Global Village will display model Habitat homes from 40 countries and house an international marketplace.

While Americus has always had an ongoing effort to maintain the appearance and viability of its downtown area, additional revitalization has occurred as a result of the SAM railroad. Several new businesses have moved into town, and the city has restored several previously-unoccupied buildings.

Downtown Americus is within walking distance of the Shortline's depot, and is a shopper's dream come true. A wide variety of consumer products are available – from upscale children's clothing at the Tot Shop to fresh produce at the Farmer's Market.

Americus may be the perfect place to turn the train ride into a weekend get-

> *This little slice of Southern Americana is located half-way between Americus and Albany.*

away too. The Windsor Hotel, which opened in 1892, is the most recognizable building downtown. Right down the street from the Windsor, you can catch a show at the Rylander Theater, built in the 1920s, which offers regular tours as well as live performances and plays.

Americus is also the boyhood home of former Atlanta Falcons Head Coach Dan Reeves and Georgia Tech Head Coach Chan Gailey. A number of other notables grew up in this story-book town.

A President In Plains

After visiting the town of Plains, it's easy to understand why a former President of the United States and his First Lady would choose to live here after having lived in the White House in Washington, D.C. With its distinctive small-town flavor, Plains is lovely to say the least. Visitors may or may not run into the Carters while in Plains, but the next best thing is meeting people that actually know them.

The SAM Shortline stops in Plains right across the street from The Plains Inn and Antiques. The inn is owned by the city and is operated under the "Better Hometown" program. It features seven suites, each decorated with items from a distinct decade from the 1920s to the 1980s, representing the decades of President Carter's life from his birth through his presidency.

The Carters were closely involved in the design of the inn. Mrs. Carter worked with a decorator designing each room in its particular furnishings – right down to the clawfoot bathtubs and the rotary dial phones.

There is also a common room where breakfast is available each morning; a television room, and the inn's most wonderful feature – a front porch on the second floor which affords a view of the entire town. The first floor of the inn is filled with antiques from over 20 dealers across the South. Sandra Walters and her husband,

The Windsor Hotel in Americus which opened in 1892, dates back to the days when this vicinity was a popular resort destination for individuals wishing to escape the harsh winters of the northeastern United States. The Windsor is quickly becoming a popular weekend getaway opportunity for riders on the SAM Shortline. (Photo by Alline Kent)

The Jimmy Carter boyhood home in Archery, Georgia on the SAM Shortline. (Photo by Alline Kent).

C.L., manage the inn for the city.

School classes were still held at the Plains High School up until 1979. Today, the building houses the museum and visitor center of the Jimmy Carter National Historical site. Visitors can see films and exhibits which depict the history of Plains and the town's famous son.

Other sites of interest are the Plains Depot, which served as the campaign headquarters for Jimmy Carter during his U.S. Presidential bid. A short distance away is

TALES OF THE RAILS IN GEORGIA

Former President Jimmy Carter is a strong supporter of the SAM Shortline (Photo courtesy of Kim Hatcher, GA Dept. of Natural Resources)

the first stop in the story of America's 39th President. Jimmy Carter's boyhood home in the little town of Archery is still a working farm where black-eyed peas, collards, squash and of course – peanuts – are grown each season between the house, barns, and other buildings. Carter lived on the farm until 1941 when he departed home for college.

As one walks around the farm today, he or she will hear – via recorded narratives – President Carter describe the childhood he spent there. Viewing the humble surroundings which include an outhouse and a hand-pump for water, visitors leave with the distinct impression that a good education and hard work can take anybody to the White House.

While riders are visiting the President's boyhood home, the SAM Shortline turns around to ready itself for the return trip back to Cordele. The train covers 69 miles of historical stops, and the entire train ride – from departure to return to Cordele – takes approximately eight hours.

Interestingly, most of the historic sites and attractions in the towns at which the train stops are free, or have only a small admission charge. The trip can be appealing to all age groups and interests. The day-long venture is also very "child friendly" with many things that reportedly will intrigue young children and teenagers.

Representatives with the SAM Shortline say there are many special events planned with the train in the months ahead, including a ride on the train with Santa and a series of special shopping excursion trips.

(Times, schedules and ticket prices vary, but the SAM Shortline has an excellent web site at www.samshortline.com. Interested persons may also call for more information about the Shortline at (800) 864-7275. The web site offers links to each town and attraction on the route.)

the United Methodist Church where Jimmy and Rosalyn were married. Even Billy Carter's Service Station and the business district which dates back to the 1890s have been preserved.

On Sundays, when he's in town, Jimmy Carter teaches Sunday school at the Maranatha Baptist Church. This attractive church has a membership of approximately 150, but it receives over 10,000 visitors a year.

Aiming At Archery

The final stop on the SAM Shortline is

Early Railroads In Lumpkin And Dawson Counties

Though no vestige of a railroad exists today in either Dawson or Lumpkin counties, rail lines at one time crossed both these areas around the turn of the century. Town fathers sought (and subsequently failed) to sustain the growth begun decades earlier by the vigorous gold mining industry in both areas.

It began as a grand vision in the mid-1870s...the advancement of the railroad to Dawson and Lumpkin counties. It was progress in its finest form of manifest destiny, but for some mysterious reason, the dream was never consummated in either of these two areas, and today, no one seems to know exactly why.

With the exception of a brief shortline (which no longer exists) constructed to the old copper mines north of Dahlonega, and a temporary logging track (which also no longer exists) constructed to Turner's Corner in north Lumpkin, no railroad has ever functioned for any substantial length of time in either Lumpkin or Dawson, making them two of the few counties in the state never to have profited growth-wise from the phenomenon of the railroad.

The railroad has always been a subject which strikes a fanciful note in many hearts. It is the stuff from which legends are made, and from which an extensive folklore of Americana has sprung.

To many people today, the absence of the railroad in Lumpkin and Dawson counties is a blessing. It has - to some extent - restrained the development and population of these regions (despite the growth afforded by modern-day Georgia 400 Highway), making these two counties all the more attractive and desirable to present-day residents grown cautious and fearful of the crime and congestion or urban sprawl elsewhere. However, to the residents of the 1870s, the railroad was an overwhelming opportunity for growth and employment, and a sense of increased civilization for a backward, semi-pioneer region.

What then happened to the railroad in these two counties? Rights-of-way and rails were constructed most of the way from Gainesville to Dahlonega, and similar efforts were expended across Dawson County. But before either of these two projects were productively operational, they died aborning.

Were they an altruistic undertaking, or

just another bold scheme to parlay invested stockholder monies into a fast buck? Perhaps we'll never know for certain. Few records exist today, and most persons involved with the projects - or even persons who might merely remember them - have long since departed this earth in days of yesteryear.

Our research on the railroads of Lumpkin began in Dahlonega, the Lumpkin County seat of government. The late Madeline Anthony, a long-time native of Dahlonega, remembered the Gainesville and Dahlonega Railroad from old newspaper clippings she had once preserved, but was not certain of the actual circumstances surrounding the railroad. Another resident - the late Ida Mae Phillips - remembered excited talk during her childhood of the railroad's construction, but little else. Former Lumpkin County Commissioner J.B. Jones, usually a well-stocked reservoir of information on past occurrences in the county, was equally at a loss. Even the normally reliable reference - Andrew Cain's *The History of Lumpkin County* - contained only a smattering of references on the subject.

The next possible reference resource for this information - the late Sybil McRay of Gainesville, Georgia - had served as head-librarian at Chestatee Regional Library in Gainesville for many years.

"Yes, I have several references to it," Sybil replied matter-of-factly, when asked about the railroad in the late 1980s. "At one time, you could still see the pilings across the river for the railroad trestle there," she smiled. "It (the railroad) never made it any further to Dahlonega than that point."

Whatever the circumstances, when the first railroads were being constructed across America, it apparently was not unusual for speculation to cloud the realities of financing a venture of this nature. Such quite possibly was the case with the Lumpkin and Dawson railroads, and also was probably at least partially responsible for their ultimate demise.

These railroads, although they were two entirely separate and distinct projects, apparently were related in some manner. They both began in the late 1870s, and several newspaper accounts discuss them as a combined project.

The Lumpkin County railroad apparently was initiated first in 1877-78. According to Cain's *History of Lumpkin County*, on March 7, 1879 at about 4:00 p.m., the townspeople and local residents of Dahlonega marched out to where the depot was to be located (the article does not state exactly where), to witness the completion of what was then called the Gainesville and Dahlonega Railroad.

A description of the day reads: "When the cannon had performed its part in the joyous occasion, Col. (W.P.) Price came forward with an appropriate little speech; Col. R.H. Baker set the last stake which was driven deep down into the ground by Miss Willie Lewis amid great applause." The crowd then dispersed, with plans to meet again when the first train arrived, which apparently was expected in the near future.

One can only speculate at the site of the Gainesville and Dahlonega Railroad depot today. Accounts indicate that it was somewhere in the vicinity of the Chestatee River, since there was no known construction beyond that point. Logic dictates that the depot be located nearer the city of Dahlonega for obvious reasons, but accounts indicate that either a spur line, or quite possibly even the

The Lumpkin County railroad apparently was initiated first in 1877-78.

main line was planned to extend to Auraria south of Dahlonega, possibly making a depot in downtown Dahlonega impractical.

According to records, the railroad crossed the Chestatee River at what was then known as Leather's Ford (not far from the present-day Ford automobile dealership on Georgia 400 Highway in Lumpkin County), and as such, was apparently destined more directly for Auraria and Dawson County than downtown Dahlonega. Whether a spur line from Leather's Ford directly to Dahlonega was planned is unknown. The actual site of the Dahlonega/Lumpkin County depot (if one ever existed at all), is shrouded in mystery.

Further accounts of the Gainesville and Dahlonega Railroad are sketchy, but the project appears to have suffered problems and set-backs which were insurmountable. An interview with prominent Dahlonega attorney Col. W.P. Price in the February 21, 1879 issue of *The Eagle* newspaper in Gainesville, indicates some of the uncertainty surrounding the project:

". . . . You are the president of the Gainesville and Dahlonega Railroad?"

"Correct."

"Well, ...I want some facts, and you are going around with them hid away in your bosom. . ."

". . . . Well," said the colonel, as he settled himself in a chair, "we did not want to raise any fuss about it, or excite hopes, until we knew what we were about; but since you force me, I will give you all the facts in my knowledge."

"What then are your plans," (the reporter asked).

"The road can be graded by convict labor," (Col. Price continued). "On the first of April, there will be some changes in existing arrangements, and then I can get what convicts I want."

"But you know they must be fed and clothed," (the reporter countered).

"The farmers of Lumpkin, Union and

Dawson County resident Mike Miller stands in the roadbed of what originally was graded as a railroad across Dawson. The route however was never completed. (Photo by Olin Jackson)

Dawson and other counties will advance me the provisions. One man alone said he would advance $500.00 and more if necessary in this way."

"Precisely," said the doubting reporter, "but they must eventually be paid."

"Well, you see, with those advances, we will issue scrip, good for freight and passage. These we will make in various denominations. The consequence will be that will be as good as money anywhere contiguous to the (rail) road, and the merchants of Gainesville and Dahlonega will take them (the scrip) because they will be cash to them," (Col. Price explained). "Why, one man – Mr. Hand, of my town (Dahlonega), pays $2,000 a year to get his goods here to Dahlonega."

"Then you will have no stock?" asked the reporter, as he looked ruefully at the nicket which he had saved up to invest.

"None whatsoever," the victimized answered promptly. "All we ask of the people of your city is to buy enough of the scrip, good for freight or passage, no matter into whose hands the road may fall, to give me a few thousand dollars to pay incidental expenses, guarding the convicts, etc. If they will do this, the road will be built."

With no stock, and the apparent lack of funds and backing, the construction of the Gainesville and Dahlonega Railroad no doubt continued, but it was a precipitous existence at best, a reality which must eventually have assisted in its downfall.

On July 4, 1890, an advertisement describes the outright sale of the rail line venture to Col. William P. Price. Up until this point, Price had apparently been involved in the endeavor with other individuals. He bought the railroad for $4,000 because, according to newspaper accounts at the time, he "owned judgements and other liens on the property amounting to more than $40,000, and he was compelled to protect this large interest."

A significant problem in the project seems to have been centered in Gainesville, from which a substantial portion of the railroad's funding was to have been raised. The March 4, 1879 issue of *The Eagle* carried a letter to the editor from W.P. Price, which, among other things, stated "There is no indifference to this enterprise, except in the city of Gainesville. The people of Lumpkin and Hall counties, outside of Gainesville, so far as I could judge, are all favorable to it. A few only of the citizens of Gainesville have expressed any desire for the road. This ought not to be so, and perhaps will not be so, after they fully understand their interests in the premises."

Other references to the railroad through the remainder of the 19th century are few and far between. Some accounts indicate that it actually provided service for the region for a short while; others suggest that it was never completed.

At some point in the construction process, a decision apparently was made to construct the railroad to Auraria, instead of Dahlonega, possibly in an effort to provide renewed legitimacy to the project as a connector to a similar railroad project being planned and constructed at the same time through the prosperous Etowah River Valley section of Dawson County. The May 7, 1880 issue of *The Eagle* carried an article announcing the fact that "After several experimental surveys, Col. Sage (a surveyor for the Gainesville Airline Railroad) has located the line of the Gainesville and Dahlonega Railroad to Aurora."

On May 20, 1899, *The Eagle* carried a notice indicating that Col. Price had apparently admitted the obvious – Gainesville, for the most part, was not interested in investing in a railroad venture to Dahlonega. The article explained: "Application was made for charter for the Dahlonega Railroad Co. (as opposed to the 'Gainesville and Dahlonega Railroad'). It is to be 30 miles in length, and is to be built from Dahlonega to Gainesville or Lula. The capital stock of the company is to be $300,000, all of which is to be common stock. It is the intention of the company to go forward at once with the work."

And then on June 1, 1899, *The Eagle* carried this brief notice: "We are reliably informed that the promoters of the Dahlonega Railroad scheme have been tendered by Col. W.P. Price, free of cost, the right-of-way of the old Gainesville and Dahlonega Railroad." The death-knell for the Gainesville and Dahlonega railroad had apparently been sounded.

With the advent of electricity, the age of the "electric" railway was ushered in. The opportunity for water power (and thus electricity) via a dam and generator at Leather's Ford in Lumpkin County, coupled with the opportunity to inexpensively obtain the then defunct Gainesville and Dahlonega Railroad right-of-ways/etc., apparently gave rise to the creation of an electric railway system which operated between Gainesville and Dahlonega.

The October 15, 1903 issue of *The Atlanta Constitution* carried an article describing the situation: "The power now used in the city of Gainesville comes from the dam on the Chestatee River, 15 miles northwest of the city. This dam is no little one, itself. It is owned by the Gainesville and Dahlonega Electric Railway Company, and furnishes 1200 horsepower, this compa-

Early Railroads in Lumpkin and Dawson Counties — Dawson County

ny being a twin companion of the North Georgia Electric Company (which also furnished electric power for Gainesville via a dam and generator at the Chattahoochee River near present-day Riverside Military Academy), General Warner being at the head of both."

"The Chestatee dam is two hundred feet long, and twenty-seven feet high. The power is brought to the city on heavy copper wires strung along the right-of-way of the old Gainesville and Dahlonega Railway, an enterprise which ex-Governor Candler headed, and over which road trains at one time ran from Gainesville to a point beyond the Chattahoochee River. The old road-bed has been reworked by the new company, and it is the intention to have cars running over this line in another year to Dahlonega. The road is graded as far toward Dahlonega as the Chestatee dam and power house, leaving only eight miles of grading necessary. The Chestatee dam cost $100,000, and was completed more than a year ago."

How long and to what extent the Gainesville and Dahlonega Electric Railway Company operated is unknown. It apparently was not cost-effective however, because it was only operational for a few years before it too was abandoned. The railroad rights-of-way have long since reverted back to ownership by the owners of the real estate along the former route, and the rest, as they say, is history.

In Dawson County, the story was much the same, however, many of the problems with this rail line seem to have centered around "too much," rather than "too little" interest in the railroad.

An article in the *Dawsonville Mountain Chronicle* of January 27, 1880, announces: "If our people would grade a railroad and lay the ties to intersect the Gainesville and Dahlonega at Auraria, there would be no difficulty in finding capitalists who would lay the iron and put the road in operation... Owing to the natural advantages, a railroad bed can be graded from this place in Auraria at a less cost than has ever been the case with any railroad for the same distance."

Numerous investors apparently were available for the Dawson County railroad, and Dawson County apparently was a more desirable destination than Lumpkin County, because not one, but several railroad companies were apparently considering a railroad to it from the late 1800s up to the early 1900s.

One of the first was the Macon and Cincinnati Air-Line Railroad. An article in the February 24, 1880 issue of *The Mountain Chronicle* announces "We received yesterday a letter from a gentleman of Brunswick reminding us of the projected Macon and Cincinnati Railroad, which will pass directly through this section. It passes Monticello, Covington, Lawrenceville, Cumming, Dawsonville or Dixon, up the Amicalola and on to Knoxville. Whilst this may not be the very best road for our people, there is more probability of it than any other now. A strong company has been organized for a long time, and have only waited for the Macon and Brunswick Railroad matter to be settled, as there was some contingency connected with that road that would affect this. But the M.&B. road matter has been satisfactorily settled, ... and may now be set down as a probability."

Another account on June 14, 1881 in *The Mountain Chronicle* proclaims: "Less than $400,000 will grade and lay cross-ties and iron for a narrow gauge railroad from

The railroad rights-of-way have long since reverted back to ownership by the owners of the real estate along the former route, and the rest, as they say, is history.

45

In 1886, three separate railroads were planned across Dawson County. The two individuals in this photo stand at the end of one of the roadbeds graded for the lines. A trestle originally planned for this site would have extended this railroad across a deep ravine near the Etowah River in Dawson County. Due to a lack of funding, bad economic times and other factors, however, no railroads were ever completed across Dawson County, including the one in this photo which ended at this ravine. (Photo by Olin Jackson)

Dawsonville to Atlanta via Cumming and Alpharetta."

In March of 1882, the Articles of Association for the Gainesville and Dalton Short-Cut Railroad Company were carried in *The Chronicle*. The Gainesville and Dalton was intended to operate in Hall, Dawson, Gilmer, Murray and Whitfield counties. Stockholders were: Robert F. Williams (Auraria), Jacob P. Imboden (Dahlonega) and John L. Summerour (Amicalola, Dawson Co.). It (the railroad) was to connect Gainesville and Dalton, a distance of about 85 miles, and provide a shorter route between Cincinnati and Charleston.

In September of 1884, the rights-of-way for the Gainesville, Dawsonville, and Cartersville Railroad Company in Dawson Co. were announced, and are carried in *Deed Book D* in the Dawson County Courthouse records. This railroad, based upon the land lots cited in the records, would have roughly followed the route of present-day State Road 53, east from inside the city of Dawsonville, and turned in the vicinity of the Etowah River, following the river north into Lumpkin County. Graded portions of the railroad are still visible (as of this writing) along State Road 53, and along the northern bank of the Etowah River.

By December of 1884, the exact location of the railroad and its depot appear to have been decided; subscriptions to the railroad had been made by some Dawson Countians, and some reservations among the subscribers had developed. The date of the completion of the line had been set as January, 1886, which was the same completion date as named for the Dahlonega railroad venture.

In 1886, three separate railroads are mentioned for Dawson County: 1/ The Augusta and Chattanooga Railroad Company. This project reportedly had a capital stock of $4 million, however, the board of directors, as a group, had agreed to purchase only $6,000 of the corporation's stock. It appears that the directors expected most of the money to come from "subscriptions at the county level" (which in today's language would be known as "a highly leveraged deal."). 2/ "Another railroad to Cartersville, perhaps by Georgia Marble Works. . . ." This reference could possibly have been to the Cartersville, Dawsonville, and Gainesville Railroad. 3/ A branch railroad to Dahlonega.

Judging from the amount of space dedicated to articles in the *Chronicle* on the possibility of railroad construction to Dawsonville, much of the talk was mere speculation and idle chatter, hoping to drum up support for any number of several potential opportunities. Dawson County was much more accessible from several different directions, than was Lumpkin, and as such, had more suitors.

The editorials, speculation, and wishful thinking may have had an effect on developments in Dawson, for by August

26, 1911, the Etowah Valley Railway Company was a reality - at least on paper. The *Dawson County Advertiser* of August 26, 1911, carried the petition for incorporation by ten men: G.R. Glenn, H.D. Garley (sic) (Gurley), John H. Moere (sic) (Moore), T.J. Smith, J.M. Brooksner (sic?), J.F. (sic) (J.E.?) Tate, H. Head, J.F. Sargent, W.H. (sic?) (W.B.?) Townsend, and Craig R. Arnold – and reads as follows: "Shows that they desire for themselves their associates successors and assigns to be incorporated for the period of 101 years with the privilege of renewal as a railroad company under the name of Etowah Valley Railway (sic) Company, the length of said road will be about 75 miles, as nearly as can be estimated. The general direction of same will be from a point on the Louisville & Nashville R.R. at or near Ballground Cherokee county, Ga., thence along the Etowah River thru Creighton, Cherokee county, Ga. to the Northern State line of Ga. in Towns county passing thru the counties of Cherokee, Forsyth, Dawson, Lumpkin, White, Towns all in the state of Ga. Said company proposes to construct and build or purchase and acquire a railroad between the points above named along private right of way and on public roads, either or both."

Although the Etowah Valley Railway Company was one of the few officially incorporated for business (at least on paper) in Dawson County, there is considerable confusion as to which railroad company actually owned the rights-of-way and railroad line constructed in Dawson County. Some references refer to ownership as belonging to the Etowah Valley Railway Company, and some refer to the Gainesville Dawsonville and Cartersville Railroad as owner.

Although there was considerable interest (as in Dahlonega/Lumpkin County) in bringing the railroad to Dawson, three major factors seem to have caused the demise of the railroad in Dawson County. These causes included a strong inclination for bickering and competition among the prospective builders, an inherent lack of available capital on the local level, and a fundamental lack of stable industry and livelihood necessary to lend legitimacy to the project and its construction. The only industry of any significance in the area at this time was gold mining, and it peaked in intensity some years ahead of the development of the railroad.

If one knows where to look along the Etowah River valley in Dawson County today, the graded and elevated railroad bed can still be seen. The grade in Dawson ended not far from the point at which Highway 136 crosses the Etowah River today.

In the waning years of the late 19th Century, the explosive growth of the Lumpkin and Dawson County areas had been reduced to a fraction of that enjoyed prior to the California gold rush. The Lumpkin and Dawson County railroad ventures - however ill-managed and ill-fated they may have been - presumably were envisioned as a means to staunch this negative growth trend, and cultivate continued development in the region.

The road-bed for one of the railroads partially constructed in Dawson County in the 1880s is still faintly visible through the trees along the right side of the Etowah River in this photo. Though the route was graded, the rails were never laid. Sketchy records indicate this construction project was the work of an enterprise known as the Gainesville, Dawsonville and Cartersville Railroad.

Historic Railroad Into The Mountains

The Blue Ridge Scenic Railway

The old rails from the Louisville & Nashville Railroad had languished for years, and were being threatened with extinction when a group of stockholders in a small north Georgia railroad came up with a plan to revitalize the line.

The Blue Ridge Scenic Railway (BRSR) is actually part of the Georgia Northeastern Railroad (GNR). The Georgia Northeastern is owned by stockholders of which the largest is an individual named Wilds Pierce, president of the line.

The idea for the scenic passenger service was hatched after a substantial number of Georgia residents made known their desire for a scenic line back into the mountains. Passenger service into the little north Georgia towns was discontinued long ago, and even the railroad tracks were removed from many of the old railroads such as the famed Tallulah Falls Railroad. Former passengers have mourned the loss of this romantic (and useful) form of transportation for decades, and even younger individuals have expressed an interest in rail transportation to the quaint and attractive north Georgia mountain towns from yesteryear.

The old Louisville & Nashville (L&N) line from Marietta to McCaysville, was an exception. It, somehow managed to survive the years. The line is owned today by the Georgia Department of Transportation and is leased to the Georgia Northeastern Railroad.

Following a feasibility study and some cooperative efforts with the city of Blue Ridge, Georgia, the Blue

Passenger service into the little north Georgia towns was discontinued long ago, and even the railroad tracks were removed from many of the old railroads such as the famed Tallulah Falls Railroad.

The Blue Ridge Scenic Railway — Fannin County

Ridge Scenic Railway was born, and is fulfilling the dream of travelers who wish to get back to the "good old days" of rail travel. It is fast-becoming a popular weekend activity for Atlanta-area residents.

The train leaves the recently-restored turn-of-the-century L&N Railroad Depot in Blue Ridge. As it travels northward through the Fannin County countryside, passengers are treated to some of the most beautiful scenery in the state.

The train is typically composed of a commissary car (where snacks and drinks are available) and a number of coach cars, all pulled by vintage 1960s diesel locomotives. Each coach features traditional upholstered seats (arranged in pairs), and many of the seats face each other, a situation which facilitates and enhances conversations with other passengers.

Each coach also has a restroom, and all the cars have picture windows for unrestricted viewing of the scenic beauty one experiences along the ride. The coaches also all have air-conditioning to keep the cars cool in summer and toasty warm in the fall and winter months.

The coaches were all built in the 1940s and '50s, so they offer a true opportunity to savor a vintage railroad ride. One of the coaches was built in the 1950s for the Santa Fe Railroad of New Mexico and Colorado fame. It was purchased from a chapter of the National Railway Historical Society in Greensboro, North Carolina. The commissary car was built in 1951 for the Northern Pacific Railroad in Washington state. Two of the cars are being leased from the Atlanta Chapter of the National Railway Historic Society headquartered in Duluth, Georgia.

There is also one "open air" car which features padded bench seats facing to the outside and running the length of the car. This option provides an even better view of the scenery for riders who prefer the great outdoors.

The Blue Ridge Scenic Railroad begins at Blue Ridge, Georgia in scenic Fannin County. The historic Blue Ridge Depot dispenses tickets and other items for the trip.
(Photo by Martin K. O'Toole)

The town of Blue Ridge once was a vibrant north Georgia railroad community. When passenger service was discontinued, however, the town's prosperity suffered dramatically.

The BRSR passes through the tiny scenic railroad communities of Murphy Junction and Curtis enroute to Copperhill, Tennessee, where a variety of gift shops await patrons.

The trip is particularly popular with individuals and groups who wish to spend a day in the mountains. The Scenic Railway began service in June of 1998, and approximately 17,000 riders made the trip during the inaugural season.

Elderly people, especially, who feared they might never have a chance to ride trains again, have expressed appreciation for the experience. "People find themselves in a gently-rocking car, with the sun shining through the windows, and the clickety-clacking sound as the train moves along the jointed track (in contrast to the continuously-welded rail used on modern lines), and it takes them back in time," one official remarked.

Passengers on the one-hour ride enjoy both scenery and a bit of history along the old rail line. Mile markers (which can still be viewed along the western side of the track) were installed when the L&N Railroad first acquired the track at the turn of the century. The markers all show the mileage from the L&N's corporate headquarters in Louisville, Kentucky.

Approximately three-quarters of a mile north of the historic depot in Blue Ridge, the railroad passes the site of the old engine shops which once existed in Blue Ridge. This facility was operated between 1887 and 1906, and was once a strategic service center for the locomotives on the route.

Approximately two miles north of Blue Ridge the BRSR passes Murphy Junction. In earlier days, the line was split at this point. A branch which continued on into North Carolina (Murphy) angled off to the right, and the main line (angling off to the left) continued (as it still does today) on to Tennessee (Copperhill).

Today, the old Murphy branch-line ends at Mineral Bluff, Georgia. The rails between Mineral Bluff and Murphy, regrettably, were taken up long ago. Had they remained in place, the Blue Ridge Scenic Railroad might have had a direct connection with the Great Smoky Mountains Railroad which is so popular with vacationers in North Carolina today.

Also at Murphy Junction, there is a "Y" in the tracks – or, in railroading parlance, a "wye"– which allows a train to turn around or reverse the direction in which it is heading.

On the northern side of the wye, an old family home which has long existed on the route can still be viewed today. A family by the name of Panter (pronounced "painter") built the home in the 1880s, and helped lay the track on the original rail line. Today, descendants of these railroading pioneers still live in this home.

Part of the route of the scenic line follows the beautiful Toccoa River. At one spot in the river near Curtis Switch Road, a historic landmark – an ancient fish-trap built by Native Americans in prehistory – can sometimes be seen during periods of drought or low water (requires a brief walk across private property).

The fish trap consists of a series of rocks placed in a "V" formation on the riverbed. When the Indians still inhabited this region, they periodically drove fish into the large opening of the "V"

On the northern side of the wye, an old family home which has long existed on the route can still be viewed today.

and gradually forced the fish down the length of the "V" until they were forced to pass out through the small end where they were caught in woven baskets.

The scenic train continues northward until it reaches the Tennessee State Line (which divides McCaysville, Georgia from Copperhill, Tennessee). The train stops just a few feet short of the state line to allow passengers to disembark.

After leaving the train, all passengers have one hour to browse the many shops in McCaysville. Tourism has replaced copper as a major industry in this scenic mountain town – the county's largest – incorporated in 1902.

One unique aspect of McCaysville has marked it as a fun spot for youngsters for a long time. Smart community promoters have painted a line across the community to mark the boundary between Georgia and Tennessee. Children just love to straddle the blue boundary, enjoying the opportunity to "stand in two states at one time." On the Georgia side, the town is called McCaysville. On the Tennessee side, it's known as Copperhill.

The blue-painted boundary line interestingly slices through the Hometown Foods IGA in McCaysville and its adjacent parking lot, then continues diagonally across the street before scaling the yellow brick building which houses the Copper Emporium furniture store. One has to wonder how these businesses know to whom they must pay their taxes.

Folks in McCaysville like to tell the

Smart community promoters have painted a line across the community to mark the boundary between Georgia and Tennessee. Children just love to straddle the blue boundary, enjoying the opportunity to "stand in two states at one time.

story of how the boundary line is actually not quite accurate, since the surveyors back in the 1800s reportedly spent too much time sampling from a moonshine still they had chanced upon at the time.

Whether that's the reason for the erroneously-marked boundary or not, the state of Georgia contends its border with Tennessee should actually lie farther north - at the 35th parallel, as specified in the laws of both states. "But if the boundary is corrected, it will shift a mile-wide strip of south Chattanooga and most of Copperhill into Georgia," says Edwin Jackson, co-author with Marion Hemperley of *Georgia's Boundaries: The Shaping Of A State*, "and that's just not likely to happen. Even though a suit could be filed in the U.S. Supreme Court, the rulings of that court in similar situations have suggested that a boundary line which has been recognized and accepted in the past will stand, even if later found to have been drawn in error."

Aside from the interest of the boundary line, there are numerous shopping opportunities in McCaysville. Everything from crafts, to antiques, to novelty gifts and tasty treats can be found aplenty!

It is noteworthy to point out that the former clinic of Dr. Thomas J. Hicks – who quietly operated a baby-selling practice in the 1950s and whose story was told to a nationwide audience on programs such as ABC Television's 20-20 – once existed in the space occupied today by the shops in the Toccoa Center.

Origin Of A Town

The Railroad Through Blue Ridge

A number of tiny north Georgia mountain communities sprang up in the 1880s as a direct result of the railroads which passed through them. And as the years went by, if the railroad languished or died, so also did the town.

Back in the 1880s, railroads such as the line between Marietta and Mineral Bluff allowed timber to be more easily harvested in the mountains of north Georgia. Lumber and other building products were in high demand as a result of the state's burgeoning population. In those days, instead of the prefabricated building materials used today, almost everything was built of wood.

The town of Blue Ridge had its beginnings in 1887 when Colonel Mike McKinney built the first house in what then was the wilds of north Georgia. Only 50 years earlier, Cherokee Indians still inhabited the region.

Col. McKinney's partner, C.R. Walton, a civil engineer, laid out and mapped the town. Its elevation at 1,751 feet above sea level made it the highest railroad town in the state at that time.

And just as was also customary in those days, this rail line between Marietta and Tennessee was built with convict labor. The men graded the route with little more than axes, picks, shovels, wrecking bars, wheeled dumping carts, horses, mules and black powder. As a result of their harsh lifestyle, the men fought, brawled and sometimes even killed each other during the construction. It was a hard way to live, but the work of these men ushered in a new era of growth as the railroads expanded.

In 1886, steam engine Number 1, called "Little Mary," chugged into Blue Ridge. It was owned and operated by the Marietta & North Georgia Railroad (precursor to the Louisville & Nashville Railroad which would later purchase the same route) which had constructed its repair shop – the only one between Atlanta and Knoxville – in Blue Ridge.

In short order, the railroad brought about major growth in Blue Ridge, even causing the county seat to be moved there from Morganton (the oldest town and original county seat) in 1895. By the late 1890s, Blue Ridge was the bustling business center of the area.

Blue Ridge was also a resort community of sorts, and the railroad facilitated this growth as well, transporting hundreds of visitors to the site during the spring and summer months every year. Three mineral springs which had concentrated amounts of magnesium, iron and sulphur – all healthful minerals – had been discovered in the vicinity.

The Railroad Through Blue Ridge   Fannin County

As word spread of the healthful waters and the attractive accommodations which were being constructed near the tracks around Blue Ridge, the railroad found itself carrying more and more visitors to the area. Interestingly, due to the concentrated minerals in the water, it smelled like swamp water, but the visitors to the spot drank copious amounts of the foul-smelling liquid, even taking jugs of it home for later consumption.

Some people took the morning train to Blue Ridge, ate lunch at the hotel, walked to the mineral springs, and then returned home via the afternoon train. It was a most unusual story, but it was one that was destined to be relatively short-lived.

Just as the railroad brought prosperity to Blue Ridge, it also took it away. The grading of a new faster route to Tennessee, coupled with the eventual decline in rail passenger service, brought about the town's decline. In 1907, a new railroad allowed trains to travel from Marietta to Etowah, Tennessee through Cartersville, Georgia. It was a route which was on a much more level terrain, and therefore faster and safer.

As a result of this and other factors, the repair shop in Blue Ridge eventually was moved to Etowah, after that route became the more heavily-traveled route. The new line was a signal that the end was at hand for Blue Ridge's railroad-oriented livelihood. It would take 45 or 50 more years before the town's commerce would die out almost completely, but it was inevitable.

The once-vibrant springs deteriorated as the years went by in Blue Ridge. By the late 1930s, few individuals drank from the waters anymore. By the late 1950s, with the demise of passenger service to Blue Ridge, few travelers even went to the town anymore, and no one – save the operators of the few freight trains which still ran on the line – even traveled by rail anymore. The automobile had conquered the railroad – at least for the time being.

Due to the sudden increase in travelers and commerce, the sizeable Blue Ridge Inn was built near the railroad tracks in the community. It burned in 1917.

This primitive photograph shows the railroad repair shops in Blue Ridge which were photographed circa 1906. Known as the Marietta & North Georgia Railroad at that time, the line was responsible for much of the early growth of Blue Ridge. When the repair shops were moved to a faster route via Etowah, Tennessee, much of the life was drained from Blue Ridge. (Olin Jackson Files)

A group of engineers with the Atlanta, Knoxville & Northern Railroad (precursor to the L&N) posed for this photograph in Blue Ridge, Georgia, in 1897. At that time, Blue Ridge was still the center of operations for the rail line. (Olin Jackson Files)

North Georgia's "Old Line" Railroad

The Last Days Of The Old "Hook & Eye?"

Railroads once criss-crossed north Georgia, providing passenger service between towns, and freight transportation for products produced by industries such as logging and mining. Today, a number of these old rail lines have been abandoned, and offer a unique glimpse into this early form of transportation in the mountains, especially on the fabled "Old Line."

Looking for an interesting weekend getaway in the north Georgia mountains? If you are one of the growing number of individuals who are purchasing the surplus railroad motor cars – commonly known as "speeders" – you can join a group of hobbyists in riding the historic rail lines. One such group – the North American Railcar Owners Association (NARCOA) – is actively involved in this growing hobby.

One of the best historic rail line riding opportunities in the Southeast is the old Louisville & Nashville (L&N) "Old Line" Railroad that winds its way through the hills and mountains of north Georgia on its way from Marietta (originally named "Elizabeth"), Georgia to Knoxville, Tennessee.

Well-known in railroading circles as the famous "Hook & Eye" line, the Tennessee portion of this scenic railroad is in danger of being eliminated. Completed in 1890, the Hook & Eye was reduced in status in 1906, when the L&N built a more direct line from Cartersville, Georgia to Etowah, Tennessee with vastly fewer curves and easier grades.

Despite its slower, more demanding route, the Old Line winds its way through many scenic north Georgia communities such as Canton, Ball Ground, Talking Rock, Ellijay, Blue Ridge and Copperhill, Tennessee. Since 1906, it has been the marble and poultry feed industries in Georgia, and the copper industry in Tennessee which have kept the Old Line in service.

Saving The Line

In 1996, the track on the Old Line north of Ellijay was put out of service. The blizzard of 1993 had brought down numerous trees across the track, giving the owner – CSX Transportation – a good excuse to discontinue service. Fortunately, the track south of Ellijay had been taken over (and thus saved from extinction) by the Georgia Northeastern Railroad, a profitable enterprise headed up by entrepreneur Wilds Pierce of Atlanta.

Today, the Georgia Northeastern has

The Last Days Of The Old "Hook & Eye?" — Fannin County

continued service to the marble and other industries on the line. In yet another innovative endeavor, Pierce also purchased and leased period railroad engines and cars and began a tourism railroad excursion service into the north Georgia Mountains. Called the "Blue Ridge Scenic Railroad," this vintage train has become highly popular, operating regularly from Blue Ridge, Georgia to McCaysville, Georgia, and giving its patrons a taste of what passenger rail service was like in the old days.

Meanwhile, a new hobby has been sweeping North America. Private individuals have been buying up surplus railroad motor cars (the small cars used to service railroads). The riding of these little machines – called "speeders" – on abandoned or nearly-abandoned rail lines, has become extremely popular.

One group of these hobbyists – the North American Rail Car Owners Association (NARCOA) – has been instrumental in helping to preserve endangered rail lines. NARCOA, which requires that its members be covered by an insurance policy and rigidly enforces the inspection of the cars, has helped to keep obstructions from abandoned or nearly-abandoned lines, offering the hope of salvation to endangered historic routes. They make arrangements with railroad companies for the occasional use of these branch lines for scenic railcar excursions.

It was during the pursuit of one of these excursions that members helped to temporarily save the Hook & Eye line north of Ellijay by clearing years of undergrowth and fallen trees from the all-but-abandoned tracks. In a number of spots, mud slides had completely covered the tracks, necessitating an excavation of the rails so that they again became serviceable.

In 1998, the state of Georgia, the Georgia Northeastern Railroad and CSX Transportation worked together to save the entire Georgia portion of the Hook & Eye. Recently, the Tennessee portion has been purchased from CSX by a consortium of local businessmen, but the future use of the track is still in doubt.

On March 2 & 3, 2002, NARCOA members from 10 states helped write a new chapter in the history of the Hook & Eye. The big Tennessee Copper Company in Copper Hill and Ducktown, Tennessee, had ceased mining copper in 1963, but the Copper Hill plant had remained open until 2000, producing sulfuric acid. With the closing of this plant, CSX Transportation no longer had customers nor any reason to keep the line open from Copper Hill to Etowah Tennessee.

Taking a Final Ride

On March 1 of that year, NARCOA members (who are hard-core railroad enthusiasts and preservationists) realized that time was running out to experience a ride on the old Hook & Eye. They brought in some 38 railcars in vans and on trailers, and put them on the track in Mineral Bluff, Georgia, for the final ride.

At Mineral Bluff, the railcars were carefully inspected, and, following a safety meeting the following morning, the men and women began assembling for a historic ride into Tennessee and around the famous "Hiwassee Loop," the only place in the East where a railroad track makes a complete circle around a mountain and then crosses over itself. This loop is the "Eye" of the old Hook & Eye.

The "Hook," a fish hook-shaped sharp curve around a mountain spur

The riding of these little machines – called "speeders" – on abandoned or nearly-abandoned rail lines, has become extremely popular.

Author Ruddy Ellis with Al & Karen Wilber's rail car on the "Old Line." The Wilbers came all the way from Hartville, Ohio for the ride. (Photo courtesy of Ruddy Ellis)

A group of engineers and other officials with the Atlanta, Knoxville & Northern Railroad at Blue Ridge, Georgia on the Old Line in 1897. (Olin Jackson files)

Engine #10, an American type passenger locomotive, came to the Atlanta, Knoxville & Northern Railroad in 1892 and is typical of the early trains which used the Old Line and the "Hook & Eye." This photo was made in Blue Ridge, Georgia in 1898. Fireman E.C. Howell is sitting on the rods and Engineer Bill Garwood is in white overalls with the oil can. (Olin Jackson files)

at Talking Rock, was bypassed years ago by digging a deep cut straight through the spur. This straighter portion of the track, however, did not substantially improve the time it took to traverse the route.

Early Saturday morning, our "train" of railcars left the historic 1887 brick depot in Mineral Bluff, Georgia and headed southwest toward Blue Ridge. Part of the enjoyment of riding an ancient rail line such as this is all the history experienced along the way.

For instance, just beyond Mineral Bluff, we crossed the Toccoa River. A little upstream, we could see the aged steel skeleton of the bridge which once carried the old Blue Ridge to Mineral Bluff highway. This road was re-routed after construction of the dam on beautiful Lake Blue Ridge.

The dam itself is also visible a little farther along, as is the abandoned roadbed of the construction railroad spur used in the building of the dam from 1924 to 1931 by the Toccoa Electric Power Company (subsidiary of the Tennessee Electric Power Co.). Toccoa Electric was sold to the Tennessee Valley Authority in 1939.

At this point on our little train ride, the track on the Old Line runs alongside Hogback Mountain, a narrow ridge almost completely encircled by "Hogback Bend" on the Toccoa River. Robert Ripley (of *Ripley's Believe It Or Not* fame) once said the top of the narrow portion of Hogback Mountain was the only place in the world where one could see the same river flowing in both directions at the same time!

Another interesting aspect of this mountain is that the famous Dickey Cemetery is located on top of it. It contains the graves of the Dickey family as well as many of their slaves.

When our railcars reached the "wye" at Murphy Junction, it was necessary for the lead car – operated by Assistant Trip Coordinator Bill Stringfellow – to stop, unlock and throw the switch to the track leading northwest towards McCaysville and Copperhill. Being the lead car, Bill carried a chain saw and other tools to clear obstruc-

The Last Days Of The Old "Hook & Eye?" Fannin County

tions from the track ahead.

Leaving the Junction, our cars ran along the scenic Toccoa River again to the bridge crossing over into McCaysville. There, we stopped at the unloading platform of the Blue Ridge Scenic Railroad. A photographer and other guests were picked up for the ride around the Loop.

As we left McCaysville, we passed the now-empty rail yard and the big Tennessee Copper Company plant which also is now silent. Back in April of 2001, many tank cars for sulfur or sulfuric acid were seen in this historic train yard. Production at this plant, however, has ceased forever.

Early Problems On The Line

We shortly began following the Toccoa River once again (called the Ocoee River now that we were in Tennessee). Our route soon turned to the north for the run to Farner, Tennessee. It was there that the situation developed in 1890 which gave birth to the famous "Loop."

Farner is hundreds of feet higher in elevation than the Hiwassee River, along which the original track from Knoxville ran to this point. Engineers tried to find a way to construct the track down Turtletown Creek, but that route was simply too steep and curvy.

Faced with a July 1, 1890 deadline to get trains running between Knoxville and Atlanta, the engineers were forced to resort to the old trick of building a temporary "switchback" track back and forth up a gully. A switchback limits the length of trains, usually requires extra locomotives, and is very time-consuming.

In 1898, an engineer from the L&N was brought in to try to solve this problem. He devised the Hiwassee Loop, where the track circles the mountain one and three-quarter times, while continuing to climb the grade. The track was also run farther up the Hiwassee River, almost to the present Apalachia Dam, giving it even more distance in which to climb.

Soon after our train of railcars passed

Photographed September 15, 1904, this engineering party was working on the new route between Etowah, Tennessee and Cartersville, Georgia which ultimately severely diminished the value and utility of the "Old Line" through Blue Ridge, Georgia to Knoxville, Tennessee. Pictured here are: Emery Gilllam, level rodman; Jack Armstrong, front chainman; John Allen, levelman; Mack Wall, rear chainman; R.C. Logan, rodman; Spencer Furguson, transitman; and William Vineyard, axeman. The dog's name was "Spot." (Olin Jackson files)

The Blue Ridge Scenic Railroad, a popular excursion train with vintage railroad passenger cars, operates on the Old Line from Blue Ridge to McCaysville, Georgia, as does the freight-hauling Georgia Northeastern Railroad which is owned by the same company. (Photo courtesy of Blue Ridge Scenic Railroad)

TALES OF THE RAILS IN GEORGIA

Volunteer railcar owners clear undergrowth and fallen trees from the Old Line north of Ellijay, Georgia. (Photo by Ruddy Ellis)

Col. Jim Bogle (l) and other members of the group take a moment to explore the famed "Hiwassee Loop" and trestle. (Photo by Ruddy Ellis)

It's smooth sailing now after the path has been cleared. (Photo by Ruddy Ellis)

Crossing the scenic Hiwassee River in Tennessee. (Photo by Ruddy Ellis)

Farner, we crossed over a tail of the original switchback track. The old switchback is no longer visible in the undergrowth, but knowledgeable railroad men know it is there.

Soon, the TVA's Apalachia Dam, which is in North Carolina, became visible. Time has mostly erased signs of the small railroad yard once used by trains bringing in supplies to build this dam in 1941-'43, but the old roadbed of the "wye" used to turn the steam locomotives in the opposite direction on the track is still obvious. Also erased is any sign of the camp where soldiers guarded the dam during World War II.

A light rain began to fall on us at about this point, but it did not dampen our spirits one bit. We crossed the Loop trestle and looked down on the track below us where we would soon be riding. As we slowly circled the Loop, riders near the back could look down on cars passing beneath them.

Leaving the Loop, the track follows the scenic Hiwassee River once again. For the first miles, the river has very little water in it, since water normally flowing here had been rerouted through a long water tunnel behind the dam to the power plant downstream at Apalachia. Holes worn through large rocks at this point testify to the former strength of the river flow at this point over the centuries before construction of the dam.

The Last Days Of The Old "Hook & Eye?"   Fannin County

All along the river banks, large icicles left over from a recent cold snap attest to our winter weather. It won't be long, however, before springtime will reign once again.

Heading Back Home

Beyond the power plant at Apalachia, the river bed is full of water once again. At Reliance, the track crosses the river on a long trestle and deck-girder bridge. After crossing the river, our "train" proceeds to the next paved road crossings of the track.

At this point, it is time to reverse our direction, since we have proceeded as far northward as CSX will allow us for our little outing. We must physically turn our railcars around, since the little machines were designed primarily to run in only a forward direction. Some of the cars have big handles so that they can be physically picked up and dragged around in the opposite direction. Some have what is know as a "turntable," which is a leg that comes down under the center of the car, supporting most of the car's weight, so that one person can swing it around and head it in the opposite direction on the tracks.

After all the cars were turned around, we ran back across the river bridge and stopped at the Outdoor Center facility where boats can be rented in the summer. The proprietors were nice enough to open their facility and serve lunch to us. After a bite to eat, we headed back to Mineral Bluff, running slowly around the Loop once again, to enjoy what may be the final trip of any rail car on this historic route.

Much of the Loop track in Tennessee runs through the Cherokee National Forest. Even if the track is removed, it is hoped that the U.S. Forest Service will preserve the rights-of-way and bridges on this historic scenic line for posterity. Stay tuned. The final chapter of the famous Hook & Eye has yet to be written.

The great Hiwassee Loop at Farner, Tennessee as viewed from below. (Photo by Ruddy Ellis)

Farner, Tennessee is hundreds of feet higher in elevation than the Hiwassee River along which the "Old Line" ran just prior to entering the town. When constructing the Old Line in 1890, railroad engineers built what is known as a "switchback," (above) in order to quickly reach the higher elevation. Later, when the Hiwassee Loop was constructed, the switchback was abandoned. (Photo by Ruddy Ellis)

The repair shops in Blue Ridge, Georgia, circa 1906. The "Old Line" railroad was responsible for much of the early growth of this town. (Olin Jackson files)

The Calhoun – Williamson Duel, And The CR&C Railroad

A well documented formal duel between two angered men degenerated into comic adventure before becoming the last such event in the state's history.

On August 8, 1889, two men in Atlanta, Georgia, exchanged words that threatened to change their lives forever. The events that led to the duel between Pat Calhoun and Captain John D. Williamson are virtually forgotten today, but they caused quite a stir at the time in north Georgia.

Captain Williamson was the president of the Chattanooga, Rome and Columbus Railroad Company. Pat Calhoun was general counsel and a director of the Central Railroad and Banking Company of Georgia. Young Pat enjoyed the added distinction of being the grandson of famed South Carolina statesman and former vice-president of the United States John C. Calhoun. Both men were highly respected in their professions.

At the time of the incident, Captain Williamson resided part-time in Rome at the Armstrong Hotel, located on Howard Street (present-day Second Avenue) in Rome. Pat Calhoun was from the Atlanta area.

The trouble between the two men began at a legislative committee hearing at the Georgia state capitol in Atlanta. Williamson was in favor of a bill that would prevent the consolidation of competing railroad companies. He assured the committee that his Chattanooga, Rome & Columbus Railroad was and would remain an "independent line."

Pat Calhoun, however, representing a company that was actively consolidating railroads in the South, strongly opposed the bill. At some point in the discussions of the new bill, Calhoun, referring to Captain Williamson, reportedly remarked, "The gentleman knows that the first project he had in the building of this road was to unload it on the Central. That would have been done had I not stood in the way."

Captain Williamson took umbrage at the remark, bounding to his feet and countering, "When Mr. Calhoun states that it was my purpose to unload on the Central, he states what is unqualifiedly false. . . I never had any talk with Mr. Calhoun on the subject, and never made any proposition of the kind he indicates."

With this dangerous charge of falsehood, a deafening silence fell over the committee room. In times past, it had not been uncommon for words of this nature to be followed with the challenge of a duel, and this day would prove to be no exception. Without any further exchange and in an attempt to stem the anger between the two men, the committee meeting was immediately terminated, but the fateful words had already been spoken.

After leaving the meeting, neither man hesitated to obtain a representative – known as "a second" – to handle any correspondence between them. Mr. Calhoun sent for his friend Captain Henry Jackson, while Captain Williamson telegraphed Jack King of Rome, Georgia, to represent him.

If there had been any hope that this confrontation between the two men could be halted, it was soon shattered. On the evening of August 8th, Pat Calhoun sent a letter to Captain Williamson which read as follows:

Dear Sir:

Before the railroad commission of the house of representatives this afternoon, in the discussion of the Olive bill, you characterized certain statements which had been made by me as false. I request an unqualified retraction of this charge.

This communication will be handed to you by my friend, Mr. Henry Jackson, who is authorized to receive the reply, which you may see proper to make.

Respectfully,
Pat Calhoun

That same evening, Williamson responded to Calhoun's letter as follows:

Dear Sir:

Your note of this evening has been delivered to me by Mr. Henry Jackson. You stated before the committee that I had solicited you to act as a general counsel of the Chattanooga, Rome and Columbus Railroad Company, and that my purpose was to unload that road upon the Central Railroad Company of Georgia through your influence.

This statement carried with it a reflection upon myself. It was without foundation, and I promptly pronounced it false. So long as this language, used by you, is not withdrawn, I must decline to make any retraction, which you request.

This will be handed to you by my friend, Hon. J. Lindsay Johnson.

Respectfully,
J.D. Williamson

After several additional communications, the last written correspondence between the two men names the time and place for the duel.

Dear Sir:

My friend, Mr. J. King of Rome, Georgia, has arrived and has been put in possession of contents of the correspondence between us. In conformity with your request in your last note delivered at 1:05 p.m. today, I will meet you in Alabama, at Cedar Bluff, on the Rome and Decatur Railroad, tomorrow (Saturday) afternoon at 5 o'clock. Unless I hear to the contrary, I shall expect to find you there at that hour.

My friend, Mr. King, will deliver this note.
Respectfully,
J.D. Williamson

Word had gotten out that there was to be a duel, and a substantial attempt was made by government officials to intercept the principals to avoid bloodshed. Governor John B. Gordon of Georgia, sent telegrams to the governors of Tennessee and Alabama asking them to stop the duel and arrest the principals. The same request was sent out to law officers at Rome and Cedartown, as well as to Anniston, Alabama. Alabama's Governor Tom Seay did the same for likely points in his state.

The *Atlanta Constitution* as well as the *Atlanta Journal* (separate newspapers at that time) eventually learned of the details of the duel. E.W. Barrett from the *Constitution* was assigned to the Williamson party and Edward C. Bruffey was assigned to the Calhoun group. Gordon N. Hurtel from the *Journal* was given orders to stick with Williamson and his party until a resolution was reached or until the duel had occurred.

As a result of the publicity surrounding the scheduled duel, the task of actually reaching the appointed meeting place was no easy chore for either party. Friday night, August 9, Captain Jackson met Pat Calhoun and both departed on a sleeping car from Union Station in downtown Atlanta. They overnighted at the Anniston Inn in Anniston, Alabama. The next morning, they slipped out the rear door of the inn.

According to Bruffey's newspaper account of the incident, while Williamson and his party were making their way to the duel site, Jackson had taken Pat Calhoun out for some target practice. Jackson reportedly tossed a coin in the air and instructed Calhoun to hit it. After five shots had been fired, the results showed three of the rounds had hit the mark – a somewhat amazing feat.

After witnessing Calhoun's accuracy with the pistol, Jackson reportedly remarked, "That's good Pat. Now, if we can't have peace and must have war, and you can do that – well, you will come home alive."

Calhoun spent the next couple of hours napping at a friend's house. The two men had sent for their luggage at the hotel, but reportedly were forced to abandon the property when they saw lawmen following the carriage conveying the luggage.

When they went to catch the 11:00 o'clock train, Jackson recognized the Anniston city police chief at the depot, so a quick decision was made to backtrack through the woods to nearby Leathertown to board the train there. After having lunch in Gadsden, the men boarded a Rome and Decatur train to be on their way to the site of the duel.

Meanwhile, Captain Williamson's trip to the meeting place was turning out to be quite an adventure as well. Gordon Hurtel, the *Journal* reporter, was able to give a detailed account because he faithfully followed the Williamson party.

Hurtel left Union Station in Atlanta at 8:00 a.m. He boarded a west-bound Western & Atlantic train to find that Williamson and his party were occupying the parlor car. His party consisted of Mr. Jack King, Williamson's second; Judge H.B. Tompkins; and Major C.B. Lowe. Dr. Henry Battey boarded the train in Rome.

The men then set out for Kingston, Georgia, where Williamson's private car was waiting. The private car was coupled to the engine and the train set out for Rome.

Hurtel, the *Journal* reporter, was a determined news correspondent, but he suspected that his ride would be short-lived because he had been spotted. He believed that Rome would be his place of departure from the group and he was not far off the mark.

"As I expected," Hurtel explained in his article, "the special car was uncoupled from [the other cars behind it] and run through town at the rate of twenty miles an hour. Two miles the other side of Rome, Mr. Jack King discovered me hiding on the steps [of the car]. The train was stopped and I was put off like a tramp, and had to count the cross-ties for two miles through the hot sun [back to Rome]."

Little did Williamson and Hurtel know, however, that fate would bring them together again where they would become allies. With the help of E.W. Barrett, who had been put off the train along with Hurtel, the two men were able to get an engine and engineer (W.T. Dozier) to drive a locomotive for them.

After procuring the locomotive "Daniel S. Printup" from the Forrestville Station in north Rome, the men set out in hot pursuit of Williamson and his party. They encountered them sooner than expected.

Roughly two or three miles down the track, Captain Williamson's train had been sidetracked at the Rome & Decatur junction for lack of an engineer who knew the route. Seizing the opportunity, Hurtel offered the men his engineer in exchange for the privilege of riding along with them. Williamson took Hurtel up on the offer and the men were welcomed into his private car.

While in the private car, Barrett and Hurtel were given a fine lunch, cigars and champagne. Hurtel later noted, "This was the same car from which I had been fired like a tramp an hour earlier."

While Williamson was awaiting the departure of his party, the men went into the nearby woods in order to allow the captain an opportunity to practice with his revolver. The target practice was short-lived, however, because a runner alerted the men that a sheriff from Floyd County, with a deputy, was coming down the tracks. In order to elude the sheriff, Captain Williamson and Jack King ran through the woods to a point a couple of miles down the track where they re-boarded the private car.

After picking the two men up, the train was once again on its way to Cedar Bluff, Alabama. It reached its destination about 4:00 p.m. in the afternoon. At Cedar Bluff, the train was side-tracked for an east-bound passenger train, and no sooner had the cars come to a halt when someone called out, "Here comes the sheriff!" The men all scrambled to get back on the private car.

According to a vivid description provided by journalist Hurtel, "We were in Cherokee County, Alabama, and the sheriff was one of those bushy, black-whiskered fellows with a broad-brimmed hat who meant business."

Hurtel went on to explain that Williamson's private car did not get far before it was caught and returned to the sheriff. Williamson, however, was nowhere to be found.

Meanwhile, Pat Calhoun and Henry Jackson had been on the regular passenger train coming from Atlanta by way of Anniston. The train stopped and Calhoun got off and was promptly arrested by the sheriff who said "Mr. Williamson, consider yourself under arrest."

If not for Captain Seay – who was known by the sheriff and attested that Mr. Calhoun was not Captain Williamson – the situation might have become even more confusing. Calhoun, however, was released and the Chinese fire-drill continued.

The sheriff would not give up easily, however. He swore he would find Williamson, never realizing he had just released the other principal, Mr. Calhoun. Both trains were searched, but the men were not found. Pat Calhoun and Captain Jackson were locked up in a closet in the private car. Captain Williamson and Jack King were hidden in a closet on the regular passenger train. These two men were determined to end the day with a duel, come hell

Patrick Calhoun as he appeared in later years.

Despite John D. Williamson's accomplishments in life, little more than a coarse illustration of him is known to be in existence today.

or high water.

When the passenger train was finally released, it carried Captain Williamson, Mr. King, Dr. Battey, Captain Williamson's private secretary, Captain Seay and Gordon Hurtel. The train continued down the tracks to Raynes' Station, five miles closer to Rome. Calhoun's train also arrived at Rayne's Station and it seemed the two

At the time of the duel, Captain John D. Williamson, president of the Chattanooga, Rome & Columbus Railroad Company, resided part-time at the Armstrong Hotel on Howard Street (present-day Second Avenue) in Rome, Georgia. (Photo courtesy of Rome Area History Museum)

The Armstrong Hotel burned in 1932, and was rebuilt. The stonework around the lower level of the new structure in this photo is from the orginal building. (Photo by Deborah Malone)

duelists might be about to effect their stated mission.

The bushy-bearded sheriff, however, was a determined man, and also proceeded to Raynes' Station. He was then led to believe that both of the dueling parties were on the train and that apologies had been made and everything was settled.

After the sheriff – being convinced that everything was alright – had departed, the men all got off the train. The seconds were arranging preliminaries and Hurtel was wiring the *Journal*. About that time, four men, believed to be deputies, riding mules and brandishing shotguns, came clamoring up and one of them shouted, "If anybody moves, I'll shoot." One has to wonder at this point if the lawmen were going to kill someone to avoid a killing.

Taking their chances, the men scrambled for the train. The engineer ducked down in the cab and pulled the throttle wide open. The previously somber preparations for a duel were quickly taking on the appearance of comical hijinks.

The train sped away from the lawmen. Three miles down the tracks, the men once again disembarked and the seconds began conferring. It was already beginning to get dark. As Jackson and King were talking someone yelled, "Look out! Everybody on the train!"

The warning had come just in time. The four men with the shotguns seemed to be just as determined as the black-whiskered sheriff. Once again, everyone jumped aboard the train which again headed down the tracks. About four or five miles nearer to Rome, the men stopped again to prepare for the duel.

The final destination for the duel was Farill, Alabama, on the Farill Plantation (about three miles east of the location where General Nathan Bedford Forrest captured Col. Streight's men in the battle of 1863). A small natural clearing in an oak grove was selected for the duel.

Captain Seay made one last futile attempt to stop the affair, but the men had come too far to abandon the fight now. Captain Williamson, having the choice of weapons, chose the hammerless Smith & Wesson five shooter. By this time, it was well into dusk, and the light was fading as the moon rose over the treetops in the east.

The two seconds, Mr. King and Captain Jackson, were attempting to load the pistols for their principals. Captain Jackson, being unfamiliar with this pistol, was having trouble loading his. Mr. Bruffey, a journalist with the *Constitution*, spoke up, "I can help Cap."

Within seconds, an explosion broke the silence in the dark woods. "There, my finger's gone!" Mr. Bruffey suddenly shouted, walking off and holding up a bloody hand. A part of the third finger of his right hand had been torn away by the ball.

"Let me dress it," said Dr. Cooper who was standing by. "Oh, go on with the fight," Bruffey huffed as he wrapped a handkerchief about his wounded finger. "A finger don't amount to anything."

Captain Jackson then loaded Mr. Calhoun's pistol and handed it to him. As the two men were preparing to face off with each other, Captain Seay made one last desperate attempt to put a stop to the duel. "As a citizen of Georgia and in the name of the Governor of Alabama" cried out Seay, "I call upon you to stop!" Seay obviously didn't know which state he was in, so he was covering all the bases.

His pleas, however, fell upon deaf ears once again.

"Gentlemen, are you ready?" called out Mr. King. The men acknowledged their readiness. The paces were counted off and the command to "Fire!" was given.

Six rapid shots followed the command. The deed was done. All the men held their breath, waiting to see which duelist crumpled to the ground. Both seconds ran to their principals to see if they were injured and discovered they were not.

There had been some confusion as to the procedure that was to be used. Captain Williamson had thought that all shots were to be fired in succession, so he had fired all five of his shots at once. Pat Calhoun, however, had fired only once, thus leaving four balls remaining in his weapon. What would Calhoun do with those remaining shots?

"Mr. Williamson," Calhoun intoned, "I have four remaining balls which I have the right to fire at you. I now ask if you will withdraw the statement you made before the legislative committee."

"I will," Williamson responded, "pro-

Both Pat Calhoun and Capt. John D. Williamson departed for the dueling site from old Union Terminal in downtown Atlanta, pictured here in 1889. In time, bridges and viaducts were built over this railroad gulch, hiding it from sight. The buildings to the right in this photo lay dormant for decades, until a popular entertainment complex known as "Underground Atlanta" brought them renewed life. The buildings on the left, however, including Union Terminal in the distance, have all long since disappeared from the Atlanta landscape.

The Farill homeplace in Farill, Alabama, just over the Georgia state line, was the site at which the duel took place. The Rome & Decatur Railroad tracks once existed beside this structure. A depot (demolished in years past) once was located to the left of the home. (Photo by Debbie Malone)

vided you will say that you meant no personal reflection upon me."

It quickly became apparent that despite the circumstances, Captain Williamson was still refusing to unequivocally retract his statement. And even though he had braved the hail of bullets from Captain Williamson, Pat Calhoun, to his credit, had no further

TALES OF THE RAILS IN GEORGIA

E.W. Barrett, a reporter with the *Atlanta Constitution* and Gordon N. Hurtel, reporting for the *Atlanta Journal*, were able to secure the locomotive "Daniel S. Printup" (above) from the Forrestville Station in north Rome, to chase Captain John Williamson and his party to the site of the duel.

Author Debbie Malone stands on the former roadbed of the Rome & Decatur Railroad at Farill, Alabama. The duelists traveled on the line to this site.

desire to fire at his opponent.

After a short additional verbal exchange between the two men, Pat Calhoun spoke these words: "Mr. Williamson, in my remarks before the legislative committee you personally did not enter my mind." Calhoun then raised his pistol in the air and fired his remaining four balls into the air.

"Since you have stated you meant nothing personal in your remarks," Williamson said, "I now withdraw the statement I made before the committee." The two men shook hands and ended the matter.

The party retired to the train and celebrated with cigars and champagne. They arrived in Rome a few minutes after 9 p.m.

News of the results was telegraphed to Atlanta.

According to records, this duel was the last such formal incident associated with Georgia, and since it actually occurred in Alabama, it may have been the final such occurrence there as well. If so, it was a dramatic final curtain for an old custom, despite the somewhat comical circumstances under which this incident took place.

Several of the sites mentioned in this incident still exist today. Captain Williamson's residence – the Armstrong Hotel – burned in 1932, but was rebuilt as the Greystone Hotel. The Greystone, which still exists today, boasts some of the original stonework from the Armstrong, and is listed on the *National Register of Historic Places*.

Much of downtown Rome remains the same as it was in 1889, with many of the buildings being from that era. Howard Street, known today as Second Avenue, does not have a trolley track down the center any longer, but it is just as busy as it was a hundred years ago.

The Forrestville Station no longer exists, but the Rome & Decatur junction where Williamson's car was side-tracked is still in use today.

A trip to Farill, Alabama, to the dueling site can be an adventure. Judy Smith and her husband live next to the old Farill homeplace. Judy had once lived in the Farill house, and can still show interested parties the roadbed where the railroad once existed beside the house. Even though the exact location of the duel is unknown today, it was quite near this vicinity.

It is unknown today if Captain Williamson and Pat Calhoun lived long fruitful lives, but it is known that on a hot August night in 1889, their lives were spared that day, and happiness reigned supreme once again – at least for the moment.

Endnotes

1/ Battey, George Magruder; "A History of Rome and Floyd County;" Cherokee Publishing Company, Marietta, Georgia, (1922).

The Old Roswell Railroad

It once transported a U.S. President for a visit to his mother's family home in Roswell many years ago. By 1999, the Roswell Railroad was little more than a fleeting memory in the minds of a few old-timers in swiftly-growing north Fulton County.

Some long-time Roswell residents still remember an old railroad called the "Roswell Railroad" from many years ago. Evidence of this old grade, as well as the grade of the rail line which had once provided access to Georgia Power's Morgan Falls Dam during its construction, is still visible.

Persons interested should read a book written by a historian named Michael Hitt. The publication, *The History Of The Roswell Railroad*, has excellent maps and information.

It was the Roswell Manufacturing Company which, in 1853, first realized the need for a rapid and dependable method of transportation. In 1863, the large mill underwrote the cost of grading the roadbed for a rail line southward toward Atlanta. A charter was granted by the Georgia State Legislature and slave labor was used for the early grading.

Interrupted by the U.S. Civil War, it wasn't until 1881 that the railroad was finished, equipped and in operation. And even though it was operating, the builders had elected to build the Roswell Railroad Depot on the south side of the Chattahoochee River. The construction of a trestle across the river, was prohibitively expensive at that time.

Explorers interested in retracing this historic old railroad should begin at the corner of Peachtree Road and Chamblee-Dunwoody Road in Chamblee. This was once the site of the Chamblee Depot, serviced by Southern Railway. It was also the beginning (junction) of the Roswell Railroad as it was originally graded in 1863 and used until

Interrupted by the U.S. Civil War, it wasn't until 1881 that the railroad was finished, equipped and in operation.

67

"Old Buck" on the Roswell Railroad provided reliable service for many years. The Roswell Railroad Depot was on the south side of the Chattahoochee River near present-day Roberts Drive.

The old Roswell Railroad Depot (Southern Railway) pictured here once stood near Roberts Drive just south of the Chattahoochee River in Roswell.

finally abandoned in 1921.

Today, at the original site of the Chamblee Depot, there is no evidence of the old grade. Modern construction (the grade once existed through what today is the site of a Woolworth store on Peachtree Industrial) has erased most signs of the rail line. Despite this fact the cautious observer can still spot the grade running through the backyards of houses in the 3800 block of Ensign Drive.

At Nancy Creek crossing north of Chamblee First United Methodist Church, the trestle site was still plainly visible a few years ago. Today, however, there is no evidence of the grade. This is due mainly to the thick undergrowth around the creek today.

A big "cut" does still exist behind the Arby's restaurant at the eastbound ramp to Interstate 285. There is no further evidence of the old grade however, since recent construction has altered the landscape. Also, present-day Chamblee-Dunwoody Road exists on top of the old railroad grade for quite a distance.

The Roswell Railroad also once extended to Morgan Falls Dam and Power Plant in Sandy Springs. The rail line was used to transport building materials and equipment to this electrical power generation plant.

If one visits this site today, he or she will immediately notice how badly the lake has silted in since 1904 when the dam was built. An amazing amount of construction has occurred upriver since that time, not the least of which was Lake Lanier. All of this development has caused horrendous siltation, filling up the impoundment behind Morgan Falls Dam. Today, there is very little storage available in the lake. This also means there is no provision for the storage of flood waters in the lake today. The water level is already at the top of the dam.

Back down at the Chattahoochee River, explorers can see where the railroad followed Powers's Branch down to the Chattahoochee and up the river to the dam. Modern construction has obliterated almost all traces of the railroad, except for a cut or two visible along the driveway from Roswell Road (U.S. 19) into the Morgan Falls

Station apartment complex.

If one drives out Roswell Road and across the Chattahoochee River, and turns right onto Azalea Drive/Riverside Road, and then almost immediately turns left into a parking lot on the left which provides access to the National Park Service's Vickery Creek nature trail, he or she can still clearly see the uncompleted pre-Civil War roadbed for the old Roswell Railroad. It was never finished nor used on the north side of the Chattahoochee since the huge trestle across the river was never completed.

Below this amazing grade lies scenic Vickery Creek. There are hiking trails at creek level on both sides of the creek. This lovely park is surrounded by the historic town of Roswell, and the park itself has many scenic and historic sites (including remnants of several old mills).

The railroad grade has rock retaining walls in several places where it runs high above the bank of the creek. One deep dead-end cut is strongly reminiscent of those of the old Blue Ridge Railroad which had been partially constructed across Rabun County before the U.S. Civil War ceased operations on it too.

The Roswell Railroad began service on September 1, 1881, with Isaac "Ike" Martin Roberts at the throttle as engineer. Since the headquarters of the new line was located at its junction in Roswell, Ike took up residence in the Roswell area, living in boarding houses for a number of years.

In 1893, Ike married Nancy Turley (1869-1924) from Roswell. In 1895, after the birth of their first two children, Ike and Nancy moved into their own home, newly built for them on Roberts Road, across from the depot. This historic home still stands (as of this writing).

At one time or another in his lifetime, Ike owned two of Roswell's best-known

Isaac "Ike" Roberts, was photographed here as a dapper gentleman in this formal studio photograph circa 1920s. The Roswell Railroad was in operation for 44 years, and Roberts served as engineer on the line for the entire duration. His former home still stands today on Roberts Drive in Roswell which was so-named in his honor. (Photo courtesy of Henry C. Wing, Jr.)

antebellum homes – Bulloch Hall and Primrose Cottage. In 1905, when he owned Bulloch Hall, he had the distinguished honor of transporting U.S. President Theodore Roosevelt on the Roswell Railroad. The always ebullient Roosevelt had traveled to Roswell to pay a visit to Bulloch Hall, originally owned and built by his grandparents, and the place where his mother and father had been married.

Today, the historic old Roswell Railroad is little more than a dim memory for the few who experienced it firsthand.

The Day The Railroad Came To Roswell - Almost

Industry and early growth attracted railroad developers to this town in the 1880's. A line was graded and rails were laid, but the mighty Chattahoochee River proved too formidable for completion of the line into downtown Roswell.

A document from the President's Office of the Roswell Manufacturing Company in Roswell, Georgia, dated July, 1880, said: "The question of securing for this Company a better connection with Commercial centres, a quicker and more economical method of transportation than by wagon, for the production, supplies and merchandise, has received the serious consideration of every President who has charge of your interest at this point." The letter, in effect, constituted a plea for the completion and operation of a railroad line, long-planned and eagerly awaited by the community of Roswell for almost two decades.

Up to that time, as the President continued: "All freights to and from Roswell have to be transported to and from Marietta or Doraville (both of which did have railroads) over common, and in winter, very rough roads by wagons, which require ten mules, five wagons, five teamsters, one smith and helper."

A proposition eventually was made to the citizens of Roswell to pledge a bonus of $10,000 for the owners of the railroad road-bed, but "only when the road is completed and in operation." Ultimately, $7,000 was raised, and the

A proposition eventually was made to the citizens of Roswell to pledge a bonus of $10,000 for the owners of the railroad road-bed, but "only when the road is completed and in operation."

president asked the company's board to authorize payment of the remaining $3,000, with the stipulation that "not one dollar shall be paid until the road is finished and in operation." The emphatic nature of the statement dramatizes the problems which had plagued the 17-year history of the unfinished railroad line.

In 1863, the city of Roswell had obtained a charter in an Act that provided for the organization of the Atlanta and Roswell Railroad Company, and the construction of a railroad from Roswell to Atlanta (actually to connect with the Western and Atlantic Railroad). No action was taken however, until 1870, when the Atlanta and Richmond Air-Line was constructing a line from Atlanta to Charlotte. The original charter was amended to consolidate the Atlanta and Roswell Railroad Company with the Atlanta and Richmond Air-Line, and provided for the connection of the Roswell line to it.

In 1874, the failure of the Atlanta and Richmond Air-Line meant bankruptcy for the Atlanta and Roswell Railroad Company, and thus another delay in the plans for a train from Roswell to railroad lines in Atlanta.

Following a number of legal proceedings during the next year that included liens, foreclosures on liens, judgements, inheritances, various legal decrees, sales of interests, conveyances of properties, etc., a reorganization occurred, and the Roswell Railroad Company was formed. The new corporation renewed its relations with the Atlanta and Richmond Air-Line which had also been newly reorganized as the Atlanta and Charlotte Air-Line.

The Atlanta and Charlotte received 201 out of a total issue of 400 shares of capital stock of the Roswell Railroad Company, and thus secured control of the rail line. The road was then completed as a narrow-gauge line from Chamblee to Roswell.

Before the Roswell Railroad was opened for operation however, the Roswell and Doraville had succeeded to all the rights of the Atlanta and Charlotte Air-Line, and had begun operating the line. This relationship continued until 1894, when the Southern Railway Company succeeded to the same relationship because of its assumption of the Atlanta and Charlotte Air-Line.

The Roswell Railroad began service on September 1, 1881, with Isaac Martin Roberts, better known as "Ike," at the throttle as engineer. With Ike at the helm, a unique era in Roswell history began.

Isaac Roberts was born in Gaston County, North Carolina, on February 28, 1853. He was the son of John Morgan Roberts (1827-1865) and Lucinda White Roberts (1823-1895).

Lucinda was the daughter of Isaac White (1798-1850) and Polly (Mary) Falls White (1800-1871). Isaac White was the son of James White (1743-1823) and Sarah Mary Givens White (1752-1836).

With the exception of James White, who was born in Pennsylvania, all of the others were born in North Carolina.

When Ike Roberts was 19, he left home and walked 45 miles to Spartanburg, South Carolina, where he joined a construction gang which was building the Atlanta and Charlotte Air-Line. When the road was completed, he secured a job as "wood-passer" on one

The right-of-way of the Roswell Railroad was 9.8 miles.

of the engines.

In 1874, Ike went on the road as a fireman on a freight train between Atlanta and Charlotte. In three years, he had advanced up the ladder, becoming an engineer on that line.

Early on, Ike became involved with the construction work for the road-bed of the line extending to Roswell; he also worked as an agent to secure the rights-of-way for the Atlanta and Charlotte Air-Line. Since the headquarters of the new line was located at its junction in Roswell, Ike took up residence in that town, and lived in boarding houses for a number of years.

The right-of-way of the Roswell Railroad was 9.8 miles. Its route, along what are today's automobile roads and streets, began at the Chamblee Depot. It went to Peachtree Industrial Boulevard, where it angled up North Peachtree Road, which became first North Shallowford (under I-285) and next Chamblee-Dunwoody Road. From there, the line went through Dunwoody to Roberts Road, and then up the long incline to where it ended just short of Roswell Road.

The Roswell Depot, ironically, was not in Roswell. It was located across the Chattahoochee River on its southeast bank. The grading of road-bed up the banks of Big (Vickery) Creek to extend the rails into Roswell was begun, but never completed.

During its days of operation, the train would leave Roswell at 7:00 a.m., and arrive back at 10:00 a.m. Then it would leave again at 3:00 p.m. and arrive back at 5:00 p.m. The train was called "the Dinkey" by most people, and "Old Buck" by others.

If flagged, the Dinkey would stop at any place along the line to pick up passengers or to let them off. However, there were four regular stops between Roswell and Chamblee: "Powers," near what is now the intersection of Pitts Road and Spalding Drive; "Morgan Falls Junction," where Roberts Drive crosses Spalding Drive; "Dunwoody Station" and "Wilson's Mill" near Peeler Road. A branch line was built from the Morgan Falls Junction to what is now Morgan Falls, to carry materials to build the Georgia Power Company dam and plant.

The train had an engine with tender, a combination baggage car and coach for passengers, freight cars, and flat cars. The passenger compartment had a restroom, a heater, and a water cooler. A glass case at one end held a saw, an axe, a crow-bar, and tools for emergencies.

On the run to Chamblee, the train hauled a number of cars loaded with lumber, stove-wood, vegetables, and fruit. On its return to Roswell, the cargo would consist of supplies, manufactured goods, and fertilizer. Horse-drawn buggies ("taxis") would meet the train at the depot, and take passengers across the covered bridge into Roswell.

In addition to engineer Ike Roberts, there was a crew consisting of a fireman, a conductor, a brake-baggageman, and a flagman. But it is Ike, whose name - even now - is almost synonymous with the train itself.

In 1893, Ike married Nancy Turley (1869-1924) from Roswell. In 1895, after their first two children were born, they moved into their own house, newly built for them, on Roberts Road, across from the train depot. Ike owned about 700

If flagged, the Dinkey would stop at any place along the line to pick up passengers.

acres of land in that area.

Ike and Nancy had five children, all girls: Lula, Laura, Edith, Sarah, and Alda. It has been said that, even though Ike had no sons to carry on his name, he had eternal connections with many of the prominent families of Roswell through his daughters' marriages to a Foster, a Lyon, a Wing, and a Bowden.

At one time or another in Ike's lifetime, he owned two of Roswell's best-known antebellum homes, Bulloch Hall and Primrose Cottage. He also owned a lumber company, a dairy, and, in a partnership – the Civil War-era Laurel Mill complex – including the manager's office which still stands today. He was also at one time chairman of the board of the Roswell Bank.

In 1903, heavier rails were installed on the Roswell line, thus eliminating the original narrow-gauge tracks.

In 1905, when Ike owned Bulloch Hall, an event of unsurpassed historic significance occurred in Roswell. The president of the United States – Teddy Roosevelt – journeyed to Roswell to pay a visit to Bulloch Hall which was his mother's ancestral home where she and his father were married. He not only arrived on the train "the Dinkey" with Ike Roberts at the throttle, but was visiting his mother's former home, now owned by Ike.

In 1921, service on the Roswell Railroad was discontinued. Ike Roberts made a trip to Washington and somehow came away with the deed to the Roswell Depot property, paying only $1.00 in the transaction. Afterwards, he used the depot as a barn.

Ike continued on in the railroad business until his death. He went from the Dinkey to the "Air-Line Belle," a line with daily runs between Atlanta and Toccoa.

When he died in 1930 at the age of 77, Ike Roberts was the oldest engineer in the Charlotte division of the Southern Railway, both in age and in length of service. The heart attack which felled him occurred at old Terminal Station in Atlanta soon after he reported for work.

Ike's obituary claimed that he was "one of the fastest and smoothest engineers in the service of the road." The obit continued by explaining that even in his last years, Ike "would set a passenger train in motion without a perceptible jar, and he would nurse it to a stop again with the smoothness of an automobile slowing down."

During his 58 years of service on Southern locomotives, Ike was never involved in a single major accident.

As of this writing, reminders of Ike and the Roswell Railroad still exist. Well-known Roberts Drive on the southeast bank of the Chattahoochee River was the site of Ike's residence for many years, and bears his name. His imposing home on that road still stands, well-preserved and in continuous use since it was built.

Occasionally, during the past few decades, new home builders and/or road construction crews have unearthed a piece of track or some other artifact from the Roswell Railroad. And perhaps, if it was an old-timer from the area who came upon the bit of railroad memorabilia, Ike Roberts and "the Dinkey" inevitably were remembered in a nostalgic moment or two.

References

Fairfax Harrison, A History of the Legal Development of the Railroad System of Southern Railway Company; Washington D.C.: Southern Railway Company, 1901

Elizabeth L. Davis and Ethel W. Spruill, The Story of Dunwoody, Its Heritages and Horizons, 1821-1975; Atlanta: Williams Printing Co., 1975

Lois Coogle, Sandy Springs - Past Tense; Atlanta: Decor Master Co., 1971

Darlene Walsh, Roswell: A Pictorial History and Roswell, Georgia: Roswell Historical Society, 1985.)

The Southeastern Railway Museum

Take a ride on a vintage locomotive or explore memorabilia involving everything from Casey Jones to a luxury Pullman coach from yesteryear. It's all there at the Southeastern.

Railroad enthusiasts are gradually discovering an interesting way to spend a Saturday morning or afternoon in Duluth, Georgia, where the Southeastern Railway Museum is picking up steam - no pun intended. The Atlanta Chapter of the National Railway Historical Society (NRHS) was organized in 1959 with the goal of collecting, preserving and displaying items and data historically significant to our nation's railroads. As a result, the Southeastern Railroad Museum, a project of the Society, has evolved into a bonafide entertainment complex and repository for railroad memorabilia.

Accomplished mostly from the donated time and labor of former and current railroad employees, virtually all the displays at the museum (including many vintage and historic locomotives and railcars and memorabilia) are well worth a visit. All of the equipment and machinery are authentic, surviving from a day long departed. Much of the memorabilia has been donated, but a significant

All of the equipment and machinery are authentic, surviving from a day long departed.

The Southeastern Railway Museum

portion has also been purchased.

According to Atlanta resident Rutherford "Ruddy" Ellis, many times, the easy part is obtaining old equipment. The hard part is finding volunteers willing to endure the heat, long hours and hard labor necessary to reclaim the old engines and railcars from the rust and rot of years of neglect.

The cost involved in new or refurbished parts is no small matter either. Still, the museum is making steady progress. Today, visitors are treated to everything from an authentic train register with Casey Jones' signature, to tours of retired passenger coaches, aged steam and coal-fired locomotives (over 40 units of railroad rolling stock), and much much more.

One example of the items of interest here is a special Pullman coach called "Superb," which was operated during the golden era of railroad travel. Sometimes referred to as the "Cardinal's Car," this special conveyance once transported President Warren Harding to San Francisco, and, following his death, returned his body home to Washington, D.C.

The museum's library contains over 7,000 catalogued items of railroad memorabilia. Rail fans can leaf through train and railroad magazines dating from the early 1930s, old railroad posters, actual railroad company time-tables, and endless additional memorabilia.

In the active "Comer Shop," visitors may witness engine and rail car restorations in progress.

And as a special thrill for youngsters, rides on a full-size commercial steam locomotive are available during special hours from April through October.

This "hands-on" working museum is located at the intersection of Pleasant Hill Road and Buford Highway (U.S. 23). For admission rates and more information, contact the Southeastern Railroad Museum.

A historic engine and Pullman cars offer rides around the rail yards of the Southeastern Railway Museum to interested youngsters. The museum includes a wide range of railroad memorabilia and over 40 historic railroad locomotives, passenger cars and cabooses available for viewing by patrons. The vintage trains and associated memorabilia are carefully restored and maintained at a repair shop staffed mainly by volunteers at the facility. (Photo by Olin Jackson)

Recollections Of An Engineer From Yesteryear

Hoyt Tench And The Old "TF"

He rode the precipitous rails between Cornelia, Georgia, and Franklin, North Carolina, on the famed Tallulah Falls Railroad for many years. Today, his memories of those experiences are the stuff of legends.

Railroading gets into your blood. If you don't believe it, just examine the career of the late Hoyt Tench of Cornelia, Georgia, who spent thirty-eight years keeping the engines fired and the trains rolling.

Tench and his bride, Catherine Dalton, were married May 27, 1939. In an interview prior to his death he admitted to being only eighteen years of age at the time. "And you're not supposed to ask how old my bride was," he said.

Her father, Beecher Dalton, was employed by the Stewart and Jones Company and Doubletrack, and worked in railroad construction. Mr. Dalton's work on the Tallulah Falls (TFRR) Railroad made it possible for Tench to be one of the first to know when an employment opening existed.

In 1942, an engineer transferred from the Tallulah Falls Railroad to the Southern Railroad. A fireman was promoted to engineer and an opening was suddenly available for a new fireman. Hoyt Tench "hired on," beginning a railroading career which lasted until 1980, a total of thirty-eight years.

Early Disaster

The first day on the Tallulah Falls Railroad almost became the last for young Tench. It began with the new fireman shoveling coal into a cart which he then rolled to the train and dumped into the engine tender (coal car). This effort was repeated four or five times until enough coal was loaded to make the trip from Cornelia, Georgia, to Franklin, North Carolina and back.

Once the coal loading was completed, the engineer next began teaching young Tench all the things he needed to observe and do during the trip. The duties included watching the tracks ahead to make sure no obstructions were on them, as well as looking backward to insure that none of the boxcars had jumped the track or developed "hot boxes" in the wheel bearings.

Shortly thereafter on his first trip, Tench found himself making numerous interesting stops along the way at spots like Clarkesville, Demorest, Lakemont, Tiger, Clayton, Mountain City, Dillard, and on and on until they reached Franklin, North

Carolina. There, the engine was turned around, the box cars were disengaged and parked for removal by another later train, and new cars were hooked to the engine for the return trip home to Cornelia.

As the train moved southward, it soon passed back through the little hamlet of Mountain City in northern Rabun County, Georgia. The train picked up speed, entered a curve, and then suddenly began to shake and rattle terribly.

A backward glance by the new fireman revealed a sight which would strike terror in the hearts of even the most inveterate of railroad men. Dust was flying, cars were bouncing, and a derailment seemed imminent.

Tench immediately alerted the engineer who gradually slowed the train to a halt. Miraculously, only one boxcar had jumped the track, and it had remained hooked to the other boxcars. The task now was one of getting the heavy derailed boxcar back onto the tracks.

Crew members, accustomed to the chore, began removing huge jacks – specially designed for this purpose – from the train. It took hours of "jacking and chocking" the errant boxcar before it was righted and the train was allowed to proceed.

By the time the train reached Cornelia, Hoyt Tench had just about decided that railroading was a job he'd be happy to let someone else do. The work was too hard. The hours were too long. There was too much to learn, and it was very dangerous. After a good supper at home and a much-needed night of rest, however, he decided to give it another try.

The second day was much less eventful. The instructions and duties didn't seem quite so formidable this time out either. Thus began a railroad career spanning a time period from the second World War to the 1980s.

Hospitality On The Rails

Neighborliness has long been a characteristic of Southerners, particularly north Georgians. This sense of camaraderie and compassion was demonstrated many times by the people who lived along the rails, as well as by the railroad men themselves.

When a wreck or derailment occurred, citizens living nearby rushed to the scene to render whatever aid could be given. In cases of injury, neighbors along the tracks were the first to summon help and render first aid.

Sometimes the roles were reversed too. Train workers on one occasion noted that certain families living near the tracks were clad in threadbare clothing and some children didn't have shoes, even on the coldest days of winter as they waved to the train crew.

Inquiring about the children, crew members learned that they were not in school because of inadequate clothing. The good-hearted trainmen discreetly learned the number of children, the ages, sex and approximate sizes of each, then purchased clothing and had it distributed to the children. Santa Claus was an exciting event that year – both for the parents and children at this spot.

Dealing With Danger

During the years the Tallulah Falls Railroad was in service, numerous frightening events occurred. Hoyt Tench, though much more fortunate than most, witnessed his share of accidents and natural disasters.

One disaster in which he thankfully was not involved, occurred on February 7, 1927, when one of the Tallulah Falls trains was passing across the high trestle over Hazel Creek. This wooden railroad bridge had been invisibly weakened over the years, and collapsed beneath the weight of the train, spilling the engine and its crew to the ground. Three people were killed.

The accident undoubtedly would have been even more disastrous had not a piece of timber fallen across the whistle arm, releasing steam from the engine. It otherwise, undoubtedly would have exploded, according to Tench, almost surely killing additional personnel. The engine – though

TALES OF THE RAILS IN GEORGIA

The late Hoyt O. Tench, sporting his aged Southern Railway engineer's hat, spent thirty-eight years as an employee on the railroads of north Georgia, including the Tallulah Falls Railroad. He is joined by his wife, the former Catherine Dalton.

"They always said the Panther Creek trestle was the highest," Tench said, "but I think the Wiley trestle (photographed here in 1939) was the most dangerous. It had five decks."

The engineer was killed and the fireman badly injured when the TF derailed south of Tiger, Georgia, on August 23, 1920. The train was carrying summer camp children. Because of accidents such as this, passenger service was eventually discontinued on the Tallulah Falls Railroad.

severely damaged – was retrieved, rebuilt and placed back into service. Hoyt Tench was fireman for this rebuilt engine (#73) for a period of time.

On a return trip from Franklin on another occasion, Tench and his crew experienced a scare similar to the trestle-spill of Engine 73. As they approached the high trestle just north of Dillard, everything appeared to be in very good order, but in the middle of the trestle, a loud pop sounded as the train was passing over. The engine gave a lurch, but the entire train passed over safely.

A repair crew sent to examine the trestle discovered that a large main supporting timber had indeed snapped under the huge weight. If the train had been heavily loaded as it crossed, the entire trestle would no doubt have collapsed, spilling the train and causing a loss of life as had occurred with #73.

Another experience vivid in Hoyt Tench's memory happened during a severe thunderstorm one summer afternoon. "The train was returning from Franklin," Tench explained, "and lightning was flashing constantly. Suddenly, a huge bolt struck some distance ahead of the train, then began traveling up the rails straight toward the engine. It (the tremendous electrical charge) passed over the driver wheels on the engine and continued along the entire train as if it followed the rails until it reached a wheel. It flashed up, over and down the wheels, and on over the rails, continuing until it had run the entire length of the train and continued on beyond. Neither engineer nor fireman was injured."

At the next stop, Tench and the engineer talked to other crew members. They, too, had witnessed the phenomenon and were equally amazed that no one was harmed by the lightning nor was the train damaged by the huge charge.

Pranks On The Rails

"Boys will be boys," as the saying goes. Some who lived along the railroad tracks delighted in a pastime that was as dangerous and troublesome for the train crew as it was fun and exciting for the young tykes who engaged in it.

The deed was usually performed on a portion of the rails that were slightly inclined up a slope. Such places were easy to find along the mountainous terrain of the Tallulah Falls Railroad.

Once the spot was located, the mischievous perpetrators applied grease to the rails for some distance. If the next train traveling the tracks was heavily loaded or proceeding slowly, the engine would immediately lose traction on the grease and stall.

In order to extract the train from the slick rails, the engineer had two choices. He could either reverse the engine, back it up a considerable distance on the tracks and then try to gain enough momentum to pass over the grease, or he could stop the train so that the crewmen could wipe the grease off the rails and place dirt on them for traction.

Runaway Engine

Cold weather always presented special problems on the Tallulah Falls Railroad. Crew members had to check equipment to insure that it was in tip-top shape. They examined signal lights, signal flags, switch controls and the mechanism of the engines as well.

When bitter cold weather arrived, it was necessary for a crew member to remain on duty at night to keep all the engines fired so the water in them would not freeze (antifreeze being still somewhat in the future in those days). One man was assigned to watch over all the engines parked in the yard at night.

On one particularly cold night, Hoyt Tench had railroad yard-watch duty. About halfway between midnight and dawn, he returned from checking each engine and was warming himself by a coal-fired heater. Suddenly, he heard a strange sound and opened his door to listen. All, however, seemed quiet. He closed the door and returned to his heater.

Sometime later, the sound came again. Tench said he opened the door again and walked a few steps into the train yard. Then, as the sound came a third time, Tench recognized it immediately. One of the engines, amazingly, was moving out of the yard!

Somebody's trying to steal an engine, he thought, trying to decide what to do. But then, as he peered closer at the engine, he realized there was no one at the controls.

Tench then made a quick dash, climbing into the cab as the engine gained momentum. He applied the brakes immediately, and the engine slowed to a stop. Once it was halted, Tench released the brakes as was customary, and was amazed to see the engine lunge forward again, even though he had not touched the throttle.

Quickly checking the device, Tench saw that the throttle had been moved from the park position. He repositioned it back into park and waited. After a few moments, the engine again moved forward, and Tench realized that a valve in the throttle mechanism was leaking, thus allowing the engine to move.

As he made temporary repairs to the controls, Tench broke out into a cold sweat. He realized what havoc might have occurred had the engine moved onto the main line and met another train, or had it struck a vehicle or person at a crossing or derailed while advancing too swiftly into a curve.

Other Dangers

"Blow-up" can be a somewhat confusing railroad term. As a fireman, Tench's job was to keep the firebox hot enough to produce steam to run the train. On steep grades like those from Lakemont to Tiger, the train sometimes had to be stopped so the fireman could "double". To stop and get up steam is known as "blowing up" (building up the steam for steep inclines).

79

A fireman's reputation hung on how few times he had to stop the train to blow up steam. Fireman Tench remembers one such instance in which he almost overdid his responsibilities.

"One day, Jim Brown and I got Engine 75 too hot," he recalled. "The engine walls never did cave in, but back in the yards at Cornelia, Noah Ward, the boiler man, had to fix all the stay bolts because they were so weak from the excessive steam (pressure) from that Tiger (Georgia) pull.

"You see, there were spaces, just like a wall (on the inside periphery of the big boiler on the engine)," he explained. "The fire was on one side, the jacket was on the other, and in the middle (in the spaces) was the water that was making the steam. Water and steam were around that stay bolt, too, that went from one sheet (of metal on the outside) to the other (on the inside). We almost burned the stay bolts in the crown sheet, and water was leaking all in the firebox on my fire. That's when we almost blew up the engine – literally. We managed somehow to get it back into Cornelia without having an explosion," Tench added, smiling weakly.

Traveling over the many trestles between Cornelia, Georgia and Franklin, North Carolina was a perilous experience too. "They always said the Panther Creek trestle was the highest, but I think the Wiley trestle was the most dangerous and boogerish-looking, because it had five decks," Tench explained.

It was on the Wiley Trestle that the cab on the TF once jumped the tracks. It went on running right across the crossties according to Mr. Tench. "We just braked it light and let it come to a stop," he noted with another smile. "It never did get off the trestle.

"Mr. John Snyder was the conductor that day; Brawner Walker was the brakeman and Alec Dillard was the flagman. We used the re-railers to get the cab back on the tracks. As you might imagine, there was very little room to work on that trestle - it was so narrow. And one mistake could have sent men and train plummeting down into the gorge. It was scary and dangerous as all get-out."

Another danger to the railroading men, especially to the fireman, was what was known as "getting a monkey." At the peak of the summer months, the heat in the engine and near the firebox could reach horrendous proportions, causing a condition known today as heat exhaustion or heat-stroke. Symptoms included delirium, hallucinations and other serious disabilities. "That's why we called it 'getting a monkey,' I guess," Tench remembered. "You might see snakes, monkeys or all manner of other things."

Changing Times

Hoyt Tench eventually worked himself up to the position of engineer. Technology was changing about that time, and steam power was giving way to diesel.

On March 25, 1961, the Tallulah Falls Railroad ceased operation – a victim of its own good service. Highways, built with materials hauled by the railroad, eventually snaked back into the mountains allowing trucking firms to move products and merchandise more inexpensively and more precisely. The timber had all been harvested and transported to mills by the TF until the supply was exhausted. Finally, in the 1950s, passenger service was discontinued, and the fabled railroad was unable to generate enough income to support itself.

Hoyt Tench moved on, working as an engineer for the Southern Railroad. He also became an ordained minister in 1948, managing two careers until his retirement from the railroad.

Today, railroad enthusiasts everywhere never tire of learning of his experiences on a little 58-mile mountain short-line railroad once called the Tallulah Falls.

Fabled Shortline From Yesteryear

Retracing The Route Of The Tallulah Falls RR

Though it went bankrupt and disappeared decades ago, the route of the fabled Tallulah Falls Railroad is still sought out today by history enthusiasts and hiking buffs in northeast Georgia.

Railroads sometimes die, but their histories quite often live on indefinitely, especially if they were the route of a passenger train. For 54 years, the Tallulah Falls Railroad (TFR) ran through some of the most rugged and beautiful mountain scenery in the Southeast, connecting Cornelia, Georgia, with Franklin, North Carolina. Though many people are not aware of it, the north Georgia region lost one of its best friends, as well as a unique way of life, when the rails on the old "TF" were taken up a few months after the last train whistled its way into oblivion on March 25, 1961. Today, some history and railroad buffs like to retrace the route of this historic line, imagining what life in northeast Georgia would be like if it were still in existence.

Many oldtimers – and some not-so-oldsters – in northeastern Georgia speak almost reverently of the famed shortline whose familiar and dependable trains made daily runs through the tiny mountain towns of Demorest, Clarkesville, Hollywood, Turnerville, Tallulah Falls, Lakemont, Wiley, Tiger, Clayton, Passover, Mountain City, Rabun Gap, Dillard, Otto, and Franklin, North Carolina. They include TF veterans like Roy Shope of Rabun Gap, former trestle foreman, and Carl Rogers of Dillard, former agent at Clayton.

Though now faded and hidden by the sands of time, most of the former locations of the 42 wood trestles which once dotted the 58 miles of track are easily pointed out by the likes of Shope and Rogers. The expense of the maintenance of these trestles, coupled with other factors, was a major cause for the demise of the line.

Long stretches of roadbed, in various states of erosion or almost erased completely by new development, can still be seen across three counties, clearly visible in some spots, and virtually lost in the underbrush and overgrowth in others.

The Tallulah Falls roadbed, sadly, was never embraced by such preservation-minded groups as the Rails-To-Trails Conservancy which has turned hundreds of other rail roadbeds nationwide into hiking and bicycling trails. Ironically, the old TF undoubtedly would have provided one of the most scenic Rails-To-Trails opportunities in the Southeast.

Remnants more tangible than faded roadbeds can still be found at numerous points along the old route. Just behind the

Photographed in the 1990s, caboose #5 was forlorn and almost forgotten, side-tracked behind the old Southern Railway depot at Cornelia, Georgia. It, however, was luckier than most of the rolling stock from this historic line, since it reportedly was still being maintained at the time by a railroad equipment dealer with railroading roots.

A section of the TF track which was not taken up in 1961 still stretched for about two miles outside Cornelia toward Demorest, Georgia, when this photograph was taken in 1994.

neat former Southern Railway station at Cornelia, the bright red TF Caboose # 5, is maintained (as of this writing) by a railway equipment dealer with TF roots. Even a portion of now-unused weed-choked TF track still stretches for about two miles out of Cornelia toward Demorest. Much of the remainder of the line between these two communities has been buried beneath new state highways. The old TF station in Demorest silently awaits an entrepreneurial investment to bring it back to life.

Tallulah Falls, at one time one of the most splendid resorts in the eastern U.S., was the namesake of the rail line. Today, the substantial tile-roofed depot standing alongside U.S. Highway 441 in this scenic little burg is one of the most visible, as well as best-preserved landmarks of the railroad. At the time of construction, the TF tracks came north, clinging to the very rim of the Tallulah Falls Gorge – north Georgia's answer to the Grand Canyon – before it pulled up to the station. Although many of the tiles were ripped off the roof by the disastrous tornado in March of 1994, the Tallulah Falls Depot, thankfully, was quickly restored. The old building still boasts its station sign, and even the chalkboard announcing the arrival and departure times of the trains.

North of the Tallulah Falls station, the railroad leaped over the village on another wooden trestle, before plunging into the woodlands ahead. A short distance beyond the village, the five towering concrete piers and abutments remain in what once represented the only steel and concrete bridge on the line – 585 feet long and 100 feet high – built when Georgia Power impounded the Tallulah River and formed Tallulah Falls Lake.

A marker with old photos of the TF has been placed on the roadbed overlooking the north end of the high bridge piers across Tallulah Falls Lake. From there, the roadbed twists around several hills as it climbs upgrade through Lakemont and Tiger on its way to Clayton.

At north Clayton, the body of the gasoline-powered motor car which performed yeoman service as the railroad's passenger train when the steam locomotives were not running, has been recycled, serving as a private residence today.

A phantom railroad also played a vital role during the building of the TF. Near Clayton, the TF encountered – and used a short stretch of the roadbed – of the legendary Blue Ridge Railroad (a.k.a. the Black Diamond Railroad). The Black Diamond/Blue Ridge was financed by John C. Calhoun, the fiery senator from South Carolina and once vice president of the United States.

Calhoun wanted the rail line – begun in

the 1850s – to connect Charleston, South Carolina with Cincinnati, Ohio. Though most of the infrastructure of the rail line was completed, bankruptcy and the U.S. Civil War succeeded in killing the Black Diamond in the tri-state area before any rails were laid. Today, several partially-completed railway tunnels from this pre-Civil War line can still be found near Clayton.

Though now long-departed, the Tallulah Falls Railroad also enjoys the unique distinction of having been preserved for future generations on the silver screen via the Walt Disney production of *The Great Locomotive Chase*. In 1956, Disney and his actors and motion picture crew came to the north end of the Tallulah Falls Railroad to film the action-adventure, complete with three vintage locomotives shipped in by rail on the old TF line.

One of the "Disney boxcars" imported for the movie can still be found south of Clayton. Inside the city, buildings now crowd in on the old rights-of-way of the line which has been bulldozed aside in a number of spots.

Disney, who had a definite appreciation for railroads, reportedly considered buying and preserving the scenic TF. Had that idea reached fruition, tranquil Rabun County might today resemble the likes of Anaheim, California or Orlando, Florida, instead of the current sleepy community.

Roy Shope worked for the TF for 21 years, much of it as the bridge foreman and as a brakeman. "We could have filled in many of those (42 trestles) for less cost than it took to maintain them," he asserts. "I don't know why the railroad never did that.

"We had seven men who worked on the trestles between Cornelia and Franklin," he continued. "Toward the end, they cut them all off before they stopped running, (and that left only me)."

Roy says he'll never forget the time several boxcars loaded with heavy pulpwood derailed atop the trestle just south of Mountain City. "Two or three cars went off, but they didn't hurt the bridge," he explained. "We didn't have a wrecker like the big railroads, so we had to use man-

The many wooden trestles of the TF contributed to its demise from financial insolvency. The only steel and concrete trestle on the line crossed Tallulah Lake, evidenced by the large piers which still stand in the lake today.

power and Norton jacks to raise them a few inches at a time."

At Rabun Gap, a remarkably well-preserved piece of roadbed embankment – kept in top-notch condition by its owner as a memorial to the TF – still exists across a field on its way to Mountain City.

From Mountain City to Franklin, the TF roadbed parallels the east side of Route 23. However, in many places, it swings far from the highway. At other spots, new development has shaved the roadbed down to the point that it is barely recognizable.

The Georgia Power Company played a large role in the life of the TF. Five separate branch lines off the TF were built by the big utility company to reach the new hydro-electric power plants being constructed to take advantage of the waters dammed behind the Tallulah River. Georgia Power was also responsible for the construction of the railroad's only non-wood trestle – spanning Tallulah Falls Lake.

As previously mentioned, the maintenance of the many trestles along the route were a financial drain on the TF. On most larger railroads, trestles were laid across low spots during the initial construction of the lines, then were gradually filled in to create a permanent raised roadbed. That practice apparently was too much of a luxury for the TF. Even more damaging were the wrecks which often occurred as a result of collapsing trestles.

The Tallulah Falls Railroad station at Demorest is one of the few depots from the historic line which still remains intact as of this writing. It once served as a location site for the filming of the major motion picture "I'd Climb The Highest Mountain," starring Susan Hayward, William Lundigan and Rory Calhoun.

Photographed in 1994, the aged Tallulah Falls Railroad Depot in Tallulah Falls had just survived the onslaught of a destructive tornado (notice the missing shingles) which caused considerable damage across north Georgia. As of this writing, this structure was being used as a shop for the sales of mountain crafts.

Another remnant of the old TF line (photographed in 1994) just north of Clarkesville, Georgia. Abandoned in 1961, the Tallulah Falls Railroad, a mountain shortline, once extended 58 miles from Cornelia, Georgia to Franklin, North Carolina.

Despite the fact that passenger service played an important role in the lives of area residents and travelers in the area, its financial impact upon the rail line, surprisingly, was minimal. As late as 1946, a passenger train left Cornelia at 11:00 a.m. and reached Franklin at 2:00 p.m. The southbound left Franklin at 2:30 and reached Cornelia at 5:20. That same year, passenger service was abruptly discontinued following a crossing accident with a truck that broke several coach windows, spraying the startled passengers with broken glass. For the next fifteen years, the TF operated without passenger service income.

The TF flirted with several brief insolvencies before it finally slipped into its final bankruptcy in 1923 – well in advance of The Great Depression. It continued in financial limbo for the remainder of its life – another 38 years. Eventually, the money ran out.

In 1961, the TF suffered its final indignity. Instead of using a train to remove the line – as was customary – the scrap dealer ripped the rails from the ties, then trucked them out.

Aside from its high maintenance costs, the TF ironically was victimized by its own efficiency. Over the years, it had methodically and laboriously brought in the building materials for the construction of highways which snaked into the northeast Georgia mountains, allowing trucking firms to take over the commercial freight opportunities. The TF also hauled out all the pulpwood from the mountains, effectively running itself out of business.

Sometimes, on bitterly cold nights, the wind can be heard blowing through the Tallulah Falls Gorge. If one listens real close, interspersed with the whistling wind, the dull staccato chant of a steam locomotive can almost still be heard.

By all accounts, the old Tallulah Falls Railroad is dead and gone, but according to some grassroots research, there are a lot of folks that sure would like to see it return. Who knows. Maybe someday, the need for rail transportation into these rugged mountains will occur once again, and another "TF" will rise from the dead.

The Tallulah Falls Disaster Of 1921

In the early 1900s, Tallulah Falls in northeast Georgia rivaled such attractions as Niagara Falls in popularity. In one fell stroke on a cold winter night in 1921, however, the entire town was virtually erased and its tourism industry destroyed – quite possibly forever.

"Oh my God! How could this have happened to us?" The thought raced through Cora Ledbetter's mind as she witnessed the devastation wrought by the terrible fire that burned the mountain community of Tallulah Falls to the ground in 1921. It was a devastating blow to the acclaimed resort - one from which it has never recovered.

Cora, interviewed for this article in the early 1990s, was a student at Tallulah Falls School at the time. During the night of the fire, she was at home in Toccoa. She saw what was left of the community the next afternoon. Perhaps unaware of it at the time, she unwittingly also witnessed the end of an era for the once-mighty falls.

The Early Days

No description of the devastating fire of 1921 would be complete without an accounting of the four decades of immense development which had preceded the fire. Tallulah Falls had blossomed as a tourist mecca from 1882 - the year the Tallulah Falls Railroad first chugged into town - until 1921, the year of the fire. Though other factors were already negatively impacting the town's tourism economy by 1921 (such as the dams built on the Tallulah River by Georgia Power Company), the community of Tallulah Falls had continued to persevere because of its grand hotels which had beckoned invitingly from the mountainsides.

Tucked away in the northeast corner of the state, the popularity of Tallulah Falls had grown progressively, thanks to word-of-mouth publicity and writers such as David Hillhouse whose account of the falls was widely published in the United States. Additionally, a new trail cut through the forested mountainsides of northern Habersham County, had gradually attracted increasing numbers of visitors curious about the phenomenal stories of a huge gorge and mighty falls emptying into the precipice.

Despite the lure of the site, many travelers found they needed a guide just to help them find their way to the falls, but still they came - in droves. According to

TALES OF THE RAILS IN GEORGIA

Photographed in 1921 shortly after the huge firestorm which destroyed the town, Tallulah Falls, as is evidenced above, was devastated. The Tallulah Falls Railroad trestle (foreground) had been quickly rebuilt by the time this photo was taken, but it too was also completely destroyed in the conflagration. It was the maintenance of the many trestles and bridges on the Tallulah Falls line which contributed to its ultimate demise in 1961.

The Cliff House, contrary to some modern-day acounts, was one of the few large hotels at Tallulah Falls to survive the terrible fire of 1921. It, nevertheless, fell victim to another fire a few years later which was attributed to cinders from the smoke stack of a locomotive. The Tallulah Falls Railroad passed directly in front of the Cliff House.

researcher and educator Dr. John Saye in his *The Life And Times Of Tallulah.... the Falls, the Gorge, the Town* (available in shops in Tallulah Falls), "By 1840, visits to the falls by groups of men, women, and even children had become quite common." By conservative estimates, nearly 2,000 visitors reportedly had journeyed to the falls in the remote corner of north Georgia by 1877.

Perhaps Tallulah Falls' resort era actually began in 1870 with the construction of the Shirley Hotel on the brow of the gorge. Just a year later, the hotel began expanding to handle the increasing numbers of visitors. With two more hotels built during the 1870s, the resort's popularity as a travel destination began in earnest.

Arrival Of The Railroad

The next decade witnessed the arrival of a convenience which brought "boom-times" to the town of Tallulah Falls - the railroad. By the 1880s, travelers no longer were required to brave the rough trip to the falls via a mountain trail. The Tallulah Falls Railroad had been completed to the rim of the gorge, making the destination even more appealing.

Travelers came by train from Atlanta and Athens to Cornelia, Georgia, where they boarded the Tallulah Falls train. An hour and fifteen minutes later, they stepped off at Tallulah Falls.

A variety of hotels offered accommodations for travelers. Author John Saye describes it this way:

"At its peak, there were seventeen hotels and boarding houses in and around town. Guests could stay in a large, grand hotel, or in a small, intimate establishment. They could stay in the heart of the bustling little town, or in the peaceful forest surrounding Tallulah Falls."

Until 1904, the railroad ended at Tallulah Falls, and the area's tourist industry thrived. However, some seventeen years later in 1921, the lifeblood of the community literally went up in smoke.

A Fire In A Windstorm

"I have never seen nor heard the wind blow so hard as it did that night," said Bertha Burrell, a Tallulah Falls resident. "That wind carried burning bark and shingles as far away as Tugalo." Bertha had arrived home from Athens Normal School for the holidays and hadn't even unpacked.

The Tallulah Falls Disaster Of 1921

Drucy Turpen remembered the fire all too well too. "We lived on a hill on the other side of town. I was sleeping in the front room. Granny Harvey lived just below us. She came up to the house hollering that the town was burning," Drucy said sadly, tears filling her eyes at the memory. "We stood on the porch and watched it. It was just awful. It even burned the railroad trestle and my daddy's store."

Valiant town residents and businessmen did what they could to save their community. Some rang dinner bells to awaken the sleeping citizens. Others fired shots from rifles and pistols.

"Most everybody lost everything," recalled a still-distraught Gussie Harvey. Her father lost a store and a car in the fire. The Maplewood Inn and the Robinson Annex and some dozen other hotels went up in flames - reduced to ashes in a matter of hours.

Terrible Devastation

The actual cause of the inferno is still a matter of conjecture today. Several differing accounts exist.

One story maintains that a man whose car had become stuck in the mud had stopped at a local garage for help. The garage was on the street level of a three-story building. The owner, who lived upstairs, reportedly told the chilled stranger to come back later.

It was shortly after those remarks that the town went up in flames. Apparently angry at the lack of help, the stranger with the mired car is suspected of having torched the town.

"He broke into the garage to steal what tools he needed to repair his car," says Drucy Turpen. "He set fire to the garage to cover up the break-in."

Ironically, according to local sources, some years later, this same individual was himself consumed by flames when he mistakenly used gasoline instead of what he thought was kerosene to start a fire.

Regardless of the cause of the conflagration, the results were horrible by all

The corner of the Cliff House is just visible in this photo (far left), as is the corner of the Tallulah Falls Depot (far right). Engine #77 in this photo was purchased for the Tallulah Falls Railroad quite near the year 1923, meaning this photo was taken after the fire of 1921, and confirms the continued existence of the Cliff House following the 1921 holocaust.

The Tallulah Falls City Hall was photgraphed in the 1990s. This structure stands where a three-story garage stood in 1921. The fire which destroyed the town that year reportedly began in this garage.

The J.D. Harvey store, one of the many businesses which were destroyed in the fire, once existed on this site.

accounts. A barn with livestock was consumed. "I remember the screaming, mooing, and braying of those poor animals," recalled Bertha Burrell. "It was terrible." Most of the animals perished. Some were more fortunate, breaking out of the barn and racing up Main Street.

"There was no fire department in those days, and certainly no water mains," Bertha added. "People had spring water for their own use, but little else. There was nothing to do but watch the town burn. We saved our house by putting bags of cottonseed meal on the roof."

Gussie Harvey recalled the destruction of the railroad. "About half of the trestle was burned, stopping passenger service to Clayton, Georgia and Franklin, North Carolina," she explained, still wide-eyed at the memory. "There was a freight train that came down from Franklin, so benches were put in some of the freight cars for passengers.

"I remember," continued Gussie, "my father went to town in his bare feet. He came back the next day with badly blistered feet. To try and save the store, he had poured Coca-Cola syrup on it, but the fire was just too hot for the syrup."

Gussie's sister remembered that the livestock ran up and down the street - many until they dropped dead from exhaustion. "Some of the animals were on fire," she said.

After The Fire

Little, if anything, was rebuilt after the fire. None of the hotels were reconstructed. Although the fire was a death blow to the town, other factors contributed to its ultimate demise.

The extension of the railroad to Clayton and Franklin, North Carolina, inevitably lured visitors deeper into the mountains, causing many of them to bypass Tallulah Falls. "Many people had been coming here from South Georgia for health reasons," explains Jim Turpen, a local Methodist minister. "Once they realized they could go even further into the mountains, they did."

The construction of the massive dam just above the falls and at other sites farther upriver also changed the town's character. The once-mighty falls were virtually extinguished, eliminating much of the original attraction and beauty of the site. The focus of leisure pursuits then shifted from the falls to fishing and lifestyles around the various lakes created behind the dams.

Cost was another reason for the town's demise. In those days, few people had insurance coverage on their homes and property, and the cost of rebuilding the hotels was prohibitive.

By the mid- to late-1930s, all of the grand hotels had completely disappeared from the brow of Tallulah Gorge. If the 1921 fire didn't get them, another fire or destructive element did.

By the 1950s, passenger service had been discontinued on the Tallulah Falls Railroad, further depleting service. And in 1961, the railroad itself ceased to exist - a victim of its own success. The transportation system which had made all of the original growth at the falls possible, had outlived its usefulness. It had made possible the construction of the dams which choked off the beautiful falls; it had transported the felled trees from the area until the logging industry expired; and it had brought in the building materials necessary for the construction of U.S. Highway 441. With the advent of the highway, trucking firms could then transport products and materials more economically and precisely than the railroad. Each year, the revenues from the Tallulah Falls Railroad became less and less until bankruptcy was inevitable.

The Future

Today, despite its decline, Tallulah Falls still vies for a slice of the tourism pie dollars in Georgia. Travelers still want to view the beautiful gorge and the remnants of the scenic little town.

A new state park was established within Tallulah Gorge in the 1990s, to preserve as much of the gorge as possible for posterity. Area residents are hopeful the new park will facilitate new growth in the little town.

The Tallulah Falls Disaster Of 1921 — Northeast, Georgia

Photographed prior to 1928, Glenbrook Hotel was located on a ridge a short distance behind the downtown district in Tallulah Falls, but it survived the fire of 1921 because the high winds fanning the flames were blowing away from the Glenbrook. This captivating structure managed to survive almost to the 21st century before being demolished. It was the last surviving hotel built during the golden age of Tallulah Falls in the early 1900s.

Photographed circa 1950s, this birds-eye view of Tallulah Falls offers a perspective of the dam on Tallulah Lake and the former route of the Tallulah Falls Railroad through the community.

The Cliff House at Tallulah Falls endured at the resort town longer than virtually all of its counterparts. It, however, ultimately suffered the same fate - destruction by fire - reportedly ignited by cinders from a passing locomotive. Guests were captured in this photograph prior to the fire during happier times.

Pictured here is the view of Tallulah Falls encountered by travelers on the Tallulah Falls Railroad as they entered the community from the south. The immense Cliff House appears on the right. Today, Georgia Highway 441 occupies this stretch of the former railroad bed.

The community of fewer than two hundred residents still welcomes tens of thousands of visitors who pause to admire the gorge, and perhaps reminisce a bit about the glory days of the town of yesteryear.

The old Tallulah Falls Railroad depot, which somehow survived the firestorm of 1921, also escaped serious damage during a devastating tornado in the 1990s. It serves today as a crafts store, displaying the wares of local mountain craftspersons.

Tallulah Falls School still attracts students from throughout Georgia and other states for its excellent programs. The area also boasts a rehabilitation center and an adult education center.

However, unless the falls are freed once again to crash and roar unrestrained into the gorge, recreating the wonderland which caused Indians to anoint the site as a sacred place and tourists to flock to the falls by the trainload, it is highly unlikely that this scenic spot will ever again be the tourism destination it was prior to a terrible fire in the winter of 1921.

Remembering The Gainesville & Northwestern Railroad

For years, it served as a medium of transportation for the burgeoning lumber industry in northeast Georgia. And when all the timber had been harvested and the mills dismantled, the little shortline struggled on for a few more years before finally dying a slow, painful death.

Today, visitors to "Alpine Helen" in north Georgia's White County may have a difficult time picturing a huge sawmill on the east side of the Chattahoochee River in what now is "downtown" Helen. That, however, is exactly what once stood on this site. And servicing it was a now almost forgotten railroad called the Gainesville & Northwestern (G&NW).

This early 1900s north Georgia rail line was completed in 1912 and began service in 1913. A typical train consisted of a steam locomotive; a coal car; a combination baggage, mail and passenger car; and another passenger car with an observation platform at the rear.

Over the years, the G&NW owned seven coal-burning steam "road" locomotives. Numbers 57, 103, & 203 were "ten-wheeler" passenger locomotives built by Baldwin, while numbers 59, 60, 101 and 102 were freight engines built by Lima.

Number 101 was later renumbered 201. The G&NW also owned number 2, a 2-truck Shay also built by Lima.

In its early years, the Gainesville & Northwestern featured excursion service from Gainesville to Escowee Falls between Helen and Robertstown, where an attractive pavilion had been built over the stream. Mossy Creek Campground was another popular excursion destination.

The Gainesville & Northwestern was originally built to provide transportation for the large volumes of lumber products produced by Byrd-Matthews (later Morse Brothers) Lumber Mill in Helen. In its hey-days, Byrd-Matthews produced 125,000 board feet per day when operating at maximum capacity.

The G&NW was also directly responsible for thriving economies in the little communities through which it passed enroute to Helen. The tracks started in downtown Gainesville where the depot and yards were shared with the Gainesville Midland Railroad which is still in operation (as of this writing) by CSX Railroad. The G&NW then ran 37 miles to Robertstown (formerly called "North Helen"). The railroad was also known as "The Nacoochee Valley Route."

The towns of Nacoochee, Yonah, Cleveland, Clermont, Brookton and others grew significantly during the G&NW's glory years, and withered and shrunk just as quickly when the rail line died. A branch line extended from Clermont to the pyrites mine in Lumpkin County.

The virgin timber stands in northeast Georgia were immense, and it took a number of years to deplete them. However, the supply finally did play out in 1928, and with it, so also did the huge lumber mill, as well as the railroad.

About 1925, after the demise of the mill, the steam locomotive and its fine cars were sold. They were replaced by what literally was a bus on railroad wheels. This contraption amazingly continued to use the old Gainesville & Northwestern tracks to provide passenger and mail service between Robertstown and Gainesville. It was nicknamed "The Yellow Hammer," and it wobbled as it ran down the tracks.

Mail service – but only a smattering of passenger service – were continued until the mid-1930s when the rails were removed completely. Today, little remains of the old line except for the faintly visible outlines of the road-bed in certain locations.

To bring the logs in from the mountain forests, the mill owners built an extensive network of logging railroads which radiated outward from Helen in all directions. By the time logging operations ended, over 150 miles of rail lines had been built into four counties in northeast Georgia!

These logging tracks off the main Gainesville & Northwestern Railroad were "narrow-gauge" in size, and temporary in nature, since their usefulness ended once the timber around them had been harvested. After the usable timber had been cut out of an area, the tracks were taken up and moved to a new location.

One unusual feature of the Gainesville & Northwestern was the use of three-rail (or dual gauge) track from the mill in Helen south to Asbestos Station. This track accommodated the normal 56 and one-half-inch standard-gauge trains out of Gainesville, as well as the 42-inch narrow-gauge logging trains on their way to

Turner's Corner & Blood Mountain

A completely different locomotive was also used to haul the heavy log-train cars out of the mountains. These engines typically were the Shay, Climax and Heisler engines, all of which were used in the Helen operations. These locomotives had all of their wheels driven by shafts and gears, making them very slow, but very powerful, and capable of operation on very uneven track.

Perhaps the last area to be logged – circa 1925 to 1927 – was a tract of land northeast of Helen. Morse Brothers ran the company's railroad across the Chattahoochee River at Bell Branch, a little southeast of the Helen mill, then roughly along what today is Georgia Highway 356, then up the right fork of the Soque River, across a gap in the ridge between Habersham and Rabun Counties, along the side of the mountains west of Lake Burton, and finally up the Tallulah River to Tate City.

From this "main line," the loggers ran spur tracks up the left fork of the Soque River, Wildcat Creek and Moccasin Creek (to name a few) which are still visible today. Here, they made the last timber harvests of this era.

Despite their temporary nature, these

This photo of a new locomotive and tender is believed to have been taken shortly before delivery of the two to Gainesville. The platform on which they are positioned has a "Baldwin Locomotive Works" identification across the front.

Among the locomotives pulling the logging trains through the north Georgia mountains were 50-ton two-truck Shay engines with a top speed of 16 miles per hour. They were quite slow, but extremely powerful.

The dilapidated remains of the Gainesville & Northwestern Railroad depot at Brookton, Georgia, were photographed on the "wagon side" in 1972. (Photo by Grant Keene, Cleveland, GA)

railroad beds were of excellent quality in the days when north Georgia highways were quite primitive. Some rock retaining walls are still serviceable in the Duke's Creek Falls area. The many trestles necessary for this area were built of untreated native timbers, so most are in various states of decay today, but the rock retaining walls are quite sturdy.

After the logging rails were taken up, local residents probably carried off most of the re-usable timbers, so only the roadbeds of these interesting trails are visible today. As recent as 1987, a collapsed trestle across Goshen Creek below a beautiful waterfall still existed in Habersham County just west of what once was LaPrade's Fish Camp on Lake Burton. Back in the early 1900s, the loggers had built square log cribs on each side of the creek, then had laid huge chestnut logs on the cribs to support the tracks. This, of course, was prior to the time that the chestnut blight destroyed the chestnut trees in the Southern Appalachians.

Another interesting area to explore is an old logging railroad in the vivinity of Wildcat Creek. The grade in this area is essentially clear of undergrowth, and is a fine "rail-trail." It follows the border of what today is a Wildlife Management Area patrolled and cared for by the Georgia Department of Natural Resources.

Little remains today of three trestles which once provided transport for the trains across the creeks, so a walk along this route today will require some climbing down to the creek beds and then back up the other side. At one of these creeks, a side road leads up to the spring which once supplied water to LaPrade's Camp.

As you approach Wildcat Creek, the trail becomes much more overgrown, but is still quite serviceable. The grade eventually joins Forest Service Road 26 (FS-26) which branches off Georgia Highway 197 and

Remembering The Gainesville & Northwestern Railroad — Hall County

The Gainesville & Northwestern was built to provide transportation for the wood products produced by the huge Byrd-Matthews Lumber Mill (later Morse Brothers Lumber) in Helen, Georgia, photographed here In 1912.

runs up Wildcat Creek. This road is built on the bed of the railroad branch which once existed along Wildcat Creek.

Just downstream from where the railroad grade crosses Wildcat Creek is the ruins of the small dam and waterwheel supports for the electrical generator that once provided LaPrade's with electrical power in the days prior to rural electrification. John LaPrade's son-in-law, the late Vernon Castner, once described the building of the power plant in vivid detail.

Mr. Castner explained the plant was constructed by local craftsmen, not by the Georgia Power Company as has been rumored over the years. One tall tale maintains the plant was built by Georgia Power for Mr. LaPrade in return for his help in acquiring land for Lake Burton.

Clark Meyer, a professional backpacking guide at Blue Ridge Mountain Sports, is knowledgeable of other trestles in a remote mountain area off the Soque River that might still be in relatively good condition.

(Directions: To find the most accessible logging railroad trail, take Georgia 197 to Lake

Byrd-Matthews Lumber Mill produced 125,000 board feet of lumber per day when operating at maximum capacity. The railroad was vital in moving this product to market.

Burton. Just north of the former location of Laprade's Fish Camp, turn west on Wildcat Creek Road (Forest Service Road 26). You are now driving on the old railroad grade. After approximately one mile, look for a grassy meadow leading to a footbridge across Wildcat Creek. Park, cross the creek, and you can find the slightly overgrown railroad grade. Hike the grade south. You will encounter three old trestle locations as you hike above the LaPrade's site.)

The Railroad And The Early Days In Clermont

It began life as an education opportunity for mountain children, and gained additional momentum as a stop on the Gainesville & Northwestern Railroad.

The tracks from the old Gainesville and Northwestern Railroad were taken up in 1935, and sold as scrap iron to Japan. The railroad rights-of-way also were sold or reverted shortly thereafter to local landowners. By the 1940s with its lifeblood gone, the sleepy little whistlestop of Clermont, Georgia, had withered and died, but things weren't always so grim for this picturesque community which was considered a north Georgia resort in the early 1900s.

In the years preceding World War I, a group of businessmen realized the immense acreage of forest products available in the northeast Georgia mountains. This same timber products industry also spawned another tiny community which would later grow to a prominence of its own – Helen, Georgia.

The Gainesville & Northwestern was incorporated on February 9, 1912, to provide a system of transportation for the products produced by this burgeoning lumber industry. The rail line passed through Clermont (originally called "Dip") on its way to Helen. As a result, Clermont enjoyed a prime position on a thriving supply line from the more heavily populated cities of Gainesville and Atlanta to the south. It was this rail line which fostered the commerce which sprang to life in Clermont in the early 1900s, and which sustained Clermont's growth through the mid-1930s.

Another growth catalyst in Clermont which actually preceded the railroad was Chattahoochee High School, established around 1890. It became a Baptist Church-supported school which belonged to the Mercer University system of preparatory schools in 1919. It was a four-year school, with records indicating it produced its first graduating class in 1906.

Educational institutions of this nature were few in number in the north Georgia mountains at that time, and facilities such as Chattahoochee High became a strong incentive for the relocation of families interested in higher education.

"My father and mother moved us to Clermont specifically so we could have the opportunity to go to a nine-month school," said the late Essie Hudgins Jordan, who was a member of the faculty of Chattahoochee High during the 1923-24 school year, and whose family moved to the community in 1912 when she was twelve years old. "Despite the fact that it meant relocating a home and a family business, it was important to Mother and Father that we children receive a good education."

Mrs. Jordan's beautiful old family home still stands on King Street in Clermont, where her father – James Z. Hudgins – a merchant from Sugar Hill, Georgia, contracted for its construction in 1912. It is one of a number of elegant turn-of-the-century homes which highlight the architectural beauty and scenic attractiveness of the town even today.

"Father had a general store beside the railroad there in the center of town," Mrs.

Jordan continued. "Clermont was a wonderful place for a child to grow up, and we had a large family – six brothers and six sisters. All the stories you read about pioneer life which describe the little general store where saddles, sunbonnets, barrels of apples, cheeses, dry goods, traps, and all the other things one needed in that day and time, were sold in Father's store. On cold winter days, the men gathered around an old pot-bellied stove to play checkers. Father loved to play checkers. His store was a wonderful place. In 1912, Clermont and the surrounding counties were still very sparsely populated.

"Chattahoochee High School was a boarding school at that time," Mrs. Jordan added. "The dormitory which housed both girls and boys was on the campus grounds. It had space for a music room and a library, and an apartment was set aside for the school superintendent. Some of the students rented small cottages, and went home on weekends and in the summer, when school wasn't in session."

The 1923-24 "Annual Announcement" booklet from Chattahoochee High offers a glimpse back in time at the school. It describes the institution as:

". . . located near the little town of Clermont, on the Gainesville & North Western Railroad, 16 miles from Gainesville. . . This puts Chattahoochee within a few minutes of Gainesville in one direction, and a few minutes of the mountains going north. For several miles in three directions may be seen broad fields of corn and cotton and small grain. Much of this plateau section is yet wooded. . . . Clermont is a thriving town, built up since the school was established. The town gives many advantages: one bank, post office, hotel, drug store, furniture store, five general mercantile stores, express office, two blacksmith establishments, and a telephone exchange."

As might be expected, social codes at the school were strict. Boys and girls were expected to refrain from all communication with each other except "that which ordinary courtesy demands." Boys and girls were not

The first post office at the community of "Dip," (present-day Clermont) was in the home of Mr. and Mrs. William Harvey Keith. The man on the horse in this photograph is Mr. Josiah W. Blackwell, the first mail carrier for the area. Though the Gainesville-Northwestern Railroad was the impetus for increased growth in Clermont in the early 1900s, it was short-lived. The railroad ceased operations in the early 1930s.

Clermont - meaning "Clear Mountains" - once thrived as a mountain town centered around higher education opportunities and the Gainesville-Northwestern Railroad. The Clermont Hotel, pictured here, still stands (as of this writing) in the town, one of only a handful of original buildings still in existence. (Photo by Olin Jackson)

allowed the freedom of the town, except by special permission. They were expected to remain in their rooms at night. Boys were required to "abstain from smoking cigarettes, playing cards, profanity, intoxicating liquors and the keeping of firearms."

Before the railroad came through, and before Chattahoochee High School was constructed, Clermont's sole claim to fame

This rare photograph shows Chattahoochee High School, an early education center in northeast Georgia. It once stood across the highway from Concord Baptist Church in Clermont.

The original Concord Baptist Church sanctuary was photographed here sometime between 1882 and 1919. A brick structure replaced this building in the early 1920s.
(Photo courtesy of Mr. Ralph Hampton, Gainesville)

Griffin Brothers' Cotton Warehouse on King Street was photographed here circa 1926. The Gainesville & Northwestern Railroad which supplied Clermont existed along the right rear of this building. Warehouse owner John T. Griffin (far right, foreground) was remembered by one elderly resident as a stern businessman.

was its resort identity. The name "Clermont" means "Clear Mountains." It was primarily because of the railroad, and the scenic location of the town in the foothills of the Appalachian Mountains, that the hotel, constructed in 1911-12, (and which still stands today), was built.

Though not luxurious by any means, the hotel was elegant for its day. The Gainesville & Northwestern passed beside it, and a tennis court (apparently one of the first in the north Georgia area) was available to the rear of the hotel, for guests.

Chattahoochee H. S. Graduates (1906-1923)

1906 - J.T. Miller

1907 - Grover Miller

1908 - A.S. Kytle

1909 - George, Gearin, W.C. Grindle, C.W. Henderson, Fred Staton, W.L. Walker

1910 - H.W. Keith, U.A. Lawson, E.B. O-Kelley, M.K. Staton, Inez Spencer, Ruth Waters.

1911 - F.L. Brown. B.J. Head, H.G. Hudgins, U.S. Lancaster, H.L. Lawson, R.H. Thomas, Minnie Head, Exer Head, Lola Staton.

1912 - H.E. Buffington, A.B. Eberhart, Claude Grindle, Hubert Haynes, W.H. Lord, B.H. Robinson, Beulah Hudgins, Vivian Jarrard, Liccie Payne, Lillie Payne, Nellie Whelchel.

1913 - W.T. Evans, Charles E. Hawkins, W.P. Pettyjohn, W.A. Whitmire, John Haynes, A.B. Keith, C.H. Keith, F.P. Lockhart, Lena Hudgins, Mary Hulsey, Florence Ragan, Pink Standridge

1914 - C.J. Broom, H.T. Brookshire, O.G. Lancaster, G.F. Tyner, Salena Jarrard, Anna Belle Lockhart.

1915 - C.C. Jarrard, J.A. Meaders, M.D. Reed, Irene Bailey, Josephine Grogan, Chester Head, Iris Maddox.

1916 - Chesley Bennett, Harry Garrison, Richard Hawkins, Carl Lancaster, Elmira Grogan, Daisy Hudgins, Ethel Roark

1917 - W.E. Barnwell, R.L. Carter, Ernest Hulsey, J.L. Keith, D.T. Lawson, Y.W. Peck, H.H. Peyton, Beulah Greer, Myrtle Haynes, Ada Highsmith, Ethleen

The Railroad And The Early Days In Clermont — Hall County

Jarrard, Florida Mauldin, Willie Staton.

1918 - Una Abercrombie, Laurie Truelove, Maude Logan, Esther Langford, Lillie Mac Culpepper, Annie Mae Haynes, Agnes Roark, Etta Chandler, Henry Reed, Clarence Puckett, Glenn Cooper, Edward Brown, Escoe Logan, Garnett Keith.

1919 - Valera Bowen, Bertie Mae Miller, Lillie Head, Sallie Iix, Hoke Grier, Homer Keith, Roy Martin, Bertha Waters, Essie Hudgins, Idell Haynes, Essie Tanner, Hester Tanner, Lucile Roark, Dewey Patten, Frank Cain, Howard Poole, Vassie Keith, Nell Whitmire.

1920 - Ernest Abercrombie, Clifton Bryson, Wallis Bennett, D.T. Buice, Nita Catlett, Callie Chandler, Adele Head, Vallie Hulsey, Floyd Hendrix, Avie Forrester, Jewell Keith, D.W. Lord, Ralph Miller, Clyde Maddox, Russell Marlow, Nellie Mae Pierce, Charlie Staton, Adelia Joe Staton, Clarence Walker, Julius Whitmire, Paul Whitmore, Edgar Hulsey.

1921 - Jarnet Carruth, Bonnie Carruth, Hugh Brice, Annie Brice, Henry Logan, Hortense Delong, Mabel Haynes, Mae Grant, Lee Grant, Herschel McGee, Seaborn Gilstrap, Y.D. Jones, Fred Moore, Ralph Thompson, J. Henry Lackey, Albert Martin, Nell Christopher, Mary Brown, Eugenia Rogers, Maudelle Pierce, Sylvia Gailey, Mary Elder, Price Bowen, Ruth Head, Michael McNeal, Texas Wallace, Herschel Davis, Laura Belle Culpepper, June Murphy, Ralph Murphy, Pearl Truelove, Pink Culpepper.

1922 - Ruth Crawford, Lee Buice, David Hudgins, Lucas Griffin, Willie Meaders, Cladith Simpson, Mozelle Marlowe, Hassie Mae Whitmire, Cordia Mullinax, Gertrude Kytle, Clarence Walker.

1923 - Cary Adams, Ernest Brown, Ralph Buffington, Lunie Mae Coker, Winnie Chandler, Kelsey Delong, Otis Dyer, Birdie Gailey, J.E. Grizzle, Clyde Hudgins, Mae Hooper, Mary Belle Jackson, Nina Keith, Vera Keith, Cora Belle Lancaster, Myrtle Moore, Fred Orr, Turner Quillian, Emma Haynes, Marilu Hudgins, Maggie Smith, Tony Walker.

Essie Hudgins, one of the first female faculty members of Chattahoochee High School in Clermont, was photographed here in 1923. She also was an early graduate of the school. Her father, James Zacheus Hudgins owned a mercantile business which thrived as a result of its location adjacent to the tracks of the Gainesville-Northwestern Railroad in Clermont. The family's impressive former home - built by Mr. Hudgins - still stands on King Street in Clermont.

Professor W.L. Walker (l) (A.B. Degree, North Georgia College), was a professor and officer of the Board of Trustees at Chattahoochee High School in 1923, as was Professor F.C. Staton (r), (A.B. Degree, Mercer University). Chattahoochee High also profited from the railroad, as a result of the passenger transportation opportunity offered its students by the Gainesville-Northwestern.

Steam Engine From Yesteryear

Last Ride Of Old #209 On The Gainesville Midland

For years, she worked the rails between Gainesville and Athens, hauling freight and passengers to stops along the route. Though its once-powerful locomotion has been stilled today, Engine #209 still stands beside the old depot in Gainesville, allowing the curious a peek at what rail travel was like in yesteryear.

She sits there in all her glory, old steam engine #209, a powerful reminder of the classic days when railroads ruled the economy of America. She is, of course, retired today – a victim of progress. In tribute to her service, however, engine #209, a mail car, and a bright red caboose have been permanently exhibited in a Gainesville city park near the old depot, and the site has become a mecca for train buffs, as well as a constant source of excitement for youngsters adventurous enough to climb to the second-story height of the old engine cab.

Under the guidance of the Georgia Mountains Museum and the City of Gainesville, #209 (of the Gainesville-Midland Railroad) is watched over by a group of dedicated railroad hobbyists who keep the "museum" open during the year for visitors.

Not only will the volunteers enthusiastically tell you about the steam engine and the cars, but older train buffs like Forrest L. Shiver and younger ones like Jeff Puett will spin you railroad yarns just as long as you want to listen. You see, railroading is more than a hobby with them – it's their life.

Engine #209 was the last steam engine to operate commercially in the state of Georgia as the diesel revolution took its toll. The old-timers from the Gainesville-Midland, such as Jesse Gillespie, will proudly tell you she even pulled her upstart diesel replacement into Gainesville to begin its career.

Old 209 was a working freight engine, originally built for the Seaboard Railroad in 1930 by the Baldwin Locomotive Works in Philadelphia. She was bought by the Durham and Southern Railroad, overhauled by the D&S crews, and then stored as a stand-by and never used. She later was bought by the Gainesville-Midland, ending up on the short run between Gainesville and Athens.

Old #209 had some help too. Just as she was revered as a workhorse, her sister engine - #206 - was undoubtedly the "show-horse" of the steam engines operating under the Midland banner.

Engine #206, in fact, came into this world as royalty. She was built in 1916 for

Last Ride Of Old #209 On The Gainesville Midland — Hall County

the Czar of Russia. She was a sport model, a Russian Decapod, and nothing defined her personality more than her sporty 10 drive wheels which were white-walled. She was designed to haul – at 60 miles per hour – both freight and passengers across a vast wasteland on the Trans-Siberian Railroad.

Interestingly, when she was finally ready for shipment to Russia, the Czar Nicholas II was having his troubles and Russia was in turmoil. In 1905, the Russians had been defeated by Japan in the Russo-Japanese War, and the czar had effectively lost control of the Pacific end of his cross-continental railroad.

Then, in 1917, a revolution was responsible for the overthrow of Nicholas, and the Bolsheviks seized power. Nicholas ultimately was executed in 1918, and the Union of Soviet Socialist Republics (U.S.S.R.) was formed in 1922.

Back in the United States, all the maneuvering in the U.S.S.R. left #206 – an engine intended for royalty – in limbo in the rail yards at the Baldwin Locomotive Works. She eventually was sold to the Detroit, Toledo & Ironton Railroad as #310. The trucks under her tender still have the DT&I RR visible on them. Eventually, the Seaboard Airline Railroad picked up this engine, and as #544, she wandered over the Seaboard system until the Gainesville-Midland purchased her as part of their post-World War II upgrading. Today, the czar's Engine #206 can be found in the North Carolina Transportation Museum in Spencer, North Carolina.

And the 209? In 1959, she was given to the City of Gainesville, a fitting tribute considering the fact this north Georgia city was once a busy railroad center, with a major North-South line coming directly through town, another line (the Gainesville-Midland Railway) connecting to Athens, and a third (the Gainesville & Northwestern Railway) extending through Clermont to Robertstown in nearby White County.

Today, a stout old steam engine with a big "209" on its side stands in downtown Gainesville in mute testimony to one of the great eras of north Georgia's commercial history. A group of steam engine lovers maintains her so future generations of kids – of all ages – may witness, first-hand, one of the dynamic modes of transportation of yesteryear.

Photographed in September of 1959, Engine #209 of the Gainesville-Midland pulls out on an excursion run, the last trip it ever made. The last official freight run of #209 was made the previous June.

Youngsters simply can't resist climbing aboard #209 to sample the view and imagine what it was like to be an engineer on the big locomotive.

This early photograph of the Gainesville-Midland was taken when the line still provided passenger service. Notice the crowds here waiting to board. The community in the background is Gainesville, Georgia.

Bandit Bill Miner And A North Georgia Railroad Robbery

By the early 1900's, it had become increasingly difficult for outlaws in the Old West to successfully rob a train and elude law enforcement officials. One member of those desperadoes, however couldn't resist one last hold-up in north Georgia.

For generations of Americans, the exciting sagas of train robberies in the old West have fueled the imaginations of young and old alike. Despite the violence of their circumstances, these events almost invariably were added to the pantheon of American folklore, and often became the romantic subject of song, story, and motion pictures.

For this reason, the circumstances surrounding the events of February 18, 1911, in Gainesville, Georgia, are considered even more incredible. Here, in a rarely disturbed little backroads community in the foothills of the north Georgia mountains, one of the most notorious outlaws of all time committed his last robbery.

Born George Anderson in Jackson County, Kentucky, in 1843, Bill Miner used a variety of names to get through life: George Morgan, California Billy, George Edwards, George Bud, and Louis Colquhoun, to name a few. He was the son of a schoolteacher mother and fly-by-night father who abandoned his family before the boy was 10 years old. Young George quickly earned a reputation as a dare-devil and an irresponsible youth, traits by which he would live for the rest of his life.

Shortly before the U.S. Civil War, George left home for the gold fields of California where he landed a job as a pony express rider. He apparently decided early in life, that an honest job just wasn't the method he wanted to use to make a living. He soon began robbing stagecoaches, igniting the life of crime from which he never wavered.

The nation watched in interest, as young Billy the Kid, Jesse James, Black Bart, Cole Younger, the Daltons and the other notorious outlaws of the old West rose to prominence and then faded into the mists of time. George, who gradually

Young George quickly earned a reputation as a dare-devil and an irresponsible youth, traits by which he would live for the rest of his life.

100

had become infamous under the name Bill Miner, was cut from the same mold and is considered by many modern-day historians to have been even more notorious than his counterparts. He was one of the last surviving members of this fraternity, and was still robbing trains well into the 20th century.

Early on a cold February morning of 1911, he held up Southern Railway's Train No. 36 near the White Sulphur station north of Gainesville. Because of his advancing years, Miner may have known that he was nearing his last days of crime, as this final episode of his life of theft began unfolding.

According to reports, at approximately 3:15 A.M. on the appointed morning, engineer David J. Fant of Atlanta might have cursed had he not been known as a railroad evangelist. Southern Railway No. 36 was already late when he took it out of Atlanta at 12:15 that morning. On this, of all mornings, Fant had H.E. Hudgens, general superintendent of the railroad on board in a private car at the rear, and now someone was flagging down the train, further delaying things.

As Fant peered through the darkness and rain of the early morning, someone was waving a red lantern. The engineer knew he had to stop. He assumed a lineman or a farmer had discovered a broken rail and was trying to save the train from wrecking.

As the train stopped, Fant slid down from the engine and asked if the track was being fixed. Out of the darkness, two other men suddenly appeared, brandishing revolvers. They announced the obvious. Southern Railway No. 36 was being robbed!

The three bandits, wearing masks and calling each other "captain," "number four" and "number five," ordered Fant's black fireman Rufus Johnson to "disappear." While the bandit with the lantern watched Fant, the other two robbers walked down to the express car with the intention of releasing the portion of the train from there rearward, so that the robbery could be completed without having to contend with a lot of panicky, confused passengers.

Shortly thereafter, flagman C.H. Shirley and conductor Walter T. Mooney, both of Atlanta, began walking up to the engine to find out what was happening. Seeing the man with the lantern, Mooney called out but received no response from the suspicious-looking man. The conductor later recalled that he "assumed he was dealing with a block-head," and he grabbed the man's arm and gave him a shove, demanding to know why the train had been stopped.

The man replied by sticking a revolver in Mooney's face and announcing the holdup. Thinking this was all just a bad joke, the conductor exclaimed "Cut out this foolishness! I've got to look after my train!" Only then when the masked man responded with a string of obscenities, did Mooney realize the full implication of the situation, and that he had come very close to losing his life.

Once out of the bandit's view, the conductor told Shirley to try to slip past the rear of the train and get help. The flagman did just that, running to White Sulphur Station, a small railway depot about a mile away.

Meanwhile, Walter B. Miller, in the express car, had learned of the robbery and was desperately trying to lock all of the doors to thwart the bandits' efforts. Despite his best attempts, the men entered through a door he had overlooked, and demanded the keys to the two safes. Luckily, the keys apparently were not kept on the train.

Disappointed but undeterred, Miner brought Fant and a shovel from the engine. With dirt from the outside, the bandits packed dynamite under the safes, lit the fuses, and fled the car. The resulting explosion tore holes through the roof and sides of the car, shattered the windows, and even put out the train's lights. When the smoke had cleared, only the smaller of the two safes was open.

With time running out, "the captain" filled a bag with the loot, and then he and his two accomplices ran into the woods "disappearing as if the earth had swallowed them up," according to a subsequent newspaper report.

Fant started up his train and took it to the nearby community of Lula where he telegraphed a report of the robbery. Ten minutes prior to Fant's report, Shirley had reached the White Sulphur Station, where he hurriedly reported the news of the robbery to local authorities.

As could be expected under the circumstances, initial reports of the robbery became twisted and distorted as the news was passed from person to person. Two mythical additional bandits were included in early reports as having been passengers on the train. The gang's escape was described in various accounts as involving an automobile, a buggy, and even as involving a ride hitched on the underside of the very train they had robbed.

No complete account of the items/money stolen was ever made, but at the very least, $800.00 in U.S. currency, $770.00 in Mexican money, an unknown amount in several foreign currencies, a number of legal papers of no value to the robbers, a pair of pearl ear screws, and a watch were taken. Left behind in the safe that they had failed to blow open was $65,000 in gold and cash - an amount which would have been considered a fortune to many people in 1911.

Miner recruited his two accomplices for the Gainesville robbery - Charlie Hunter and James Handford - in Pennsylvania and Virginia respectively, in 1910. Hunter, a thirty-year-old Irishman from Michigan agreed, after some persuasion, to accompany the old bandit to a locale in the South, "to try holding up a Southern train." The pair worked for two months in a Virginia sawmill where they completed their group by recruiting thirty-three-year-old Handford from Nebraska.

The trio moved on to Georgia to prepare for what was almost unthinkable - a Wild West-style train holdup in the East. The week before they finally struck Southern Railway No. 36, Hunter pawned Miner's watch in Atlanta, using the money to buy whiskey and a lantern later used in the robbery. A track wrench later found at their camp indicated that they had considered derailing and wrecking the train.

The first reports of the incident were met with incredulity by a disbelieving Gainesville populace. According to newspaper accounts of that day, most of the townspeople dismissed the news of the robbery, thinking it was a joke. Most were dumbfounded when they learned the truth.

"The truth dawned at last," the newspaper said, "and they were confronted with the fact that here in a free, civilized, God-fearing, and law-abiding community, a train robbery was committed that would abash the most God-forsaken Wild West country to be found. That such a daring hold-up could take place right at our doors was inconceivable."

The Atlanta newspapers had a field day with the event. The *Atlanta Journal* filled the first two pages of the February 18 issue with the news. The train crew, all of whom were Atlanta residents, were interviewed and their photographs published.

When the report of the robbery reached the Hall County Police Office in the early morning hours of February 18, Sheriff W.A. Crow was at home sick with the mumps. He arose from his sick bed to organize a posse by telephone.

Assembling his deputies, Crow gave them a pep talk: "I want you to go out into the country and mountains now, and don't come back here until you bag these train robbers," he instructed. "Bring them back alive if you can. . . . But if not, just bring them along anyway."

These initial efforts in locating the bandits proved futile. Deputy Sheriff Little, with the help of county officials and railroad detectives, began a search of Gainesville, to see if the robbers might have been in town all along.

The posse sent to the robbery site was delayed, waiting for the bloodhounds to be brought from Gwinnett County. By the time the dogs arrived, the rain and pepper and snuff reportedly scattered by Miner and his two accomplices had obscured the trail.

To Sheriff Crow's posse were added the Pinkertons, a deputy U.S. Marshal, and detectives of the Southern Railway and Express. All local law enforcement officials also went into the field, using the promise of a $1,500 reward (almost more than the bandits actually took) offered by the State of Georgia and the Southern Railway, to enlist men and boys for their posse. Despite all these efforts, the ultimate capture of the train robbers was accomplished, as the editor of the 1911 *Dahlonega Nugget* explained, "by mountaineers skilled in tracking."

Only a few days after the robbery, the search efforts were losing steam. Officials conducting the man-hunt were sitting around the main room of the old Dixie Hunt Hotel - their headquarters in Gainesville - so despondent, that they hardly noticed when the telephone began ringing. When one of the lawmen finally picked up the receiver, the caller turned out to be ex-Lumpkin County Sheriff Jim Davis calling from Dahlonega to announce that he believed he had found the train robbers in an abandoned house nearby.

Davis had learned of the men earlier, and both he and Lumpkin County Sheriff John Sergeant began having doubts about them. They claimed to be prospectors and had overnighted at Sergeant's Hotel in Dahlonega. However, between them, the three strangers had no prospecting tools other than one broken and split shovel.

When Lumpkin County resident Pete Carmichael reported the three men near his farm, Sergeant became even more suspicious. He set out for the Carmichael place where he picked up two sets of tracks. The bandits apparently had split up at this point, and Sergeant decided to follow the single set of tracks. He assembled a posse which included the aforementioned Jim Davis and Davis' two sons - Rufus and Joe.

At length, the trail led the group to the Elbert Kendall farm some 17 miles northwest of Dahlonega in the present-day Nimblewill community. The Kendalls

Just as he was described by countless lawmen and victims alike, George Anderson, alias Bill Miner, never looked the part of a dangerous outlaw. He often appeared to be more of an elderly gentleman than the notorious bandit who robbed stagecoaches and trains from California to Georgia. This photo is believed to have been taken in Canada where Miner was captured following one of his many robberies. He subsequently escaped from the prison in which he was incarcerated, solidifying his nickname, "The Grey Fox." (Photo courtesy of Heritage House Publishing Company and Art Downs)

White Sulphur Road at the old Southern Railway intersection in Hall County was photographed above in 1987. In 1911, Southern Railway's White Sulphur Depot stood in the vicinity of the warning signal pictured here, and it was to this point that flagman C.H. Shirley ran to report the robbery of Train #36. (Photo by Olin Jackson)

HISTORIC CROSSING - The late Ray Shaw of Gainesville was an employee of the U.S. Postal Service in Hall County for many years, and as such, was intimately familiar with the history and terrain of the area. He was photographed above in 1987, at the spot at which Southern Railway's Train #36 was robbed by old West outlaw Bill Miner and his accomplices near White Sulphur, Georgia, on a cold February morning in 1911. (Photo by Olin Jackson)

TAKING ON SUPPLIES - This primitive print shows the Merritt M. London homeplace which once stood near the intersection of Long Branch Road and Highway 60 in Lumpkin County. While fleeing lawmen in February of 1911, Bill Miner reportedly stopped at the country store adjacent to this home to take on provisions. Pictured in this photo are: Merritt M. London (with white beard and hat in center of photo). His wife, Mary Neisler London stands beside the tree in the front yard. Sons Frank (in the wagon) and Bob (2nd from left) also appear. The identity of the individual in the overalls is unknown. (Photo courtesy of Annie Lou Dobbs of Toccoa, GA, daughter of Frank and Annie Kemp London).

reported that they did have a male boarder who was sleeping on a cot upstairs in a loft.

Davis and his sons reportedly mounted the stairs where they found a person who appeared to be asleep. As Davis pulled the blanket away, the stranger aimed a .45 revolver at him. Davis' salvation was found in his two sons who had a shotgun and a .22 rifle directed at the old man who in fact turned out to be George Anderson, alias Bill Miner.

Rufus Davis was still alive in 1987, and lived in Cartersville, Georgia. Though in his nineties at the time, Rufus still remembered details of this day. He also still possessed the set of handcuffs used to restrain Miner after his capture.

Jim Davis eventually collected the reward offered for the capture of the train robbers (Miner's accomplices in the robbery had been arrested earlier in the day prior to Miner's arrest.) Sheriff Sergeant unsuccessfully sued Davis for part of the reward, claiming the last capture was really his work.

Despite all the clamor of the event, the detectives, sheriffs, and other officials in the manhunt still had no idea who they had captured even after Miner was clapped in chains. The old bandit identified himself by his real name - George Anderson - and all the official Georgia police and criminal records relating to him identified him by that name. It was probably the first time in many years that he had used his actual name for identification purposes. Interestingly, when the name by which he was commonly known - "Bill Miner" - was learned by the authorities, it was assumed that that was his actual name, and that the moniker "George Anderson" was an alias.

While waiting in the Lumpkin County jail, Anderson (alias Bill Miner) talked of the great potential of Dahlonega's inactive gold mines in such a way that the *Dahlonega Nugget* published his remarks as if he were a prominent geologist, stroking local civic pride. It is ironic to note that Miner began his life of crime at the site of the second great gold rush in California and ended it at the site of the first U.S. gold rush in Dahlonega, Georgia. And even as he was captured, he was preaching the merits of the gold mining industry.

After his capture in Dahlonega, Miner was transported to Gainesville for trial. His arrival by automobile in Gainesville was greeted by crowds of hundreds of people, gathered as if to see a street parade, and caused Miner to remark "They must think I am a bear."

A special session of the Hall County Superior Court was held on March 3, 1911, to try the train robbers. Charlie Hunter confessed his role in the robbery, and became the state's chief witness against Miner. Hunter received a sentence of fifteen years, but escaped within a year, and surprisingly, no effort was made to recapture him. James Handford also pleaded guilty, received the same sentence, and was granted a parole in 1918.

Miner however, insisted upon a trial. He sat impassively as the state paraded witness after witness before him. Miner's almost flawlessly polite manners, some observers believed, would carry weight with the jury, but in fact, the Hall Countians quickly returned with a verdict of "Guilty." Miner's only show of emotion came when Howard Thompson, special attorney for the express company, spoke of the dynamite used in the express car potentially "blowing into eternity sleeping women and children on the train." A reporter witnessed Miner answer that charge "with a most vengeful, glaring, and hateful glance."

When Judge Sims sentenced Miner to twenty years in prison, the old gentleman bandit reportedly thanked him, stood up and turned to a group of college girls and ladies and proceeded to provide a moral for the story they had witnessed unfolding before them:

"When one breaks the law, one must expect to pay the penalty. I am old, but during all my life, I have found the golden rule the best guide to man in this world," he said. He then smiled and sat down.

Though one of the most cold-blooded and notorious thugs in the colorful history of train robberies in the U.S., Miner is routine-

The historic Merritt M. London homeplace at the intersection of Long Branch Road and Highway 60, was photographed in 1993, a few years prior to its unfortunate demolition. (Photo by Anne Dismukes Amerson)

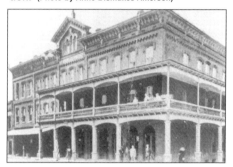

Officials managing the manhunt for Bill Miner used the main room of the old Dixie Hunt Hotel (above, photographed circa 1900) as a headquarters. This structure, a portion of which still exists today on the square in Gainesville, was built in 1882 on the corner of Main and Spring streets. (Photo courtesy of Hall County Library)

ly described as "looking less like a criminal than almost any man one might imagine." Yet, this kindly-looking old man reportedly methodically shot virtually all of a group of possemen pursuing him from the scene of a stagecoach robbery in 1881 in California, and was identified as associated with numerous other crimes throughout his life.

Though this final event in Georgia ended forever Miner's stagecoach/train robbing days, it did not bring to a close the ability of the Grey Fox as he was called, to galvanize public attention. Above and

Photographed in front of the old Lumpkin County Jail (which still stands today in Dahlonega), are: (left to right) Sheriff James M. "Jim" Davis, Gordon Davis, Joe Davis, William S. "Bill" Davis, Charles C. Davis, and Rufus Tilman "R.T." Davis. Just a few days after robbing Southern Railway's Train #36 near White Sulphur, Bill Miner was captured by Sheriff John Sergeant, Jim Davis, and Davis' two sons - Rufus and Joe. Following his capture, Miner was incarcerated in this jail. (Photo courtesy of C.C. Davis, Jr.)

Old Lumpkin County Jail - in which bandit Bill Miner was incarcerated - as it appeared in 1995. (Photo by Olin Jackson)

beyond his notoriety as a train robber, Miner was also a legend as an escape artist. He had escaped from prisons in Canada and elsewhere and often boasted that no prison could hold him indefinitely.

William Pinkerton, head of the well-known detective agency of the same name, was a spectator at the trial, and warned the press that he doubted that any Georgia prison could hold the old man. His comments proved prophetic. Miner escaped not once, but twice from prison in Milledgeville, Georgia after his incarceration there. Had it not been for his aging condition and lack of resistance to exposure and the elements after his escapes, he might not have been recaptured.

Following the trial in Gainesville, the convicted trio was sent to Georgia's huge prison camp in Newton County. Life in the camp did not suit Miner, however. A personal appeal to Robert E. Davison, then chairman of the State Prison Board, finally earned him a transfer to the state prison farm for the infirm in Milledgeville.

While at the farm, Miner recruited the services of convicted murderers John B. Watts and Tom H. Moore for an escape. Late one night, Watts somehow managed to remove the peep-hole apparatus out of the door of his cell, and squeeze through the opening. He took the keys and a pistol from a sleeping guard, and released Miner and Moore. The trio made a clean getaway.

Following his escape, Miner was brazen enough to mail a letter to Robert Davison, thanking him for giving him his opportunity for escape. "My dear sir," he wrote, "I want to thank you for your kindness in putting me at Milledgeville. My dear sir, don't trust a prisoner, don't matter how sick he is or makes out he is. Yours truly, B. Miner"

The chairman's embarrassment was also the embarrassment of the state of Georgia and the newspapers and citizens who had urged that the "sick old man be allowed to die in peace" at the lightly-guarded prison farm. The *Atlanta Journal* proclaimed that "wherever Bill Miner is, he is probably grinning and the joke is on Georgia."

It wasn't long however, before Miner was recaptured. He and Moore had headed for Augusta, Georgia. At a tiny community nearby called Keysville, a J.W. Whittle overheard a brakeman talking to two "bums" in a boxcar. When it was realized that the two matched a description of two escaped convicts, Whittle summoned help.

The boxcar was surrounded shortly thereafter by a posse, and Miner recaptured. Moore, however, chose not to return - at least not alive. He reportedly fired a single shot in the vicinity of the posse, and then in turn was killed by a single shot to the face. Inside the boxcar, members of the posse found dynamite and fuses which Miner explained "were good for catching fish." Old Bill had been a breath away from another train robbery.

Returned to his prison cell in Milledgeville, Miner boasted that he would escape again at the first opportunity. His guards, understandably, took no chances against any future embarrassment. One can only imagine their total humiliation, when on the morning of June 27, 1912, they found the Grey Fox gone again, his ankle and arm bracelets locked to his bunk, the window bars sawed out, and the bedding made into a rope which he had used to climb to the ground. It was literally the stuff from which legends are made.

Accompanied by convicts W.J. Windencamp and W.M. Wiggins, Miner was loose once again. The trio took a boat into the Oconee River this time, with the plan of reaching a port where they could ship out as deck hands. The boat capsized however, drowning Windencamp.

For three days afterwards, Miner and Wiggins were lost in a swamp near Oconee, Georgia, living on blackberries and unable to find safe drinking water. When they finally came out near Toombsboro, they offered no resistance to a posse which found them at a home begging for breakfast. Miner's escape this time had lasted only five days.

The reception the old outlaw received upon his return to Milledgeville this time even exceeded Bill's wildest imaginings. Driven in an open, heavily-guarded automobile and shackled securely, Bill was met in the downtown area by an extremely large crowd of admiring townspeople who reportedly literally applauded him and passed him money and cigars.

Always gracious, Miner stood up in the car and waved his hat to his fans. The *Union Recorder* claimed that "for a short time, it looked like a hero had come to the city instead of a man who had wrecked and robbed trains." This, however, was the last adventure for the grizzled old man who had robbed trains from coast to coast. The exact circumstances of his last days are unknown today, but it is believed the hunger, exposure to the weather, and contaminated water he consumed during his escape, apparently took their toll on him, causing him to lapse into illness.

The *Atlanta Journal*, learning that Miner was near death in September of 1913, interviewed him one last time. Before they could get the story printed, the Angel of Death visited the cell of the Grey Fox, and gave him permanent freedom at last.

Though accounts of his actual burial site vary today, the final resting place of Bill Miner is in the old city cemetery known as Memory Hill in Milledgeville. His grave is marked with a simple headstone, and is found on the southeast side of Memory Hill where the cemetery slopes toward Fishing Creek, a place where many convicts were buried when the penitentiary was located at Milledgeville. His headstone bears his pseudonym Bill Miner, since no one was certain of his true name.

Treasure-hunters still ply the railroads and other sites suspected of holding the loot Miner supposedly left behind somewhere in Hall or Lumpkin counties in north Georgia. Interestingly, almost all of the money and valuables stolen by Miner and his henchmen in the robbery in Gainesville were recovered. Miner had personally provided Sheriff Crow (of Hall County) with directions to two caches of loot. Several other caches turned up later, satisfying most recovery efforts.

The site of the famed train robbery now bears mute testimony to the events of February 18, 1911. Today, the crossing at White Sulphur is known as "Bill Miner Crossing."

Early Rail Center

The Day Belton, Georgia "Dried Up"

As an early stop on the Richmond & Danville Railroad, Belton grew steadily until town leaders in nearby Lula found a way to best their up-start sister city.

Water is essential to the fabric of life for humans, animals and plants. The over-abundance of rain or snow, or a lack thereof, has sometimes changed the course of history. Muddy battlefields or the scarcity of water for soldiers in combat can, and has, resulted in wars being won and lost.

The same analogy can be applied to civic contests. Towns can also die due to a lack of water. Belton, Georgia is a good example.

This small unassuming town once existed approximately halfway between Gainesville, Georgia, in Hall County, and Cornelia, Georgia, in adjacent Habersham County. Today, one would be hard-pressed to realize a town once existed at this site at all.

While driving through this community today, one must search closely for a road-sign containing this town's name. As of this writing, there are approximately three: one on the "Belton" Baptist Church (churches quite often are the last structures to disappear in a dying community); another on "Belton" Bridge; and the last found by this writer on "Belton" Park.

At one time, Belton and Lula were known as "twin towns." They were each located about 14 miles from Gainesville; they both faced the railroad tracks that divided Hall and Banks counties; and they were both located about three miles south of the Habersham County line.

The story of Belton and Lula is an interesting page in our state's railroading history. It is a tale which covers topics ranging from a bitter rivalry between two wealthy men, cotton production, the railroad, and most importantly - the scarcity of water in Belton.

According to *Cyclopedia Of Georgia*, published in 1906, both towns had post offices, express and telegraph offices, mercantile and shipping industries, schools and churches – all despite the fact they were separated from each other by little more than one mile. Belton was the oldest of the two. It was also the largest in the early days.

First named Bellvue or Bellview, the name of Lula's counterpart was later changed to Bellton, and then following a change in the town's charter in the early 1900s, the name was shortened to simply Belton.

According to one account, the town was named for a John Bell who came to Georgia from South Carolina. He was one of a number of individuals who traveled to Belton as a result of early land speculation and mining activities.

The arrival of the Richmond & Danville Airline Railroad which passed through both Lula and Belton in 1873 had spurred much of the development. The railroad provided a convenient means of marketing locally-produced goods – especially cotton which was abundantly grown in the area. One old-timer, when recalling the boom-times of the town, reminisced that "sometimes I could walk from one end of the town to the other atop bales of cotton awaiting shipment."

Another account describes a Mr. Madison Buice who came to the area from Atlanta. He reportedly named the town after a Major Madison Bell, a former comptroller general of Georgia and a son of Major John Bell.

Buice took temporary quarters in the community while having timber sawed for his own home. According to reports, he planted vineyards and orchards and then shipped wine and fruit throughout the country.

Buice also reportedly surveyed and laid out the town, selling lots, running a steam-powered saw mill and furnishing lumber for construction. An entrepreneurial individual, he built and sold houses, promoted the community to other settlers, and indirectly influenced the construction of churches and an academy.

By 1880, the population of Belton had grown to approximately 500, and a variety of businesses were in operation. A newspaper – *The North Georgia* – was published weekly in the community, and chronicled the towns burgeoning growth.

Meanwhile, things were heating up in the nearby township of Lula, where visions of greater things were on the minds of the town fathers there. It seems the railroad had expansion plans in mind in the 1870s, and both Lula and Belton were contending for a planned line (to be called the Northeastern Railroad) through the area which would connect Athens, Georgia with the Richmond & Danville Airline Railroad.

Joseph H. Banks and his brother, Dunstan E. Banks, sons of Dr. Richard Banks for whom Banks County was named, came from Gainesville and played a prominent role in the development of the town of Lula. In the process, they had accumulated

Once operated by Mrs. Gussie Coffee, the rooming house pictured here provided accommodations and meals for train crews stopping over in Lula.

substantial properties in the area, and it therefore became vitally important to them that the rumored new railroad line should be built through their community – and not through adjacent Belton.

As the situation evolved, both Joe Banks and Matt Buice therefore, for the same reasons, desperately wanted to attract the planned rail line, because their property values would be dramatically increased (or devalued), according to the circumstances.

In a generous (but obviously personally motivated) gesture, the Banks brothers deeded a large tract of land for the railroad "provided the main and principal depot at the junction be located on land donated by [them] (the Banks brothers), and that the town of Lula will be laid out at the junction."

Prior to this inducement, Matt Buice had already provided his own gift of a depot in Belton, to attract the Northeastern Railroad builders. The Banks brothers, however, had offered a larger "brick" depot, winning the day for Lula.

In a twist of irony, the track was required to be forty miles in length in order to obtain the required railroad franchise, but when surveyed to Lula, it measured only 39 miles. Rather than extend the necessary extra mile of track to Belton as well, the builders extended a branch line into an uninhabited rural area instead, and this extra portion was never used thereafter.

When the railroad was completed in

1876, there was an elaborate celebration which included dinner in the diner of a train which had journeyed over the line to celebrate its inaugural run. Among the young ladies in attendance that day was a Miss Lula (or Lulah) Phinizy, daughter of Ferdinand Phinizy, a wealthy Augusta, Georgia resident and one-time owner of White Sulphur Springs, a popular resort at that time between Gainesville and Lula. The junction and new depot were christened "Lula," in remembrance of her.

The trains and train station were very important for the growth of Lula. It was reported that three freight train crews were stationed at Lula every night. They boarded there in a white frame hotel which was operated by Mrs. Gussie Coffee. (The hotel unfortunately, has since been demolished.)

The town of Lula, with its big new water tank and coal chute for the steam locomotives, became an important rail junction, and quickly usurped the railroad business formerly accorded to Belton. The Richmond & Danville Airline Railroad trains had formerly stopped at the Belton Depot where the trains were refueled by water pumped from a small branch. Lula eventually attracted the lion's share of this business.

With the demise of "King Cotton," however, both Belton and Lula suffered. Their large warehouses soon were emptied of the cash crop which had previously been such a staple commodity in the communities.

The Great Depression also dealt a severe blow to the townships. A bank in Lula, supported by Joseph Banks, closed during the depression years, and drug stores and other businesses failed as well.

With the business drought, the railroad trains had fewer and fewer reasons to stop. By 1936, they stopped only in Lula.

Despite the harsh realities of life, competition seemed to continue between the two communities. The Belton and Lula schools had consolidated in 1911. A new high school, built in 1938, was placed with one-half of the structure in the Belton city limits, and the other half in the Lula city limits.

Finally, on November 19, 1955, Lula and Belton, formerly bitter rivals, merged. Citizens of both communities voted 150 to 3 on the consolidation. Belton, it seems, was in dire need of a number of public services, if its residents were to be able to persevere, so Lula, once again, held the upper hand.

In the process, Lula was allowed to keep its name, and Belton, in exchange for its lost identity, received the much-needed resource of Lula's water system, as well as other services. Thus, the need for water, quite literally, caused Belton to lose its name.

Today, the long freight trains, as well as an Amtrak passenger train, both pass through Lula on a regular schedule – the operative words being "pass through." The trains never stop.

The old water tank still exists on the hill overlooking the streets and businesses of Lula – a vestigial connection to the community's historic past. Today, however, all the water for the little township comes from the Gainesville, Georgia water system.

Much of Lula's history today is based understandably upon the railroad. As of this writing, the town continues to conduct a two-day observance of "Railroad Festival Days," to honor the community's origin. Festivities include a parade down the town's main street, capped off by a carnival at a nearby park.

Years ago, a high rounded wooden bridge was built over the railroad tracks in the middle of town, so that traffic on the street would not be interrupted by the intermittent trains. Recently, an effort was made to remove this bridge, but the movement was quickly squelched in typical Lula fashion.

"We saved it by proving that if there was a fire across the tracks and a train was passing through at the same time, the fire trucks would be delayed, possibly causing a calamity," explained one resident.

Today, Belton, one of the state's early pioneer communities has virtually disappeared, but Lula continues to persevere.

Historic Georgia Film Site

Remembering *Fried Green Tomatoes*

It wasn't too long ago that tiny Juliette, Georgia, was a virtual ghosttown – abandoned and forgotten in the 1950s when the grist mill closed down and the railroad ceased passenger service. However, following the release of a hugely-successful motion picture filmed at the site, the little community has sprung to life once again.

I had an eerie feeling as I sat eating fried green tomatoes (of course) and barbecued ribs at the Whistle Stop Cafe in Juliette, Georgia recently. The comment Sipsey (the well-known character in the movie) made to the Georgia sheriff as he ate barbecue in the major motion picture production of Fried Green Tomatoes came suddenly to mind, and I had to remind myself that it was only a movie.

"The secret's in the sauce," Sipsey quipped, as she shuffled around in the dead man's shoes. I half expected her to serve me as I ate the delicious food in the now famous little restaurant, so powerful is the aura of the site.

Aside from the aforementioned famous entrees at the Whistle Stop, my lunch on this delightful day included coleslaw, gumbo, candied yams, collard greens, and cornbread. Peach cobbler came with the meal which cost only $5.95. The atmosphere you get for free.

The cafe uses up to 20 cases of tomatoes each week. Slices come with every order, and a five-slice side order costs $2.25.

Much of the credit for the revitalization of this once-forgotten mill-town is due to Fannie Flagg, author/producer of the movie which captured the attention of young and old alike. Miss Flagg reportedly rode up and down the railroad tracks at many sites in Georgia looking for a little town to use as the setting for her fictitious community in the movie - Whistle Stop, Alabama. Juliette finally caught her eye. It will never be the same.

In the summer of 1991, the cast and crew for the movie came to town. When the filming was completed and the movie stars departed, so also did the glamour and activity with which the quiet little community had been infused.

The movie company tore down the sets used in the production. Juliette would have returned to its sleepy forgotten status had it not been for a few entrepreneurial spirits who realized they had a real opportunity staring them right in the face.

"The director of the movie said we ought to consider opening the place as the

Whistle Stop Cafe," Jerie Lynn Williams, a resident of Juliette explained. She and Robert Williams (no relation) quickly began thinking about opening a real restaurant in the Whistle Stop. People thought Robert was crazy. "Who are you going to feed?" some asked.

Jerie and Robert started buying and renovating the old stores along the little main street. Jerie says she bought old fixtures at auctions that give the interior of the cafe its authentic look. She also maintains that she didn't know how to cook, but did have her grandmother's recipe for fried green tomatoes (which Jerie keeps secret, right along with her barbecue recipe. . .). She persuaded a cook from Mable's Table, the town's only restaurant (which recently had closed) to cook for her.

Jerie and Robert opened the cafe April 16, 1992, hoping immediately to ride the coattails of the movie's popularity. It wasn't as smooth an entry into the hospitality industry as they had hoped for, however.

"I think I cried the first ten days," Jerie continued, remembering the early days when few if any visitors traveled to the site. Eventually, however, newspaper and magazine publicity began attracting attention, and a steady stream of customers began appearing at their doorstep.

Once inside, guests are transported back to a bygone era. The restaurant looks much as it did in the movie, with overhead fans, clapboard walls, booths, and tables covered with green-checked oilcloths.

A small bullet hole still pierces one window, as was scripted in the movie, and movie memorabilia decorates the walls.

"When a Southern Railroad freight train rumbles past, guests rush outside. It's amazing," Jerie laughs. "It's as if people had never seen a train before. One woman thought we had staged the whole thing!"

The first thing to do when you arrive is to put your name on the clipboard waiting list at the cafe's front door. Don't be surprised if you have a one- to two-hour wait on weekends.

To date, visitors to the site have traveled from 44 different countries - some from as far away as Egypt and Iceland. Residents from every state in the U.S. have also visited.

As a result of the popularity of the site, Juliette has literally returned from the dead. At one time, it boasted the largest water-powered gristmill in the world, but by the 1950s, gristmills had become a thing of the past, bringing operations at Dr. Glover's enterprise to a close. When the mill closed, the town's residents abandoned their homes and stores in an almost wholesale move to find employment elsewhere.

For years, a handful of residents attempted to bring the community back to life, all to no avail. Even the construction of nearby Lake Juliette proved fruitless.

Ironically, the very quality which was working against it – its rural, scenic locale – was what ultimately appealed to the Hollywood movie-makers. The rest, as they say, is history.

Today, the big dam across the river in Juliette still offers the scenic quality that made it a highlight in a number of the movie's scenes. So also do a number of other manifestations of rural flavor which enlivened the production.

All of this, coupled with the Whistle Stop Cafe, have combined to make Juliette a popular tourism destination. And in answer to the growing visitation to the site, other entrepreneurs have opened gift shops selling everything from antiques and crafts to collectibles and candy up and down the tiny streets of the community, so be prepared for a measure of commercialism. One shop bears the name "The Ruth and Idgie House."

A little Hollywood magic seems to have worked wonders for a town that was given up for dead in 1990. For more information about the Whistle Stop Café at (478) 992-8886. To reach Juliette, take Exit 61 off of Interstate 75, one hour south of Atlanta.

Retracing The Route Of The Great Locomotive Chase

Many articles have been written over the years which described the famous "Great Locomotive Chase" which occurred on the Western & Atlantic Railroad in 1862 in Georgia during the U.S. Civil War. Very few of these articles, however, have taken the reader, step by step, back over this historic route, pointing out the remnants of the historic sites involved in this unusual incident.

The first weekend of every October, Adairsville, Georgia hosts the Great Locomotive Chase Festival. History enthusiasts today may enjoy retracing the original route of the General – the famous locomotive involved in this historic event.

This will be a very interesting and informative driving tour, so be sure to pack up the kids for this trip too. It will be a great way to have fun, see a lot of the scenic countryside in north Georgia, and make history come alive for the youngsters.

With the U.S. Civil War well underway in 1862, a group of 23 volunteers from the Union Army and one civilian, led by civilian spy James A. Andrews, planned to destroy the railroad and disrupt service between Atlanta and Chattanooga.

An account published by the Louisville & Nashville Railroad (L&N) summed it up this way:

"The basic plan of the raid was for Andrews and his men to move deep into the Confederacy, take over a locomotive and, en route north, set fire to as many as possible of the several bridges on the W&A. This would put the railroad out of commission for many weeks. Some Federal military strategists felt that such a plan, if successful, could even end the war – or at least shorten it considerably."

On April 10, 1862, the raiders were scheduled to meet in Marietta, but most of them – including Andrews – were held up, and did not arrive until April 11. This forced the men to begin their raid a day later than scheduled. This delay was a harbinger of worse times ahead for the men.

On the night of the 11th, there was a steady rainfall in Marietta. Most of the raiders took quarters at the Fletcher House, an imposing brick building which still stands today beside the railroad tracks in downtown Marietta. This structure is known today as the Kennesaw House, and we will begin our tour here.

Today, the Kennesaw House provides quarters for the Marietta Museum of History, and is an excellent place to see historic items from Civil War days in the Marietta area. Managed by Daniel Cox and wife Connie, this museum is a great

TALES OF THE RAILS IN GEORGIA

The "General" was photographed circa 1900, possibly in the rail yards in Atlanta. (Photo courtesy of Adairsville History Museum)

This sketch of Kingston, Georgia, was published in *Harper's Weekly* magazine on July 2, 1864. Andrews and his raiders, with Conductor William A. Fuller and his men in hot pursuit, raced up the rail line through this village.

Kingston Depot was photographed above in 1864. This view, facing east, shows the depot in the background and the railroad, running north to south, across the center of the photo. (Olin Jackson files)

spot to begin piecing together the details surrounding this exciting incident from the war.

On the morning of April 12, 1862, at approximately 5:00 a.m., James Andrews and 19 of the volunteers boarded the Confederate locomotive General in Marietta for the trip northward. Including Andrews, there initially were 25 men in the group. However, along the way, two of the men came under suspicion and were forced to join the Confederate army at Chattanooga. Another man never showed up at all, and two others overslept on the morning of their planned departure from Marietta. This reduced the total number of participants to 20.

The first stop after leaving Marietta was Big Shanty (present-day Kennesaw), Georgia. It was a miserably wet and rainy day, and the General made a scheduled 20-minute stop outside the Lacy Hotel at Big Shanty. The trains had no dining cars, so regular stops were necessary so that travelers could take their meals. The Lacy Hotel provided a hearty Southern breakfast which was relished by all the trainmen.

The crew and the passengers trudged inside the hotel – all except for Andrews and his men who remained with the train. William A. Fuller, conductor of the General, had seated himself by a window with Engineer Jeff Cain and machine foreman Anthony Murphy when he realized the train was moving! All three men bolted outside where they learned the General was being stolen!

Fuller, Cain and Murphy chased the train, but before they could reach it, it had moved too far down the tracks and was gaining momentum. Undeterred, the trio continued running down the tracks for two miles until they reached Moon's Station. Here, they commandeered a handcar that a maintenance crew had been using. It was slow going, but it was better than running.

If one wants to see the Lacy Hotel today, he or she will be disappointed. The Lacy was burned to the ground by General William T. Sherman's troops in 1864, and nothing remains of this historic structure today. It was located approximately 100 yards south of the current (circa 1905) railroad depot which exists today on the east side of the tracks.

If one wants to see the General, however, it does still exist. It is housed in the Southern Museum of Civil War and Locomotive History, located across Cherokee Street from the depot.

Moon's Station suffered the same indignity as did the Lacy Hotel. Nothing, save a lone historic marker, remains of this historic site from yesteryear. A road named "Moon's Station Road" crossed the tracks at this spot until recent years when it was closed in 1995.

Andrews and his raiders stopped briefly at Moon's Station to obtain tools they needed for their planned demolitions ahead. A "pull-bar," among other things, was taken and later used to pull up rails.

One might wonder how Andrews was able to stop at the many stations along the way without his ruse being uncovered. Andrews has been described as being 6 feet tall with a clear complexion and abundant black hair. He also possessed a confidence which instantly convinced others of his authority. These traits apparently served him well in this venture.

When questioned about his status and destination with the General, Andrews reportedly replied, "I'm taking a 'powder train' through to General Beauregard at Corinth." This was a plausible explanation, since the well-known battle at Shiloh in which Beauregard had been involved had occurred only a few days earlier.

Meanwhile, not far behind the General, its crew doggedly continued in pursuit. Propelling the little handcar furiously with poles, they made their way down the tracks until they reached the community of Etowah.

Interestingly, a portion of the raiders' plans included the burning of the Etowah River Bridge. For reasons unknown today, the demolition of this bridge never occurred. This was just one of several fateful decisions which ultimately led to the

The original depot at Adairsville, Georgia. It was at this site that the locomotive "Texas" was commandeered by William Fuller for use in the pursuit of Andrews' raiders who were on board the "General."

Though a portion of the image on the front of this antique postcard has peeled away and degenerated at the top, the old Adairsville Depot and the tracks of the Western & Atlantic Railroad are still clearly visible, as is a portion of the town. (Photo Olin Jackson files)

The Oostanaula River Bridge. It was here that Andrews attempted to set fire to a boxcar and burn the long covered railroad bridge which once existed on this site. The stone ramparts on the left bank (slightly visible in the photo) date to the 1862 raid.

The historic Dalton Depot on the old Western & Atlantic Railroad line still stands today. It was here that the young telegraph operator jumped to the depot platform in order to send a message ahead to General Leadbetter instructing him to deploy troops from Chattanooga. Today, this site is known simply as "The Depot," and is a popular restaurant.

Today (as of this writing), historic Tunnel Hill Depot still exists, but is sandwiched between several factory buildings along the railroad tracks, and is not available for public viewing.

The signage confirms that this historic tunnel was designated as a preservation project back in the year 2000. As one can clearly see, there is still a light at the end of the tunnel, but thusfar, the interior has not been stabilized for public viewing.

capture of the raiders.

Today, the massive stone piers of the old Etowah River Bridge still stand mutely in the river. They can be clearly seen from U.S. Highway 41, south of Cartersville. Just two miles from this bridge, visitors may also see remnants of Cooper's Iron Works, a large rolling mill and factory which once provided supplies to the Confederacy. One portion of this mill which remains today is an immense stone furnace.

Cooper's Iron Works was an extraordinary complex built by Jacob Stroup in the 1830s, and later sold to businessman Mark David Cooper. This unusual historic site must be seen first-hand to appreciate the immenseness of the development. It is located in Cooper's Day Use Area on Lake Allatoona just off U.S. Highway 41. The park has a picnic area and hiking trail, which make it a nice place to stop and take a break during the trip. A number of the old stone buildings from Cooper's Iron Works stand today on the bottom of Lake Allatoona.

Cooper's Iron Works also played a significant role in "the Great Locomotive Chase." It was here that Conductor Fuller commandeered the engine Yonah, which he used to give further chase to the General. By this time, Fuller and his two able assistants were, no doubt, very relieved to trade in the handcar for the locomotive.

Next stop: Cass Station. Very little – other than ruins – remains of Cass Station today either. The remnants of this depot are located north of Cartersville, as was the town which was burned by General W. T. Sherman. There is an old warehouse in front of the ruins. In the 1860s, however, Cass Station was an important stop on the Western & Atlantic Railroad.

Andrews and his raiders stopped at Cass to replenish their wood and water supplies for the General. While they were at this stop, a tender, William Russell, gave the Union spy a railroad schedule, thinking he was aiding the Confederate war effort. Little did he know he was actually assisting enemy espionage agents.

From Cass Station, the General proceeded on to Kingston, a busy junction on the W&A. This stop played a major role in the turn of events which ultimately led to the capture of Andrews and his men.

According to the railroad schedule, the General would be side-tracked for only one train. (The W&A was a single-track line which required periodic side tracks to allow scheduled trains to pass each other along the route.) Despite the scheduled one-train wait, Andrews watched frantically as other trains were flagged to resume access to the line ahead of him.

Finally, in desperation, Andrews demanded that any more on-coming trains be held up so he could take his "much needed cargo of ammunition" to General Beauregard at Corinth. The old switch-tender, Uriah Stephens, had reservations about the strangers on Fuller's train, but according to one account, he reluctantly threw the switch that let the General pass. (A conflicting report maintains that Andrews was forced to throw the switch himself after Stephens refused.) By the time he was able to depart, Andrews had lost a very precious hour and five minutes at Kingston Station.

The lost time gave Fuller and the Yonah just enough time to catch up to Andrews and his men. Fuller later reported the Yonah made the 14 miles in 15 minutes at speeds of up to 55 miles per hour. The only thing which saved the capture of Andrews and his men at this point was the fact that trains had been moved to let the General pass. These trains on the tracks prevented the Yonah from following.

Once again, Fuller, Murphy and Cain applied the only source of transportation left to them – their feet! They took off on foot around the southbound trains and past the station to another northbound train which was about to roll.

With her steam up and wheels ready to turn, the William R. Smith was an able locomotive belonging to the Rome Railroad. After hastily explaining the circumstances to conductor Cicero Smith and

A marble marker two miles north of the Ringgold Depot marks the spot today at which the "Great Locomotive Chase" ended.

In 1962, one hundred years after the famed "Great Locomotive Chase," the General went on tour, retracing the route of the famed incident from Marietta to Ringgold, Georgia. (Photo courtesy of Adairsville History Museum)

Known as the Fletcher House in 1862, the Kennesaw House still stands beside the railroad tracks in downtown Marietta, Georgia. It was in this structure that many of Andrews' raiders spent the night prior to the locomotive chase. Though much of the town had been destroyed by fire by war's end, the Kennesaw House managed to survive, even though a portion of it also fell victim to the flames.

TALES OF THE RAILS IN GEORGIA

The Kennesaw House was photographed here in 1867, just a few years after the famed locomotive chase occurred. Notice how near the railroad was constructed to the hotel. (Photo courtesy of Marietta Museum of History)

The late Wilbur G. Kurtz was a noted artist/historian from Atlanta, and the son-in-law of Conductor William Fuller on the locomotive "General." From conversations with and descriptions by individuals such as Fuller who were contemporaries of the Lacy Hotel, Kurtz painted this view of the famed structure at which the train crew was taking breakfast on the morning that James Andrews and his men hijacked the "General" in 1862. (Illustration courtesy of Wilbur G. Kurtz Collection, Atlanta History Center. All rights reserved)

Photographed by George N. Bernard, official photographer for Gen. William T. Sherman, the Western & Atlantic Railroad Bridge spans the Etowah River in the background. The trenches which were used to provide a defense for the bridge are visible in the foreground.

engineer O. Wiley Harbin, Fuller and his men took over the William R. Smith and continued after the raiders. Along the way, several volunteers joined the chase.

Kingston was another of the many cities destroyed by Sherman and his men. According to Emma C. Williams and Martha H. Mullinex, it was a growing and prosperous city on the W&A in 1862.

Emma and Martha are members of the Kingston Women's History Club. The ladies of the club have opened a history museum in Kingston which houses relics and photographs from yesteryear involving this community.

The original stone depot in Kingston was destroyed in 1864. Two subsequent depots were built in the same spot, but were likewise destroyed by fire. Today, the foundation of the original depot is the only reminder of the Western & Atlanta Railroad and the Great Locomotive Chase at this spot.

The lovely town of Adairsville is the next stop on our tour of the W&A. The William R. Smith was forced to stop several times so that the men could remove cross-ties placed on the railroad tracks by the raiders. A short time later, Fuller and his crew had to abandon their train once again after discovering that a section of the tracks ahead of them had been destroyed.

Without hesitation, Fuller reportedly climbed down from the William R. Smith and proceeded once again on foot. When he looked behind him, he discovered that only Murphy was still with him – carrying a shotgun they had acquired sometime during the chase. The other men had abandoned the chase.

Meanwhile, up ahead in Adairsville, Andrews had cunningly convinced Peter Bracken, engineer of the Texas, that he must get through to General Beauregard with their cargo of powder. Bracken obligingly sidetracked his train so that Andrews could pass with the General.

Having traveled on foot for a couple of miles, Fuller and Murphy were relieved to see the Texas steaming down the tracks.

They signaled for the train to stop and explained the dire circumstances to Bracken. The engineer immediately put the Texas in reverse and backed the 21-car freight train to Adairsville where he sidetracked the cars. The locomotive then continued down the tracks in reverse, chasing feverishly after the General. The Texas crew now consisted of Fuller, Murphy, Engineer Bracken and his 15-year-old fireman, Henry Haney.

If you visit Adairsville today, you will no doubt enjoy the historic personality of this quaint little town. On December 4, 1987, the entire town was listed on the National Register of Historic Places. The original depot which witnessed the Great Locomotive Chase in 1862 still stands on the town square.

Contrary to most other depots which have disappeared from the old route of the W&A, the Adairsville station not only still stands, but has been renovated for use as a history museum. A portion of the museum is dedicated to the history of The Great Locomotive Chase.

According to Col. James Bogle, an authority on the chase and co-author of the publication The General & The Texas, the town of Calhoun was the next stop for the Texas.

"The Texas made the run, in reverse, to Calhoun in some 12 minutes," Bogle wrote. "Here, the crew picked up valuable reinforcements for their cause. Fleming Cox, an engineer on the Memphis & Charleston Railroad, was on his way to Atlanta. Caught up in the excitement of the day, he climbed aboard the Texas and relieved 15-year-old Henry Haney as Bracken's fireman. Alonzo Martin also climbed on-board and assisted in passing wood to the tender."

Meanwhile, the raiders were approaching their next site of destruction – the Oostanaula River Bridge south of Resaca. They knew the Texas was not far behind them, and they realized they must destroy this bridge if they were to continue uncaptured.

To burn the bridge, the men started a fire in the rear car of the train. They intended to use the flames from this car to set the bridge aflame. Unfortunately for them, a steady rain had continued to fall, and the wood was so damp that it would do little more than smolder.

Today, the covered bridge over the Oostanaula no longer exists. The new bridge at this spot, however, uses some of the same stone pilings which once supported the covered bridge. If you stand on the modern-day bridge on Highway 41 and look over to the railroad bridge, you can still see these pilings.

By the time the Texas reached the bridge, they had already hooked up with a previous car left behind by the raiders. Now, with the addition of the smoldering car, they were pushing two additional cars up the railroad.

Between Resaca and Dalton, the General had stopped for wood and water, both of which were imperative for operation of the large locomotive. However, with the Texas hot on their trail, the men were unable to stop long enough to get the amount of wood and water necessary to continue their momentum. Time was running out. . .

At Dalton, the General sped past the depot without stopping. The Texas, close behind in pursuit, slowed down just enough to allow a young telegraph operator to jump from the train to telegraph a message ahead. According to a news account of this incident, the raiders cut the telegraph line a few miles beyond the depot, but not before most of the message had been sent ahead to Confederate forces under the command of General Leadbetter.

Today, the historic Dalton depot has been renovated and is used as a restaurant appropriately named "The Depot." A stop here is one you will enjoy. Once inside, you will be transported back in time by the décor and aura of this historic building. As you eat, you can observe trains rushing by large picture windows adjacent to the tracks. The menu is filled with delicious entrees and tasty desserts.

By this time, the raiders were merely

Author Deborah Malone stands beside a Georgia Historic Commission marker which indicates the former location of Moon's Station. Nothing remains of this station today, but in 1862, it was here that the pursuers of Andrews' raiders were able to obtain a push-car to aid in their pursuit of the saboteurs.

The immense pillars which once supported the Western & Atlantic Railroad bridge across the Etowah River still stand today, and can be seen from U.S. Highway 41. Had the raiders destroyed this bridge as originally planned, they quite possibly might have delayed their pursuers enough to allow themselves time for escape.

One of the enormous stone furnaces at the former site of the Civil War-era Cooper's Iron Works has been preserved by the park service. This extraordinary complex was built by Jacob Stroub in the 1830s and later sold to businessman Mark David Cooper. It was here that Conductor Fuller commandeered the engine "Yonah" which he used to give further chase to Andrews and the engine "General."

trying to stay ahead of the Texas just to prevent their capture. Their plan of destruction had failed. They were fast-approaching Tunnel Hill.

Just prior to reaching the tunnel, Fuller slowed down, fearing the raiders might have left their last boxcar inside the dark confines. Upon reaching the tunnel, he was able to see light from the other end, so he knew it was safe to continue on thru. From this point on, the General was in sight most of the time.

Today, Tunnel Hill is boxed between factory buildings, but it is still intact. There are several informative historical markers in this vicinity. Just beyond the Tunnel Hill depot is an old covered bridge. After crossing this bridge, the tunnel comes into sight. The area is closed off with a gate, but can be easily seen. It's hard to imagine this aged tunnel was constructed over 150 years ago.

Ringgold was the last station passed by the General. By this time, it was obvious the chase was almost over. In Fuller's words, "About two and a half miles the other side of Ringgold, we saw the engine we were pursuing apparently fagging". In other words, the General was running out of steam.

And that is literally what happened. Without an ample supply of wood and water, the mighty engine could not produce the steam necessary to drive it. It finally crawled to a stop, with the raiders scattering in all directions. According to an account at the time, Andrews reportedly said at this point, "Every man take care of himself!"

On top of a hill, the old Ringgold Depot still stands today, but it sadly has not been preserved. Just a couple of miles from the depot, a historical marker identifies the spot at which the General came to a stop.

Unfortunately for them, all of the 22 raiders eventually were caught. Eight of them – including Andrews – were executed in Atlanta, Georgia. Interestingly, eight of the men managed to escape from the Atlanta prison and make their way home. The remaining six were paroled at City Point, Virginia, on March 17, 1863.

A Driving Tour Of The Great Locomotive Chase

Kennesaw House/Marietta Museum of History

From Interstate 75 take Exit 263. Go west on Loop 120 for approximately 3.3 miles. Turn right onto Mill Street which will take you into the parking lot.

Kennesaw Civil War Museum

From Mill Street, turn right. Continue on Loop 120 for about 1.6 miles, and turn left onto Hwy 41 / Cobb Parkway. Continue for approximately 5.1 miles then angle off to the right onto Old Hwy. 41 just prior to the large Kennesaw Civil War Museum sign. Travel approximately 1.6 miles, then turn right onto Cherokee Street. After crossing the railroad tracks, the museum will be on the left. The depot and the site at which the Lacy Hotel once existed are on the right.

Moon's Station

From the museum, turn left back onto Cherokee Street and travel approximately two miles to Jiles Road. Turn left onto Jiles for approximately 0.7 of a mile and turn right onto Baker Road (at the traffic light). Travel 0.3 of a mile and the Moon's Station historic marker is on the left.

Etowah River Bridge

Backtrack to Hwy. 41 / Cobb Parkway and turn right onto the highway. Travel approximately 16.4 miles. Take the Highway 293 / Cooper Furnace Day Use Area Exit and then turn right at the stop sign. Continue for approximately 100 yards; turn left onto River Road then go approximately 50 yards and the remains of the old railroad bridge will be visible on the right.

Cooper's Iron Works

Continue on down River Road for approximately 2.5 miles and you will reach a point at which the road dead-ends at the Cooper Day Use Area Park. The remains of Coopers Iron Works at which the locomotive Yonah was commandeered by Conductor William Fuller are visible in this vicinity.

Cass Station

Backtrack to Highway 41 and travel north for approximately seven miles to Mac Johnson Road. Turn left at the traffic light. A Texaco service station will be on the left at the light. Turn right onto Highway 293. Turn left onto the first road on the left (Burnt Hickory Road). The remains of Cass Station are approximately 200 yards away on the right, behind an old warehouse just prior to the point at which you reach the railroad tracks.

Kingston

Backtrack back to Highway 41 once again and continue northward. Travel approximately one mile and turn left onto Boyd Morris Road (which is a detour to our objective which is Highway 293). Turn right onto 293 and continue for approximately six miles into Kingston. Turn left at the caution light onto Shaw Street and this will take you into downtown historic Kingston. The foundation of the old depot is on the opposite side of the railroad tracks to the right.

Adairsville Depot

Backtrack to Highway 293. Turn left onto 293 / Howard Street and travel approximately 0.4 of a mile. Turn right onto Hall Station Road. Continue on for approximately ten miles, then turn right onto King Street and travel 0.3 of a mile. Turn right onto Railroad Street and continue on for 0.3 of a mile to the old depot on the left.

Oostanaula River Bridge

Return to King Street and turn right. Go one block then turn left onto Main Street. Travel approximately 0.4 of a mile and turn right onto Highway 140. Continue approximately 1.5 miles to Interstate 75. Turn left onto Interstate 75 North and travel approximately 12.8 miles to Exit 318. Turn right onto Highway 41 and proceed approximately 1.5 miles and the old bridge will be on the right. The stone ramparts at this site date to the Civil War era and the Great Locomotive Chase.

Dalton Depot

Backtrack to Interstate 75 North. Continue 15 miles to Exit 333 / Walnut Avenue. Turn right onto Walnut Avenue and continue for 1.8 miles. Turn left onto Thornton Avenue. Proceed 0.7 of a mile and turn right onto Crawford. Continue for three blocks on Crawford and turn left onto Hamilton Street. Continue for one block and turn right. At this point, you will be in the depot parking lot.

Tunnel Hill

Backtrack to Interstate 75 North and proceed northward for eight miles to Exit 341. Turn left onto Route 201S and proceed for 2.5 miles, continuing straight onto Varnell Street at the point that 201 turns to the right. Turn right onto Main Street. Turn left onto Oak Street and cross the railroad tracks. Turn left onto Clisby-Austin Road. The old depot is on the left. There are several historic markers in this vicinity. Continue on Clisby-Austin Road for approximately 0.3 of a mile and the old tunnel is on the left. As you return from the tunnel, the remains of an old railroad bridge are visible on the right directly across from the covered bridge.

Ringgold Depot

Backtrack to Clisby-Austin and continue straight on Oak Street to Highway 41. Turn right onto Highway 41 and proceed for approximately 7.5 miles. The old depot is on a hill to the right.

Great Locomotive Chase Marker

Take a left from the depot and go under the bridge. Take a left onto Ootewah and travel approximately 1.9 miles and the marker will be on the left.

Early Northwest Georgia Railroad Disaster

The Wreck Of Train #81

In the early 1900s when rail transportation was growing dramatically in the United States, the scheduled time-tables for the trains were becoming very important. As a result, proper caution was not always observed by the engineers at the helm of the huge locomotives hurtling down the tracks. The result often was disastrous, and a route through northwest Georgia was the scene of a number of these tragedies.

They were goin' down grade making ninety miles an hour, When the whistle broke into a scream - He was found in the wreck with his hand on the throttle,
   Scalded to death by the steam."
         - From "The Wreck Of Old 97"

"Train Number 81, southbound on the Southern Railway, had a few minutes to get in the clear at Dallas for Number 18 northbound vestibule Sunday morning," according to a news report in a 1903 issue of the *Dallas New Era*. The men on board did not know it at the time, but a sizeable disaster was only a few moments away. . .

The article continued by explaining "Engineer Jim Nichols opened the throttle of his monster engine on the summit one mile south of McPherson. Engine 345 never acted better, the big machine moved forward at a terrific rate with twenty-five cars behind. The engineer looked at his watch and knew that time was precious."

What happened in the next few minutes on that autumn day of October 23, 1903, is not remembered by many people today, for obvious reasons. Most of those witnesses have long since passed on into eternity.

Pumpkinvine Creek Trestle

The disaster broke the stillness of a quiet Sunday morning approximately one mile north of Dallas with a horrendous crash. It was the type of accident that, unfortunately, was not unusual on lonely mountain trestles in the early days of railroading. It was also the type of accident which immortalized the trainmen who traveled dangerous routes – often at excessive speeds – day after day until fate finally overtook them.

Train Number 81 was a very heavy train. It included some twenty-five cars, and was hurtling down the track at approximately 60 miles an hour when the huge locomotive rolled onto the high steel bridge over Pumpkinvine Creek. The engineer later said he felt the trestle lurch from the

For reasons still unknown today, the Pumpkinvine Creek Trestle collapsed beneath the weight of Train #81 of the Southern Railway on October 23, 1903, killing the fireman of the train. (Photo courtesy of Duane Mintz & Jack Howel)

The trestle over Pumpkinvine Creek was photographed above by Gordon Sargent in 1997. Very little has changed at this site since the 1903 disaster.

weight, and he quickly throttled back, but it was too late. Behind him, six spans of heavy steel trestlework began collapsing with a thunderous roar into the creek-bed seventy-seven feet below, taking thirteen freight cars, the engine tender, and the fireman into eternity.

Then, just as suddenly as the horrifying accident had begun, it ended, bringing a deathly silence to the spot. As he brought his locomotive to a screeching stop, Nichols reportedly turned and looked desperately for his faithful fireman, John Fagala (also reported as "J.M. Flagler" in the news article), who had been standing on the tender when the collapse began. After a quick but futile search around the locomotive, Nichols next went back to the edge of the high broken trestle where his eyes landed upon the sight he feared he would find in the ravine below.

The tender had been ripped from the engine coupling as the track collapsed beneath it. It was lying far below in a tangle of trestle steel and freight cars. John Fagala (Flagler?) undoubtedly never felt the impact when he struck the bottom of the chasm. He may have jumped free of the tender, hoping for the best, or maybe he had simply been tossed off the precipice as the tender was snatched from the engine. Whatever the circumstances, his body was found in the wreckage, his neck and leg broken. He had been killed instantly.

Miraculously, the last cars of the train had remained on the track on the opposite side of the chasm. Consequently, the conductor and flagman in the caboose survived the devastation without a scratch.

The 360-foot bridge across Pumpkinvine Creek was one of the longest and highest in northwest Georgia. It had safely carried hundreds of fast trains in the late 1800s. Today, no one knows what caused the bridge to collapse, but many individuals knowledgeable of rail accidents have speculated on the cause. One report indicated the large locomotive had simply been traveling too fast and had jumped the rails on the curved trestle, leading the cars behind it to devastation.

"The first time I heard of the Pumpkinvine trestle collapsing was from Mr. Paul McDonald, Southern Railway's third trick operator at Rockmart," explained the late Duane "Cowboy" Mintz, a former conductor on Southern (present-day Norfolk-Southern) Railway, who says

Early Northwest Georgia Railroad Disaster

he passed back and forth across the Pumpkinvine Creek trestle continuously during his career. "Later, after I went to work for Southern, I mentioned the incident while dead-heading to Chattanooga on (Train) Number 32, Rockmart's four o'clock train in the afternoon. I was rebuffed by some of the veteran railroaders who seemed to be irritated at me for passing on tales they had never heard of. The old head conductor, Mr. E.E. (Emmett) Whittle, however, came to my rescue. 'The boy's right,' he told them. 'It happened not long after I went to work (for Southern). I almost quit the railroad on account of it.'"

The trestle is located on the line between Atlanta, Georgia and Chattanooga, Tennessee on the route once known as the "Georgia Division" of Southern Railway. Even today, trains pass over a steel trestle (one of the longest and highest on the division) at this same site above the creek many times a day. "I, as well as a lot of others, never did like crossing it," Mintz added. "I personally don't like any trestle that is built as part of a curve like that one is."

The Dallas to Rockmart portion of the Georgia Division has long been a dangerous one. As a part of the Atlanta to Chattanooga line in Southern Railway's network it was completed on July 1, 1882. There have been at least four major disasters on the Dallas to Rockmart segment alone in the past 90 years, and possibly numerous others.

Break-neck speed and a tight railroad time-table undoubtedly were major factors in several of the incidents. In 1902, Southern Railway obtained a contract to haul the mail between Washington, D.C. and Atlanta, Georgia, on the New York to New Orleans line. The U.S. government wanted the best means possible for quick transport of the mails, and fast locomotives were the answer. In return, Southern Railway earned $140,000 a year for this service. In those days, that was big money.

But it was a double-edged sword. If Southern Railway couldn't keep up with the

The old Southern Railway depot in Rockmart, Georgia, a short distance from the Pumpkinvine Creek trestle was photographed circa 1905. Train #81 stopped regularly at this station.

On December 23, 1926, a horrendous collision between the Ponce de Leon and the Royal Palm passenger trains resulted in one of the worst rail disasters in U.S. history. This accident in Rockmart, Georgia, occurred only a short distance from the Pumpkinvine Creek trestle disaster site.

schedule, it was penalized $100.00 for every thirty minutes the mail was late at every destination. That was more than enough incentive for rail management to put heavy pressure on trainmen to maintain schedules. This often meant exceeding the speed limit by many miles an hour more than the speed for which a stretch of rails and their supporting components (such as trestles) were designed. And the fact that some trains were traveling on dangerous stretches of track to begin with, only added to the propensity for disaster.

One such example is the stretch of tracks between Dallas, Georgia and

Rockmart. On the evening of December 23, 1926, on the outskirts of Rockmart, the Ponce de Leon passenger train, traveling in excess of 50 miles per hour, collided head-on with the Royal Palm passenger with devastating results. There were at least 19 and possibly 20 or more fatalities (the exact number is unknown today). At least 113 passengers, 4 Southern Railway employees and 6 Pullman employees were injured. This wreck remains as one of the worst disasters in the history of the railroad in the United States.

Big Raccoon Creek Trestle

Another accident (on that same dangerous stretch between Dallas and Rockmart) which caused the death of several individuals occurred nearby at Big Raccoon Creek trestle in February of 1883. The bridgework at this site was practically new at that time, and railroad historians have long pondered the reason for its collapse. "It's just another of the many puzzling events in the annals of railroading in the early days," Mintz continued matter-of-factly.

The 44-year veteran of the rails served on the Georgia Division Safety Committee of Southern Railway for ten years. "I wrote, printed and distributed a safety newsletter, and one of the articles I carried in the newsletter was a description of the Big Raccoon Creek accident," he smiled.

The trestle at Big Raccoon Creek is seven miles north of Dallas. The creek is comparatively small but the creek-bed is significantly deep with high bluffs on either side. At the time of the accident, the trestle was a three-deck trestle, spanning 1,480 feet from bluff to bluff and rising 94 feet from the creek-bed.

Mr. Mintz's newsletter article of this disaster, reprinted from a news report in the February 22, 1883 issue of the *Dallas New Era* newspaper, described the accident as follows: "Last Saturday morning, about 10:30 a.m., as Train Number 59, a through-freight of the E.T.V. & G. R.R. (East Tennessee, Virginia & Georgia Railroad) was leaving the switch at the tunnel, southbound, Conductor Bob Shoemaker boarded the engine, as it was convenient for him at the time, and (he) remarked to his engineer that he would ride with him down to Dallas rather than drop back to his caboose.

"All went well until the train, running at the rate of 7 or 8 miles an hour, ran upon Big Raccoon Trestle. . . Having passed across to within a few yards of the south side with his engine, Mr. Neeley gave her a little more steam in order to pull over the grade immediately in front. Almost immediately, a severe shock being felt, Mr. Shoemaker, (comprehending) the cause and looking back, shouted, 'Pull her open! Pull her open! The bridge is going!' . . . The terrible crash that followed left them standing upon the very brink of a yawning abyss - the bottom of which was covered with ruins, all within a moment of time."

"The (collapsed) section consisted of ten or eleven cars laden with merchandise, and the caboose. There were three men in the caboose and a Negro brakeman about midway of the train. . . The unfortunate brakeman was killed outright. Mr. R.P. Kidwell . . . was on board, enroute to Atlanta to visit his family. He too was so fatally injured that death came as a relief to his sufferings very soon after being removed from the debris to the car in waiting. Mr. John Cox . . . also in the caboose, sustained injuries that proved fatal to him, living until Saturday night totally unconscious all the while. Mr. Charles Camp, flagman . . . remained unconscious for several hours, then awoke to the realization of his remarkable escape . . . (He had) a scalp wound, a crushed ankle, and a dislocated elbow, (but he was alive!)."

The heavy train had passed across the trestle until the caboose was immediately over the creek. At that point, according to the news account printed in the *New Era*, section after section of the trestle began giving way somewhere near the center of the train. The general collapse of the trestle was very similar to the collapse of the trestle just six or seven miles away at Pumpkinvine Creek in 1903.

Common Cause For The Disasters?

The 360-foot trestle across Pumpkinvine had safely carried hundreds of fast trains over the years. The cause of its collapse is still unknown also, but the news account in the 1903 *New Era* speculates upon the possibilities. "Some think train wreckers had removed a rail causing the wreck, while others believe that the high rate of speed caused the terrible disaster," the newspaper intoned.

Duane Mintz said he didn't think a missing rail had caused the accident at all. "If a rail had been missing, the whole engine would have gone over the side of the trestle, and it wouldn't have caused much trestle damage either," the trainman explained. "I think simple structural weakness caused both the Raccoon Creek and Pumpkinvine Creek disasters."

A very similar accident, which was highly publicized across the United States, had occurred on the Southern Railway just three weeks earlier. The wreck of the "Old 97" which occurred in Danville, Virginia, became the subject for a popular ballad which is still remembered by many railroad enthusiasts today:

Steve Broady, the engineer of the Old 97, was pushing the mail train faster and faster to make up lost time. Witnesses claim the train reached ninety miles an hour as the 80-ton behemoth swept down a grade and struck the "curved" timber trestle. Reportedly, a flange on one of the wheels broke off, and the engine with its cars plunged seventy-five feet into the creek below.

Twelve of the nineteen individuals on board Old 97 were killed. The engineer and fireman were found with the skin flayed from their bodies by the super-heated steam from the crushed boiler. It was a fate from which the engineer at Pumpkinvine Creek had mercifully been spared, but there's no arguing that the Danville, Virginia and Pumpkinvine Creek, Georgia disasters were strangely similar in nature.

Whatever the cause of the wreck at Pumpkinvine, rail officials were determined not to allow the accident to keep the line out of service any longer than absolutely necessary. Service between Chattanooga and Atlanta was temporarily rerouted through Rome, while a huge work crew labored feverishly to repair the damage. Every hour the line remained out of service represented a great financial loss for Southern.

"Two wrecking crews reached the scene about 12:00 p.m., six hours after the occurrence, and more than two hundred men were clearing away the debris," the Dallas New Era explained.

Even this amount of man-power, however, apparently was not enough, and still more men were dispatched to the site to help. Working around the clock, the men had the track and trestle repaired three days after the disaster. By Wednesday morning, the first train steamed safely over the repaired bridge, heading north to Chattanooga.

Once the wreckage had been cleared away and the repairs had been made, the scene at Pumpkinvine Creek quickly returned to normal too. Previously on that fateful Sunday, sightseers had streamed out of Dallas to view the site of the disaster. And with the crowds came scavengers who dug through the wreckage in search of booty.

The atmosphere, no doubt, was like a country carnival. The crushed freight cars had spilled their cargoes of corn, oats, cotton, and apples, and according to one wag, a load of Bull Durham tobacco. It was reported with some mirth, that virtually every boy in Paulding County learned to smoke as a result of this wreck.

Meanwhile, in sleepy Varnell, Georgia, near the Tennessee state line, the festivities were not quite so lively. . . A railroader – the poor fireman at the Pumpkinvine Creek Trestle accident – had been killed. The grieving wife – with her two small children – received their loved one home from the railroad for the last time.

The Silver Comet Rail Trail

The old Seaboard Railroad ceased to exist decades ago, and the tracks in most of Polk County were taken up and sold for scrap. However, a growing phenomenon in the great outdoors has breathed new life into the road-bed of the old rail line, preserving it for future generations.

Who ever heard of the small northwest Georgia town of Rockmart? Outside of a thriving stone products industry, a championship high school football team or two over the years, and a terrible train wreck in 1926, there haven't been many other things to focus regional attention on the town. That may be changing, however, with the advent of a substantial new hiking and biking trail through the county.

Called the "Silver Comet Trail," this twelve-foot-wide multi-use byway is built on the abandoned road-bed of the old Seaboard Airline Railroad. To date, approximately 38 miles of the trail have been completed between Smyrna and Rockmart, and the trail has proven to be a big hit among exercise and outdoor enthusiasts. At its completion, the Silver Comet Trail will join other trails to stretch a total of approximately 100 miles as a scenic byway for enjoyment by walkers, bicycle riders, horseback riders and skaters from throughout the state.

On almost any given weekend (and often on weekdays as well), trail users may be seen enjoying this scenic avenue. The trail has not only attracted hikers and bikers, but nature and history enthusiasts as well, since the old railroad bed snakes through some very scenic and historic terrain in northwest Georgia.

On almost any given weekend (and often on weekdays as well), trail users may be seen enjoying this scenic avenue.

The Silver Comet

In 1947, the famous Silver Comet Train – one of the finest forms of transportation in the southeastern United States at that time – made its maiden journey. Traveling through such major cities as Birmingham, Atlanta, Washington, D.C., and Philadelphia, this passenger train was unequaled in speed and luxury, and passed through many rural areas such as Polk County along the way.

The Silver Comet consisted of three day coaches, a dining car, a tavern car, and several sleeping cars. Each of the sleeping cars was named after towns along the Comet's route, such as the "Atlantan," or the "Cedartown," and the train flourished for a decade or more.

However, with the growth of interstate highways and increased air travel in the 1960s, rail transportation fell out of vogue, and passengers on the train gradually declined. Eventually, the Silver Comet was unable to generate the revenues necessary to substantiate its existence. In 1969, the Comet made its final run, and passenger service was discontinued. The rail line between Smyrna and Rockmart eventually was abandoned completely.

Luckily for the communities along the old route, however, a movement called "Rails-To-Trails" became interested in the road-bed once traveled by the Silver Comet. In 1989, the Georgia Department of Transportation purchased the rights-of-way of the former railroad. In 1998, an organization by the name of PATH agreed to oversee the construction and completion of what was being called the "Silver Comet Trail" from Smyrna to Rockmart, and the stage was set for a whole new life for the old railroad bed.

The PATH foundation is a non-profit organization dedicated to the conversion of old railways to metro-wide trail systems. In the process, the foundation seeks to enhance community spirit and bring neighborhoods together. The Silver Comet is just one of a number of successful similar projects undertaken by PATH in the foundation's endless pursuit of "Rails-To-Trails" opportunities.

One portion of the Silver Comet Trail – the portion from Rockmart to Cedartown and on to the Alabama state line – remains incomplete as of this writing. When finished, the Silver Comet will connect with the Chief Ladiga Trail in Alabama for a combined total of approximately 100 miles of hiking and biking enjoyment.

Stops Along The Trail

From the Rambo access point in Dallas, Georgia, the first scenic stop on the trail is the Pumpkinvine Creek Trestle at mile marker 23.02. Here, the traveler passes over a 750-foot-long, 126-foot-high historic trestle. Today, this viaduct has been rebuilt with concrete and heavy steel, and, just as did railroad passengers in the late 19th and early 20th centuries, patrons on this route can again admire quite a view from this spot.

The next scenic locale on the trail is Brushy Mountain Tunnel. Here, visitors are treated to an 800-foot-long lighted tunnel nestled beneath the beautiful hardwoods and lush waterfalls of Brushy Mountain. Trail hikers sometimes pause here to explore the adjacent natural environment.

During the Atlanta Campaign in the U.S. Civil War, the Battle of Brushy Mountain occurred not far from this vicinity. General William T. Sherman maneuvered Joe Johnston's Confederate army out of several successive defensive positions in this area. The Confederates had dug in all the way from Brushy Mountain to Lost Mountain.

As a portion of the trail development, a man-made pond with goldfish has been creatively constructed in this vicinity. Frogs and turtles doze along the pond's edge, enjoying the sunlight.

Leaving the coolness of the deep forest at Brushy Mountain, it is approximately three miles to the next stopping point. Along the way, it is not uncommon to encounter abundant wildlife, including deer, turkeys, snakes and other denizens of the forest.

TALES OF THE RAILS IN GEORGIA

Brushy Mountain Tunnel once reverberated with the sounds of huge locomotives thundering through its length as the Silver Comet passenger train sped across the Georgia countryside enroute to Atlanta, Philadelphia, Washington, D.C. and points inbetween. Today, the lighted passageway is quiet as patrons of the Silver Comet Rail Trail stroll casually through its cool confines.

One of the "denizens of the deep" along the Silver Comet Trail, Mr. Copperhead is almost perfectly camouflaged as he slithers into the undergrowth to the side of the trail.

In short order, the traveler will reach the Coot's Lake Rest Stop. This local attraction in Polk County includes a lake for swimming and relaxation, a nice beach area, and a snack shop for treats. A fee is charged for admission to the lake and beach.

There is also ample parking at this stop (which is the trailhead just prior to the main Van Wert Trailhead a short distance away), and if the snack shop at Coot's Lake is closed, a convenience store at this site offers an additional opportunity for food, refreshments and supplies.

Historic Van Wert

From Coot's Lake, the trail winds down to the historic community of Van Wert. Some bikers may wish to take a side trip at this point to visit this tiny town. (Then again, they may not, since there is not a great deal to do here except possibly visit a fragment of history.)

Van Wert originally was the site of a 19th century Indian village and, a little later, an early pioneer community known as "Clean Town." According to folklore, the Clean Town name was designed to mock the somewhat uncleanly nature of the trading post and early inhabitants of this town.

As the young state of Georgia was

Though stabilized and safe today, Pumpkinvine Creek trestle was considered a dangerous bridge by early railroad men.

being settled, Van Wert existed within the confines of what then was Paulding County (prior to the creation of Polk County), and as a result, the small but growing town was named as the county seat of Paulding. At one time, Van Wert boasted a courthouse, several taverns and other mercantile businesses, all of which have burned or been torn down over the years. The only substantial historic public building left in the little community is an aged church – once the town's Methodist facility – which includes a very historic adjacent cemetery with aged headstones, some of which date back to the early 1800s. This church also enjoys the distinction of being the sanctuary at which the once nationally-renowned evangelist Sam Jones began his ministry in the late 1800s.

Van Wert remained the county seat for many years until the creation of Polk County in 1851, and the subsequent naming of Cedartown as the county seat of that county. There are a number of historic homes remaining in Van Wert, but the old Methodist church is the most historic public structure still in existence.

The Van Wert trailhead a short distance from the Coot's Lake trailhead again includes plenty of parking space. There are also portable toilets, water fountains and picnic tables at this site.

Other Historic Sites

Approximately half a mile from the Van Wert trailhead, Silver Comet Trail patrons will pass a site to which long-time Rockmart locals still refer as "Ma White's Bottomlands." Here, visitors will see the lush fertile creek bottomlands which were tilled by Indians in pre-history, and by the owners of a plantation which existed on this site in the 19th and 20th centuries. Numerous Indian artifacts have been discovered in this vicinity over the years by area residents.

The plantation at this site was owned by four previous families before the Whites came into possession of the property.

Coot's Lake, skirted by the Silver Comet Trail, has been a gathering spot for Rockmart area residents for generations. Patrons of the trail can cool off in the lake at adjacent Coot's Lake Beach in the summertime.

The tiny town of Van Wert originated from an Indian village derisively referred to as "Clean Town" by early settlers. By the time it was burned by Union army troops during the U.S. Civil War, the town included a courthouse and jail, four saloons, two drug stores, a Masonic Hall, a blacksmith shop, possibly a hotel or two, one school (Williams Academy), and a number of lovely homes. Today, the forlorn structure built as the Methodist Church (foreground) in 1846, is the only historic public building left in the town. Numerous pioneers lie buried in the graveyard at this site. (Photo by Olin Jackson)

TALES OF THE RAILS IN GEORGIA

This photograph of historic Van Wert Methodist Church was taken circa 1923. This interesting structure is just a short walk from the Silver Comet Trail. (Olin Jackson files)

Inhabited by Native Americans in pre-history and later cultivated as a plantation for many years by white settlers, the rich creek bottom lands once owned by the White family offer additional scenic beauty to one stretch of the historic rail-trail.

According to records, contingents of General William T. Sherman's troops camped across the road from the plantation home circa 1864, and even fired a cannon round through the length of the home before departing the area. Luckily, the residents of the home had taken refuge in the basement, and escaped harm.

For many years (and indeed until recently), the historic plantation home was still visible across the fields from the Silver Comet Railroad. Unfortunately, the large structure burned to the ground in 1985 during renovations.

A short distance from this spot, travelers on the Silver Comet will pass the historic Rockmart Slate Quarry at mile marker 36.8. Here, beside Thompson/Euharlee Creek, park benches offer a cool, quiet place to pause for a moment. A historic marker at this spot explains the history of the pre-Civil War slate industry at this site. This vicinity became world-renowned for its bricks, slate and limestone products in the 20th century. Many roofs on the homes in Polk County and elsewhere in the state still contain the original slate shingles installed on these homes, some over 120 years ago.

Also at this spot, the historic Seaboard Depot still stands beside the railroad (which continues periodically to be used between this spot and Cedartown, Georgia, by CSX Railroad). The date of construction of this depot is unknown, but the aged structure appears in very early photos of Rockmart, many of which date back at least to the early 1900s.

Riverwalk

Advancing into downtown Rockmart, many of the historic buildings (with slate shingles) of the town come into view. At this point, you are on the leg of the trail – the Riverwalk trailhead – used in Rockmart's annual Homespun Festival foot race. Riverwalk ends at Wayside-Seaborn Jones Memorial Park in downtown Rockmart. You might wish to take the time here to cool off in the shallow areas of Euharlee Creek near the bridge, and to visit the historic downtown section of Rockmart just a few yards away.

If not for pioneer Seaborn Jones, the Silver Comet Trail quite likely would never have come into existence. Mr. Jones donated land for the original railroad depot in Rockmart, an event which resulted in the development of the town and subsequently

The Silver Comet Rail Trail — Polk County

attracted the rail line upon which much of the Silver Comet Trail is built today.

Sometimes known as the "Father of Rockmart," Jones provided land not only for the first railroad depot, but also for several churches, the town square, a city park, and Rose Hill Cemetery. Today, his gravestone is still the most prominent in the cemetery.

Also at the Riverwalk trailhead in downtown Rockmart, many other opportunities are available for patrons, including food, picnic tables, pay phones, and commercial items at local businesses. The Silver Comet Depot shop offers bike rentals, ice cream, Silver Comet souvenirs and more.

Group activities are often on-going in the park at Riverwalk. Professional photographers are sometimes available here since this trailhead is one of the most beautiful and delightful to visit.

In the middle of the Rockmart town square, Veterans' Memorial Walk was recently created. The names of U.S. military veterans – both living and deceased – from the Rockmart area are permanently enshrined here engraved in bricks.

Departing the downtown Rockmart district and heading west, trail patrons encounter an attractive iron bridge with the Silver Comet Trail logo over Euharlee Creek. The view from this bridge back toward Riverwalk offers the opportunity for scenic photos of Euharlee Creek, the bridge and Riverwalk itself.

This short leg of the trail skirts the edge of historic Rose Hill Cemetery, the final resting place of Rockmart's founder, Seaborn Jones, as well as that of a number of other notables. At this vicinity, the trail also intertwines around one of the still active railroads on which freight trains pass daily through Rockmart.

Patrons on the trail next encounter Nathan Dean Sports Complex. Here, many athletic activities take place on well-manicured and maintained baseball and softball fields. When you reach the end of

Gold was discovered in the vicinity of Van Wert, but it was large deposits of slate discovered in 1849 on the Joseph Blance property that hastened the grown of the Van Wert /Rockmart communities. Remnants of this early industry may still be viewed along the Silver Comet Trail.

Photographed circa 1926, a locomotive idles trackside beside the little depot (left center) on South Marble Street in Rockmart. This depot still stands as of this writing, and is visible from the Silver Comet Trail which today parallels (on the far side of) the tracks on which the locomotive sits in this photo. (Olin Jackson files)

Wayside-Seaborn Jones Park is visible (far-left) along the Riverwalk portion of the Silver Comet Trail in downtown Rockmart. Jones donated the land for the park, the town square, and the first railroad depot, and as such, was responsible for much of the early growth of Rockmart.

Seaborn Jones, early Rockmart resident and businessman, donated land for many civic needs in the town, including that on which the train depot in the community was built. (Olin Jackson files)

the split-rail fence at the northwestern corner of this complex, you have also reached the current end of the Silver Comet Trail. Construction is underway to continue the trail on to Cedartown, and to the Chief Ladiga Trail in Alabama.

Rockmart Eateries & Events

The slow-paced confines of old downtown Rockmart offer a wholesome area to pass time prior to leaving the trail to depart home. The Impala Grill, a 1950s-style diner complete with nostalgic decorations of hotrods and muscle cars from yesteryear is located within easy pedaling distance (a couple of city blocks) of Riverwalk. For the classic automobile enthusiasts, a Hot Rod Cruiser Show is periodically held in front of the Impala. Elvis has been known to return from the dead and make an appearance here on occasion.

Other restaurants in the downtown area include Hometown Pizza, Bar-L Barbecue, the Chocolate Café, T's Seafood, Pizza Depot, Sidekicks, House of China and others. A short distance from the trail end at Nathan Dean Complex are fast food franchises such as McDonalds, Pizza Hut, Hardees, and Sonic. Also in this vicinity is a new Day's Inn if you want to overnight in the area.

Rockmart is also home to several local festivals, so plan your trip accordingly. The annual Homespun Festival hosted by the local Chamber of Commerce occurs the second week in July each year. Located at Riverwalk and Seaborn Jones Memorial Park, visitors to this event can enjoy a morning parade, a 5-K footrace and other festival activities right on the trail. Also scheduled is a complete lineup of entertainment from morning to night at the gazebo, arts and crafts items for sale, barbecue plates, games and rides for the children and much more. The grand finale is a late evening fireworks celebration which can be seen for miles around.

Other area events include the Aragon Barbecue held the last Saturday in June of each year in nearby Aragon, Georgia. A growing event a short distance off the trail after the Coot's Lake trailhead is "The Rock." This gathering is held the first weekend in October each year, and is home to a popular arts and crafts festival as well as substantial musical entertainment.

Take advantage of the Silver Comet Trail. You'll be glad you did.

(For more information on the above events and the Silver Comet Trail in Polk County, contact the Polk County Chamber of Commerce at (770) 684-8774.)

The Wreck Of The Royal Palm

The sleepy northwest Georgia community of Rockmart was not widely-known in the state in 1926 – that is, not until a horrible disaster two days before Christmas in 1926.

> *"I heard the shrill whistle and saw the headlights ahead, but the northbound was not slowing. . . . When I saw the collision was certain, I slammed on my brakes and called to my fireman to jump."*
> -Arthur M. Corrie
> Engineer of the Royal Palm

The Christmas season normally is a joyous occasion, replete with celebration, home-comings of family and friends, and many happy memories. The evening of December 23, 1926, however, is still remembered with horror by a dwindling number of the citizens of Rockmart, Georgia, and most certainly by the survivors of the Royal Palm and the Ponce de Leon passenger trains which collided on this date in one of the worst railroad disasters in the history of the United States.

In 1926, with the exception of the Southern States Portland Cement Plant on one side of town and a slate quarry on the opposite side, Rockmart, for the most part, was a sparsely-settled township, known mostly as a farming community in Polk County. To the surprise of many, however, despite its small size, it had enjoyed passenger rail service since the earliest days of the railroad in the county in the 1870s. This was due in no small measure to one of the community's early residents, Seaborn Jones.

According to tradition, Jones, in return for the donation of his property for railroad rights-of-way, had stipulated that the community of 'Rock Mart' (as it was known then) always be provided with railroad passenger service. It was this passenger service, and the strict timetables followed by the railroad, which quite possibly set the stage for disaster in 1926.

On that fateful day, the Royal Palm and the Ponce de Leon - both crack passenger trains of Southern Railway - were filled near

TALES OF THE RAILS IN GEORGIA

According to tradition, an early resident of Rockmart provided land for the rights-of-way for the railroad with a stipulation that passenger service always be available in the small Polk County community. Despite the stipulation, passenger service was discontinued at all towns along the route in the 1960s, but freight trains still rumble down the same track where the 1926 disaster occurred. (Photo by Olin Jackson)

Downtown Rockmart was photographed here in the early 1900s. A trestle for the Southern Railroad is visible in the distance. The large building visible below the trestle is the old Commercial Hotel, and the building in front of it is the original (first) Seaboard Depot in the middle of town. The Rockmart City Hall building exists on this original depot site today.

The site at which the Ponce de Leon and the Royal Palm trains collided in 1926 was photographed here in 1994. (Photo by Olin Jackson)

capacity with happy travelers. Both trains were renowned for their good food, accommodations - and timely schedules. December 23rd was no exception, as both trains traveled toward a date with destiny.

Leonora (Mrs. Robert Henry) Mintz was seventeen years of age on the day of the accident. As of this writing, she lives not thirty feet from the tracks of the Norfolk-Southern Railroad (formerly Southern Railroad) in Rockmart, and approximately one mile from the scene of the 1926 disaster. Though it has been over 66 years, she says she can still remember that fateful Christmas.

"We lived on our family farm (near the site of present-day East Side Elementary School) at that time," Mrs. Mintz explained in an interview in the early 1990s. "We heard the crash all the way from there. It was so loud, we thought it was thunder."

That December evening was a dark and rainy night in the foothills of north Georgia. Despite the miserable weather and gloom outside, the Pullman coaches in the Ponce de Leon must have been warm and alive with diners and Christmas cheer.

It was at a long side-track at Rockmart that the Royal Palm and the Ponce de Leon regularly passed each other. The Southern Railroad through Rockmart was not double-tracked, so the side-track at the Rockmart depot made it possible for these two luxury trains to continue their destinations in opposite directions.

According to records, Engineer Arthur M. Corrie on the Royal Palm had throttled down and was easing his locomotive southward at approximately 4 miles per hour, waiting for the north-bound Ponce de Leon to take the siding as scheduled. To his horror, however, Corrie suddenly realized that not only was the huge locomotive in the distance not taking the siding, it was bearing down on him at a considerable rate of speed.

As an experienced trainman, Corrie knew that he had just enough time to yell a warning to his fireman, pull on the whistle-cord as another warning to his passengers, and then to jump from the train. After he had jumped, he next thing Corrie heard was the horrendous blast from the collision, the grinding of metal, and the screeching of the rails.

According to reports, Corrie later told Interstate Commerce Commission (ICC) investigators that he turned and watched as the Ponce de Leon, traveling at approximately fifty miles an hour or better, crashed head-long into his beloved Royal Palm.

"I will never forget it," Corrie later stated. "It sounded like the heavens had split open. I don't want to ever hear anything like it again."

Despite the enveloping darkness and rain on the fateful evening, the noise of the crash immediately brought local residents running to the crash site. The provision of help to the injured and dying proved a challenge for the citizens of the tiny, poorly-equipped community, for the carnage at the wreck site was almost overwhelming.

"When the Royal Palm and the Ponce de Leon collided, we weren't allowed to go up there to see it, because it was just too horrible," Mrs. Mintz explained emphatically, still shaken by the tragedy. "A friend of mine told me she and some other friends went to the wreck, and she said they saw the best-looking gentleman in a car. All of a sudden, it seemed like his head just rolled off his shoulders. He had been decapitated.

"Rockmart was a very rural area back then," Mrs. Mintz continued. "People were begging for help. We had no ambulances here at that time. Some people were carried in private automobiles to Rome (Georgia); some others were carried as far away as Atlanta. It was just chaos."

One can only imagine today the misery and pain endured by the injured as they were carried out of the wrecked train cars and huddled into automobiles for a long, bumpy ride to a hospital many miles away. It is not known today how many victims died of their injuries enroute to hospitals and doctors.

The site at which the Ponce de Leon and the Royal Palm trains collided in 1926 was photographed here in 1994. (Photo by Olin Jackson)

The Southern Railways depot in Rockmart was photographed in the early 1900s. A locomotive, very similar in class to that of the Royal Palm or Ponce de Leon, is stopped at the station. Notice the old well (left foreground). (Photo courtesy of Polk County Historic Society)

With the departure of passenger service in the 1960s, the old depot building became obsolete and therefore was demolished. A replacement structure for the monitoring of freight trains was photographed in 1994. (Photo by Olin Jackson)

Arthur M. Corrie was the engineer of the Royal Palm on the night of the accident. His counterpart on the Ponce de Leon, Robert M. Pierce, was killed in the wreck. Corrie leaped from the engine cab at the last moment, and watched as the two monstrous locomotives collided. He provided much of the eye-witness testimony on the disaster.

Photographed shortly after the December 23, 1926 wreck, the heavy damage inflicted upon the Ponce de Leon (r) is visible in the photo. The Royal Palm, however, due to its slow speed, suffered far less damage. (Photo courtesy of Atlanta Historic Society)

Curious bystanders watch as a crane works at the front end of the Ponce de Leon. The daycoach pictured here telescoped into the dining car, and was the scene of many mutilated bodies. (Photo courtesy of the Atlanta History Center)

Mr. Hal Clements, a retired educator and a native of Rockmart who, as of this writing, lives in Atlanta, was a lad of 11 at the time of the disaster. He and his family resided on Bluff Street in Rockmart. He remembered traveling with his father to the wreck shortly after it occurred.

"It happened just east of the present-day Goodyear Mill complex in an area we used to call 'Barber's Woods'," Clements explained. "I was only eleven years old, so I don't remember a lot. I do recall, however, that the steam was still rising from the locomotives. And I remember later that they brought a lot of boxes down to Cochran's Funeral Home.

"My father drove immediately to the accident, because he wanted to help in any way he could," Clements continued. "As I remember, I held onto my father's hand the whole time. I knew there were a lot of bodies in those crushed cars."

Much of the horror of the disaster was caused by the Pullman cars of the Ponce de Leon which telescoped into each other when they met the immovable force of the huge locomotive which suddenly had come to a halt. The impact was horrendous - crushing and mutilating passengers as the heavy cars crashed into each other.

After the shock of the initial crash had passed, the screams of the dying and injured passengers - many of whom were trapped beneath the wreckage - horribly filled the night. The Associated Press reported "The screams of women pinned beneath the wreckage were mingled with the hoarse shouts of men and the prayers of a Negro waiter when he was released, uninjured, from a hole in the side of the dining car."

According to the *Rome*, Georgia *News-Tribune*, "The scene. . . . tested the strength of strong men. Bodies of victims crushed and mangled beyond description were . . . unreachable because of tons of weight upon them. The roof of the diner was rolled up like paper. The body of one man was hanging from a window, his legs pinned beneath the heavy weight."

Most of the residents of Rockmart were unprepared for the trauma involved in a disaster of the magnitude of the 1926 wreck. Some rescuers went about their work numbly; others found themselves unable to continue.

"After the survivors had all been removed, they finally had to get some of the men about half drunk, I think," Mrs. Mintz continued, before they'd go back into the wreck. They'd try to lift a body and it would just fall apart. Even after we returned to school (Rockmart School just across the tracks from the wreck site) following the Christmas holidays, there were still body parts in some of the wreckage. It really was tragic - a terrible thing."

Most sources today agree there were approximately 20 fatalities as a result of the collision. The official Interstate Commerce Commission report, filed January 11, 1927, reported that 11 passengers, 7 Southern Railway employees, and 1 news agent were killed (a total of 19 deaths as of that date; others may have died at a later date as a result of injuries from the disaster.). The report went on to explain that 113 passengers, 4 Southern Railway employees and 6 Pullman employees were injured in the wreck.

On December 24, the front page of *The Atlanta Georgian* trumpeted "18 Dead In Wreck." Due to the confusion which reigned at the scene of the accident and the inaccuracies in news reports of that day, several variations of the death count were published.

The dead in the Ponce de Leon included Road Foreman of Engines, Robert M. Pierce, who had assumed the engineer's duties from the regular engineer shortly before the crash. An arm and a leg were amputated from Pierce in a futile effort to save his life, but he succumbed shortly thereafter. Also dead was the fireman in the engine with him - H.R. Moss - who was killed instantly. W.H. Brewer, the baggagemaster, died a few hours later.

Others listed as dead in the December

Residents from miles away traveled to Rockmart to view the disaster for several days. (Photo courtesy of the Atlanta History Center)

Some onlookers posed for photographs in front of the battered Ponce de Leon at the fateful site. It is easy to see how the impact from the wreck severely mangled the bodies of both Engineer Robert M. Pierce and Fireman H.R. Moss, both of whom were inside this locomotive at impact. Pierce lived for a few hours following the wreck, but Moss was killed instantly. (Photo courtesy of the Atlanta History Center)

Southern Railways, in a perpetual race with time, began clearing and repairing the rail line into Rockmart as soon as possible, to allow for the continuation of traffic. Amazingly, both locomotives from the Rockmart collision were repaired and put back into service - including the Ponce de Leon, pictured here, as badly damaged as it was. (Photo courtesy of the Atlanta History Center)

Another view of the wreck was photographed across a cotton field from the approximate site at which a Goodyear Mills complex was later constructed. (Photo courtesy of Rockmart Library)

Heavy-duty railroad cranes labor to re-rail the battered Ponce de Leon locomotive. (Photo courtesy of the Rockmart Library)

24, 1926 issue of *The Atlanta Georgian* were:
* Dr. P.T. Hale, 69, a professor of evangelism at Southern Baptist Seminary in Louisville, KY.
* W.L. Dynes, 56, an Atlanta real estate developer who lived at 951 Courtney Dr.
* J.E. Frost of 509 Foster St., Chattanooga, TN.
* L.B. Evans of Lebanon, KY, Kansas City and Jacksonville, FL addresses.
* Mrs. J.W. Whitaker of Chattanooga, TN.
* Goldie Williams, the infant daughter of Mrs. Alice Williams of Detroit, MI.
* J.W. Whisenhunt of Aragon, GA.
* W.I. Dowie, Jr. of Jacksonville, FL.
* A young boy, age approximately 8 years, believed to have been the son of Mrs. George Hardy of Toronto.
* A young girl, age approximately 10 years, with the initials H.M.H. on a bracelet, believed to have been the daughter of Mrs. Hardy.
* Six other individuals were unidentified: two white and four Negro.

Those listed as injured in the same article were:
* Mrs. George Hardy of Toronto.
* J.W. Dosser of Chattanooga, TN.
* F.W. Swann of Bolton, GA.
* Will Kuhn of St. Louis, MO.
* L.I. Seibert of Chattanooga, TN.
* Corporal Gus Rusts of Ft. Oglethorpe, GA.
* Dan Lobrugh of Cincinnati, OH.
* Robert Hilty of Lansing, MI.
* Edward Wiseman of Louisville, KY.
* H.E. Bullis of Lexington, KY.
* R.L. Bateman of Macon, GA.
* Mrs. J.J. Finlay of Chattanooga, TN.

As for the Royal Palm, the injuries were much less severe, and there were no fatalities. Much of this was due undoubtedly to the slow speed of the Royal Palm as its heavy engine impacted the Ponce de Leon.

"The hand of providence guided the destiny of the Royal Palm last night," Corrie told a reporter at his home Friday morning following the accident. "I was barely moving, pulling my engine along about 4 miles per hour as I neared the switch at the siding. I was obeying orders to await the Ponce de Leon which was to pull up and go into the siding so I could pass. When I saw the collision was certain, I slammed on my brakes and called to my fireman to jump. I jumped to the ground and rolled down a steep embankment. I don't suppose I was 30 feet away when the two engines met. . . . I fully expected the engine and cars to topple over and roll down upon me, but they didn't."

The Royal Palm consisted of one club car, five Pullman sleeping cars, one dining car and two Pullman sleeping cars of all-steel construction. They were pulled by Engine #1456.

The Ponce de Leon consisted of one combination car (half baggage & half coach), one coach, one dining car, and seven Pullman sleeping cars, all of steel construction, pulled by Engine #1219.

Following the impact, both engines were derailed, but miraculously remained upright. Engine #1219 (Ponce de Leon) was badly damaged and its tender was torn from its frame and thrown down the embankment on the inside of the curve. The combination car was telescoped at its forward end nearly the length of the baggage compartment. The coach immediately following it telescoped into the dining car.

The specific cause of the accident is still not known to this day, and many questions linger. What about the switch controlling the entrance to the siding? Much speculation has centered around this device. It is not known today if it (the switch) was open to admit the Ponce de Leon to the siding, but even if it had been open, the Ponce de Leon was moving at a rate of speed much too great to have allowed it to negotiate the arc of the turn leading into the switch.

The mountain descent down into Rockmart can be a perilous route. As recently as 1961, another train - this time a freight - was derailed in almost the identical spot as the 1926 disaster, causing an immense catastrophe in its own right. Speed and a lack of familiarity with the incline from the Braswell Mountains into Rockmart quite possibly played a role in that accident, and are suspected as prime catalysts in the 1926 disaster as well.

Just a few moments prior to the 1926 accident, S.J. Keith, the regular engineer, was directed by Pierce to "go back into the train." According to Keith's later statement, Pierce was running behind time at a high rate of speed, "dropping down off the mountain below Rockmart."

According to the 1927 Interstate Commerce Commission report on the accident, "When it (the Ponce de Leon) stopped at McPherson, 11.4 miles south of Rockmart, for the purpose of meeting an opposing train, Road Foreman of Engines Pierce, who had been riding in the combination car, boarded the engine and took charge of it, Engineman Keith going back to ride in the combination car.

"Train first No. 2 (the Ponce de Leon) departed from McPherson at 6:23 p.m., 15 minutes late, passed Braswell, 6.4 miles from McPherson, at 6:35 p.m., 16 minutes late, passed the south passing track switch at Rockmart and collided with train #101 while traveling at a speed believed to have been approximately 50 miles per hour."

Some individuals have speculated that the blinding rain, coupled with Pierce's unfamiliarity with a newly-installed switch-head, were responsible for the tragedy. Others have maintained that in the driving rain, Pierce mistook a freight engineer's signal from a siding further up the line as the Royal Palm's signal that all was clear. This, at the very least, might provide a measure of explanation for Pierce's obvious decision to continue on at top speed without taking the proper side track.

The Interstate Commerce Commission report, however, concluded that the wreck occurred because Road Foreman of

> *Some individuals have speculated that the blinding rain, coupled with Pierce's unfamiliarity with a newly-installed switch-head, were responsible for the tragedy.*

TALES OF THE RAILS IN GEORGIA

Engines Pierce, who had relieved Engineman Keith, either failed to have a thorough understanding with the engineman as to the contents of Train Order #92 (requiring him to take the siding), or else forgot it.

The true reason for the tragedy may never be known, since this information departed with Robert M. Pierce when he succumbed to his injuries shortly after the wreck. However, as of this writing in the early 1990s, there are some long-time former employees who have developed interesting opinions and theories over the years.

The late H.D. "Cowboy" Mintz, a retired Southern Railways senior conductor and the son of Mrs. R.H. Mintz of Rockmart, said passenger train crews always consisted of the oldest men on the seniority list. Therefore, most of the Southern Railway employees from the Ponce de Leon and the Royal Palm who were involved in the accident were either deceased or retired by the time he was employed by Southern in the mid-1940s. A few, however, were still around, and shared their thoughts with him.

"I worked with Nath Turner, an engineer on the Royal Palm; Henry Sorrells, the conductor; and Harry Smith, the flagman," Mintz related. "Harry told me he and Henry were up in the cupola on the caboose on the rear of the Royal Palm, and they could hear the Ponce de Leon 'still working steam' as it was approaching. The whole train should have been coasting down the grade by that point. He always thought Bob Pierce was attempting to make up the lost time the train was suffering from."

But Mr. Mintz also said there have been rumors over the years of a personal

> *The true reason for the tragedy may never be known, since this information departed with Robert M. Pierce when he succumbed to his injuries shortly after the wreck.*

vendetta between Keith and Pierce. There has also been speculation regarding the possibility that this may have played a role in the disaster.

When Keith was relieved of control of the engine by Pierce at McPherson, could he (Keith) possibly have intentionally neglected to inform Pierce that the Ponce de Leon was to take the siding in Rockmart? Surely Keith would have known that failure to communicate these instructions to Pierce would have meant almost certain death or injury to himself.

The Interstate Commerce Commission report however, states unequivocally, that "After the accident, Mr. Copeland assisted in removing Road Foreman of Engines Pierce from his engine and he said the road foreman asked him how the accident had occurred. When told that he had failed to take the siding for train #101 (the Royal Palm), he replied that Engineman Keith, Fireman Moss and everyone concerned had told him that he was to hold the main track."

"Harry Smith's personal observation, Engineer Keith's statement that he explained the conditions of the orders to Pierce, and the theory of a personal vendetta between Keith and Pierce will always add to the mystery of the Rockmart wreck," Mr. Mintz added. "We'll never know the answer for certain."

Despite occasional mishaps on the railroad, it remains as one of the most viable (and safe) forms of transportation in our nation today. With any luck at all, Rockmart, with its railroad rights-of-way still intact, has a promising future, and will hopefully close the door forever on the disaster of a grim Christmas in 1926.

Recollections Of An RPO Clerk On The Tallulah Falls Railroad

A Railway Mail Service worker gained the opportunity of a lifetime when he was granted a temporary job working on the historic Tallulah Falls Railroad in the 1950s.

For many years, first as the Northeastern Railroad chartered in 1856, later as the Blue Ridge and Atlantic Railroad in 1887, and finally as the Tallulah Falls Railway (TF) beginning in 1897, a very scenic and historic railroad ran through several extreme northeastern Georgia counties. Sadly, the fabled line went into receivership in 1923, but managed to last another 38 years before finally whistling its last run in 1961. Prior to that time, however, a number of individuals experienced many adventures on this colorful railroad.

On Sunday morning, May 27, 1951, Harold Bell, the regular mail clerk on the Tallulah Falls Railroad woke up and reached under the bed for his trousers. He forgot that the last thing he had done before dropping off to sleep was to place his revolver under the bed – on top of his trousers. As he picked up his pants, the gun tumbled to the floor, discharged, and the bullet shattered the shocked trainman's shin bone, crippling him.

Bell was able to get medical attention, and no doubt was greatly relieved once the pain had subsided. He, however, would be unable to continue his duties on the Tallulah Falls Railway until his leg healed, and that assuredly troubled him considerably.

The district office of the TF immediately began assigning substitute clerks to fill Bell's vacancy, but the substitutes all requested to be relieved after two weeks, because that was the limit of time that they could draw subsistence pay for having to spend the night away from their normal jobs in the Atlanta headquarters, and money was

As he picked up his pants, the gun tumbled to the floor, discharged, and the bullet shattered the shocked trainman's shin bone, crippling him.

TALES OF THE RAILS IN GEORGIA

In this photo, a Tallulah Falls Railroad diesel-electric mail car or "Dinky" is being loaded in downtown Cornelia in the early 1950s. It was this conveyance on which Mr. Ragsdale worked in 1951. (Photo courtesy of Thomas Frier)

Train #501 with its diesel-electric engine travels north across Tallulah Lake circa 1950s. It was at this spot that Mr. Ragsdale dumped the block of ice each day. In the right foreground is the old Highway 441 bridge which still exists today in Tallulah Gorge State Park. Though the rails were removed long ago, the large concrete piers pictured here beneath the Tallulah Lake railroad bridge also still exist today in Tallulah Lake. (Photo courtesy of Buck Snyder)

money – especially in those days.

As a result of this unstable situation, the office approached Theron Ragsdale about moving back to Banks County where he had been born. They wanted him to make Cornelia his headquarters so that no subsistence pay would be necessary. So it was, that a substitute clerk with less than three years' seniority, became the Railway Post Office (RPO) clerk on the Franklin and Cornelia run until Harold Bell's one year of disability leave was up.

Learning The Job

"The work was drastically more complicated than what I had been doing in the Railway Mail Service stationary unit in Atlanta," Ragsdale explained in a recent interview, "so I wisely requested that I be allowed to ride without pay and assist the current substitute – a Mr. Sarrett – for two days before tackling the job solo. Sarrett was a good instructor, and because of the tips he gave me, I felt much more confident when I had the job to myself on Monday morning, July 30.

"There was, however, one problem that Sarrett never warned me about. The "dinky", a diesel-powered, single-unit car, the middle portion of which served as my railway post office, was to remain in Cornelia for repairs that first day. I would have to perform all distribution of mails in the unit before leaving Cornelia, and then the railroad had arranged for a local trucker to carry me and the mail to Franklin and back on the highway.

"Now in those days, railroad regulations forbade the railroad repairmen from beginning work until I had left the car. Those workmen all were well aware of this requirement too, and, as a result, they obviously had decided to have a little fun with me. As I labored to sort and organize the mail, they stood around – looking as idle as possible – every time Bob Addington, the president of the railroad, came by.

"As I worked frantically at my job, I heard Mr. Addington yelling at the men, but they simply responded with, 'We can't jack the car up, because the mail clerk hasn't finished working his mail.' Needless to say, when I finally got all the mail 'worked' and loaded on the truck, I was a nervous wreck and exhausted to boot.

"I think it was Thursday of that first week before the dinky was fixed and on the road again. When we arrived in Cornelia at 5:20 and I off-loaded all mails for transfer to Charlotte & Atlanta Train 39, a man in a brown suit came into the mail compartment and started looking in a first aid box on the wall. He was acting like he didn't notice me, but I thought I ought to at least

Recollections Of an RPO clerk On The Tallulah Falls Railroad   Rabun County

make him identify himself, so I asked him, 'Do you work for the railroad?'

"I was mildly confused when this fellow touched the tip of his finger to his hat, and said something that sounded like 'See?' The next morning I mentioned this incident to Mr. Snyder, the conductor of the dinky, and he explained that the railroad was in receivership, and that the man in the brown suit was Henry Brewer, the person appointed by Southern Railway as the Receiver of the Tallulah Falls Railroad. When he said 'See,' I guess what he really said was 'Receiver.' Maybe there was an emblem on his hat that indicated his position. I still don't know. The TF was plagued by financial problems for much of its existence.

"I believe it was on the morning of that first day of riding the dinky solo that we were passing through a woodsy area somewhere above Clarkesville, when suddenly I heard two shotgun blasts in rapid succession just outside the mail car door.

"In a flash, I thought about the one time I had ridden the Tallulah Falls train in 1941 to visit relatives near Turnerville. While crossing a trestle, I had looked out the window and seen a man in wading boots, lying on the ground beside a stream, with one of his boots actually in the stream. He evidently was drunk – or at least I hoped that was all that was wrong with him. He might also have been shot for all I knew.

"In that same flash, I also thought briefly about Jesse James and his feud with the railroads. I dropped on the floor in case the shotgun outside contained another shell. The dinky slowed, but didn't come to a stop, and a few minutes later, Mr. Snyder appeared in the doorway, smiling, and explained that the track maintenance workers had put down a couple of torpedoes (audible alert devices) to warn us that they were working on the track up ahead. The track was clear, but they hadn't had time to go back and retrieve the torpedoes.

Mr. John B. Snyder

"As I got to know John B. Snyder, I realized he was the same conductor who had taken my ticket on that trip I had made in 1941. He wore overalls and a felt hat as conductor on the dinky, but as conductor on the passenger train in 1941, he had worn an immaculate navy blue conductor's uniform and the official conductor's billed hat. His career as a conductor included some of the years when Tallulah Falls was a popular tourist attraction, and on Sundays, excursion trains to 'the falls' departed from both Atlanta and Athens. Entire cars would arrive at Cornelia – loaded with tourists – to be hooked onto the TF engine. Thus, Mr. Snyder had become an experienced tour guide as well as conductor.

"He had grown up near Sylva, North Carolina, and had started working for the TF as a young man, I suppose about 1913, at which time he was 21 years old. He worked his way up to conductor as a freight train crewman. He said that at first, he was frightened by the prospect of being conductor on a passenger train, but it was a promotion, so he tackled it. He told me that once he got into the swing of it, he had rather enjoyed conducting the excursion trains.

"Mr. Snyder always had a ready smile, and was friendly, so I thought it was a shame the railroad no longer had an opening for his services as a passenger train conductor. As it was, since the dinky did actually offer minor passenger service (passengers occasionally rode in the forward compartment with the engineer and conductor), he drew more salary than Brawner Walker, the freight train conductor.

"I don't know how much money Mr. Snyder actually made, but it's a fact that he never owned an automobile. Maybe traveling 114 miles a day six days a week left him feeling that he didn't need any additional transportation.

"Mr. Snyder would frequently inquire of people at Otto, Prentiss, and Franklin if they had any eggs or other produce to sell. I suspect that, being from North Carolina and remembering the days when the area was hungry for trade and contact with the outside world, he wanted to grab every chance available to throw some trade to his fellow North Carolinians.

Honest Hard-Working Folks

"I presume that the salaries of the railroad employees were set by railroad regulations, even though the railroad was in receivership, but one morning when I had been on the line about three weeks, I got to wondering. Shortly after I had climbed into the mail compartment and started preparing for the day's work, Earl Ward, one of the yard crew, called to me. 'Hey, mail boy! Come out here!'

"Now I didn't know what he wanted so I came to the door. There, I saw that the entire yard crew – about ten men including Mr. Snyder and Goldman Kimbrell, the engineer – were standing in a small semicircle, looking up intently at me. 'Mail boy' Earl repeated. 'Have you lost anything?'

"I examined the eyes in the semicircle, and it looked to me like they were expecting a confrontation, maybe a fight. I couldn't think of anything I might have lost, and I didn't want to admit that I was so careless that I didn't know whether I had actually lost anything or not, so I tried to sound confident when I replied with a somber 'No.'

"Earl then related to me how he had found a ten-dollar bill on the floor of the mail compartment the previous evening when he was sweeping it out. He said he just wanted to be sure it wasn't mine before claiming it for himself. I nervously repeated my denial that the money was mine, and as Mr. Snyder walked away, he said, 'Well, it couldn't be mine, because I don't have that much.'

"The next morning I was to discover just how honest and good these folks could actually be. Earl came walking up to me that day and said he just didn't feel right about keeping the ten, and I admitted, 'Well, I did a little figuring, and I believe I am about ten dollars short.' He handed me the ten and that was that.

"Another time, the dinky broke down near Franklin, and we had to wait for the freight train to come along so it could pull us back to Cornelia. As we headed back, some of the stops we made were mail stops, and some were freight stops, involving the shuttling to and fro of cars onto sidings. This made the freight train even slower than it normally would have been.

"By the time we got to Clarkesville, it was pitch dark, and a hard rain had set in. Broughton Ward, who usually worked with the yard crew in Cornelia, was in the passenger compartment with two other yard crewmen. I don't know why they were on the train, but they must have been on duty, because as soon as the train came to a stop, they ran out into that pouring rain to get the mail from the Clarkesville Post Office. The mail messenger who normally passed the mail to me at the mail car door had left it with the station agent, who in turn had locked it up with a railroad lock before going home for the evening. I guess the agreement between the Post Office Department and the railroad required that the railroad guarantee that the mail would be brought to the mail car door. Apparently Mr. Ward and the crewmen knew about the mail requirement. They had allowed me to stay warm and dry while they got soaked to the bone carrying the mail to the dinky.

"Many of the rules which governed the RPO clerk's interactions with the railroad had been drawn up many years earlier. I'm sure that Mr. Brewer's inspection of my first aid kit was a standard operating procedure to make certain the kits were in compliance with the rules.

"Another of these rules was surely a carryover from the days before refrigerators were invented: Every morning the yard crew placed a five-pound block of ice in my lavatory so that I could have the luxury of a cold drink at lunch time every day. I wish I had told them not to bother, because it actually was a nuisance to me. The drip from the ice itself went down the lavatory drain, to be sure, but the condensation that formed on the outside of the lavatory

Recollections Of An RPO Clerk On The Tallulah Falls Railroad — Rabun County

dripped on the floor, and I had to carefully avoid storing any mail in that area, or it would get wet. Those railroaders however, didn't ask me what I wanted. They just blindly fulfilled the requirements of the postal contract.

"At the stationary unit in Atlanta, I had carried a thermos of coffee in my lunch box every day, but I found where I could get a pint of buttermilk in Cornelia every day, and the ice in the lavatory kept it good and cold. I usually finished my buttermilk about the time the train was crossing the high concrete-pillared trestle across Tallulah Lake, and to stop the incessant drip from the ice, I would throw the remainder of the block out the door and watch it splash into the lake waters far below.

Mail Call

"Improperly addressed mail was a problem on the TF, just as it was throughout the Post Office Department (the nomenclature 'U.S. Postal Service' didn't come into use until 1972). Some guy named Pasquale in Hollywood, California, was always getting mail in a blurred type that made it difficult to determine whether the state was CA or GA. Harry Dover, a WW I veteran Hollywood Postmaster would simply dispatch these letters to me without making any notation. It was up to me to surmise that there was no Mr. Pasquale in Hollywood, GA, and that I needed to write 'Calif' under the address and then place this mail in the slot for Western States.

Outside my mail car door was the notation 'United States Railway Post Office,' and underneath was a slot for receiving letters to be mailed. One day, just before the dinky started moving out of Mountain City, headed north, Mr. Snyder happened to notice a fat boy starting to insert a letter in the drop slot, and he stopped him, saying, 'Let's give it to the mail clerk.'

"I came to the door, and took the boy's

The distinctive Tallulah Falls Depot was photographed in this peaceful setting circa 1950s. The dinky on which Mr. Ragsdale worked stopped here daily. Today, modern U.S. 441 Highway passes beside the depot near where the railroad tracks exist in this photo. This depot, the most ornate of all the Tallulah Falls Railway structures, was expected to provide service for a substantial portion of the mail and passengers on the line, but after the tragic fire in the town of Tallulah Falls and the disappearance of the massive hotels along the brim of the gorge, this depot was little used. (Photo courtesy of Bob Whittaker)

Photographed March 25, 1961, the final year the Tallulah Falls Railroad was in operation, engineer Goldman Kimbrell smiles forlornly down from the cab of one of the line's diesel-electric engines. (Photo courtesy of Goldman Kimbrell)

The dinky was photographed in 1953 on Queen's trestle just south of Mountain City in Rabun County. (Photo by R.D. Sharpless, from the collection of Frank Ardrey, Jr.)

This somewhat dramatic photograph shows a Tallulah Falls train at Wiley Junction in 1939. Today, the immense trestle - just like most of the rest of the Tallulah Falls Railroad - has disappeared from the landscape.

letter. It was for his girlfriend in Rabun Gap, just three miles up the road. If he had put it in the slot, it would have silently landed on the floor under my work table, and I probably wouldn't have noticed it until the next morning – on my work table – where Earl Ward would have placed it when he was sweeping up. The drop slot on the RPO car was grossly unworkable.

"One of the entrepreneurial opportunities which opened up with the construction of the railroad was the illegal removal and sale of shrubbery from the nearby National Forest lands. Someone would occasionally have fairly large shipments of laurel, rhododendron and other shrubs from the post office at Tallulah Falls. The shrubs were tagged with the return address of 'Nature's Greenhouse.' I was told that state inspectors would occasionally come to inspect this business at 'Nature's Greenhouse,' but this individual apparently always either bluffed or bought his way out of the situation.

"A sawmill run by Ritter Lumber Company in downtown Mountain City had about done all the logging that was practical in the area by 1951, but at that time, it was still in operation. The home office of the company was in Cincinatti, and the mill would send reports in a cardboard cylinder about once a month. Earl Dotson, postmaster, would hand me these cardboard cylinders outside the pouch. I thought he did this because they wouldn't fit inside, but after letting one or two of them get by me, I realized they were registered mail, and required my signature as well as the recording of their dispatch.

"The mail messenger at Franklin was John Pennington. He used a ton-and-a-half truck to carry mails between the train and the Franklin Post Office. He was always in a hurry to get to the post office with his mail. Maybe his girlfriend was timing him. . . I never knew.

"One day when Mr. Pennington backed his truck up to the mail-car door, I had a crate of baby chicks, and I wanted to give them to him first thing, to be sure I didn't forget them. John said, 'Save those dern chicks for the last; otherwise, I'll be having to work around them.' As I started handing him the other stuff, I said, 'Well, help me remember them.'

"We spent about ten minutes loading his truck with outside parcels, parcel post sacks, newspapers, pouches, rose bushes, tail pipes and whatever, then he said hurriedly, 'Is that all?'

"As was my habit, I quickly replied, 'Yes,' and he was off like a bullet. I had already passed Prentiss – the first post office south of Franklin – when I heard the first 'peep peep' coming out of the crate with the baby chicks. They had been making a continuous racket prior to the time I set them out of the way for John, but had become silent thereafter – until I had left the station. I was just angry enough with John for not taking the chicks when I first handed them to him that I put them off at Otto, North Carolina, and told the mail messenger to call John Pennington in Franklin and tell him to come get them.

Tornado Tales

"On February 29, 1952, a tornado hit the Banks County house where I was living with my parents, and in order to have some protection from falling timbers in case the house collapsed, I had crawled under an oak table. As I sat there, I could feel the floor shaking as the wind whistled and growled outside. For weeks afterward, whenever the dinky would go down a grade, the vibrating floor of the mail car frightened me so that I became nauseated.

"Compounding my problems with this phobia, was the fact that at this same time the dinky actually did jump the track on one of those dangerous grades. Luckily, the rear truck twisted, straddling the rails, so that two wheels were on the right and two wheels on the left of each rail. This kept the dinky from leaving the roadbed and turning over, but it really was a bumpy ride on the cross-ties till we came to a stop.

"We soon discovered the cause for the wreck. A rail that wasn't sufficiently spiked down had leaned to the outside and caused the truck to twist. I thought we would have to wait for a railroad crane to come and set us back on the track, but as it turned out, Mr. Snyder had what was known as a 'derail' in his compartment up front. This was a piece of metal that fitted onto the rail. It had a groove that would catch the flange of a railroad wheel and force it off the rail as the train passed over it. They simply turned this derail around backwards so that it became a 're-rail,' forcing the wheel back onto the rail. We were on the go again in about thirty minutes, but what a scare for a guy who had recently been in a tornado.

"One day, there was a thick large brown envelope on which I just happened to notice the return address. It read 'Lillian Smith, Old Screamer Mountain, Clayton, GA.' I was struck by the name of the sender. I knew she was the well-known author of a popular novel at that time, *Strange Fruit*. This package was evidently another manuscript on its way to a publisher, and I felt honored at being in the position of providing her with a service.

"Also at this time there were lots of airmail letters to and from Oregon and Washington State. Harold Bell explained to me that the local boys had been sent out there by the Civilian Conservation Corps, and they had

They simply turned this derail around backwards so that it became a 're-rail,' forcing the wheel back onto the rail.

married females from that area and had remained there, but were keeping in touch with their northeast Georgia relatives. The longer I worked the TF line, the more attached I became to the local people of the area.

Tango Uniform (Time Up)

"It surprised me how fast time passed. One day I noticed that Harold Bell's registry book was still in the drawer of the letter table. His last entry bore the date 'May 26, 1951.' I knew that as that date approached in 1952, I would have to be reassigned back to the Atlanta, Georgia Terminal RPO, and I wasn't looking forward to that.

"Today, as I record these memories, I am surprised to discover that all my recollections from my days on the old TF are of bad things that happened to me. But in retrospect, a part of me actually died the day I had to leave the old dinky for the last time.

"After I went back to Atlanta, my old-timer co-workers in the Terminal related to me how, when the RPO was discontinued on the Toccoa & Elberton Line, the mail clerk there had committed suicide to keep from having to return to the Terminal. I knew the feeling. Being the sole representative of the Post Office Department on a one-man run gave a man an independence and prestige that was not to be had in a larger facility.

"For example, on one of the days back on the Tallulah Falls run I was carrying the mail in the truck. There was an auto accident on the highway between Habersham Mills and Clarkesville. Gawkers had lined the shoulders of the road with their parked vehicles, and then had filled both lanes of the highway itself, just so they could get out and take a close look at the poor unfortunate souls in the wrecked vehicles.

"I was already behind on my schedule, and it looked like the accident was going to cause a long delay. I swung down from the cab of the truck and started walking toward the wreck, thinking I would ask the sheriff or patrolman – whoever was in charge – for some help getting through.

"As soon as I got six feet in front of the truck, the teenager who was driving the truck gunned the motor loud enough to get the attention of the entire crowd. I suddenly saw people pointing at me and murmuring to each other.

"In order to appear non-confrontational, I looked down at the ground as I walked. When I looked back up, I saw the highway was almost completely clear. Those gawkers who had parked in the middle of the road had seen my shiny RMS badge and the RMS revolver on my belt, and they immediately had assumed I was in charge. They had gotten into their cars and moved on. I felt like Gary Cooper in *High Noon*.

"A large part of my love for the TF Line was from childhood conditioning. From my earliest recollections, watching the trains cross the Hazel Creek trestle was a highlight of every visit to my grandparents' house in Demorest. I followed the smoke coming up through the trees before and after the crossing, and the loud Huff! Huff! Huff! which told me the train was moving again after stopping at the depot.

"My mother told me the train went to Franklin, North Carolina, and to me, that sounded like some wonderful enchanted land, where I probably would never have the good fortune to visit. So, getting the RPO clerk's job was virtually the realization of a life-long dream.

Bell/Snyder Last Days

"The last time I saw Harold Bell, he was still using crutches to get around. I feel sure he was still using them when he reported to work on Monday morning after I had put in my last day on the route on Saturday. Despite the crutches, Harold loved the route too, and I'm sure he didn't want to retire, so he gave it a good try.

"Harold's regular clerk's schedule called for three weeks on and one week off. The off-week would be filled by a substitute clerk. When Harold's three weeks were up, I was asked if I would like to go back to the

Recollections Of An RPO Clerk On The Tallulah Falls Railroad   Rabun County

Franklin and Cornelia route (called the Frank & Corn in RMS parlance) on the old TF and do Harold's off-week. It was a temptation, but at that time, Ethel and I had been married just one week, and I would have been ashamed to leave her for a week as a newlywed.

"I later had second thoughts about the offer, however, and the next time I thought Harold Bell was due for a week's layoff, I inquired about the substitute's job. To my disappointment, I learned that Harold had been granted another one-year disability leave, and John Carroll, the substitute who had taken the first layoff fill-in, was now assigned to Frank & Corn for the one-year period.

"Much to his despair, I'm sure, Harold Bell ultimately was forced to retire. I don't know if he ever even reported for work again. Interestingly, shortly after Harold retired, the dinky was discontinued forever. Harold was a good friend of the district supervisor, Mr. Stevens, and I suspect he had been using his influence to keep the Frank & Corn RPO going just to accommodate his old friend.

"With his seniority, Mr. Snyder obtained a freight conductor's job. This was shortly before Walt Disney began filming *The Great Locomotive Chase* on the Tallulah Falls route. Walt Disney promoters had learned of the scenic railroad and had gone to a great deal of trouble to ship in a vintage locomotive and build sets to use to film the movie on the TF line.

"With filming in progress, the freight train had more than normal difficulty moving along the tracks. Mr. Snyder was exposed to the rain and cold more often than normal. Tragically, he caught pneumonia and died. I don't remember what year it was, but if it was 1956, he would have been only 64 years old. His last thoughts probably involved the railroad which he loved dearly.

"As long as I live, I'll never forget my days on the Frank & Corn RPO job, nor the colorful Tallulah Falls Railroad either."

–Theron Ragsdale

A Tallulah Falls freight train was photographed near Demorest, Georgia in 1951. It was on this train that Mr. John B. Snyder and many other friends of Mr. Ragsdale worked.
(Photo courtesy of Goldman Kimbrell)

Though virtually all the rails from the Tallulah Falls line were removed and sold for scrap almost half a century ago, short stretches still existed in recent years. This photograph was taken outside Cornelia in the mid-1990s.

Searching For Clues To The Historic Blue Ridge Railroad

Four individuals embarked upon an odyssey to locate remnants of a pre-Civil War railroad partially constructed in northeast Georgia in the 1830s, 40s and 50s.

By Ruddy Ellis

It was with a great deal of anticipation that I and a group of friends decided to explore the old grades and infrastructure of what was once known as the Blue Ridge Railroad, a pre-Civil War-era rail line originally designed to connect the seaport of Charleston, South Carolina, with Knoxville, Tennessee. It seems that the concept of connecting eastern seaports with the inland great lakes and major waterways was a high priority among early developers and financiers.

The Blue Ridge line was originally conceived by South Carolina statesman John C. Calhoun, and promoted by him almost to the day he died in 1850. The line was meant to give Charleston an advantage over what then was a developing port at nearby Savannah, Georgia.

Rabun countians of that date, such as Henry T. "Colonel" Mozeley and James Bleckley, welcomed the idea of the railroad. Mozeley was one of the incorporators in the Georgia Charter of 1838, while Bleckley was a director. These two gentlemen also obtained a charter for the Northeastern Railroad of Georgia from Athens "so as to strike the Blue Ridge RR at or near the town of Clayton." The portion of this railroad from "Rabun Gap Junction" (present-day Cornelia) on into Rabun County became, of course, the Tallulah Falls Railroad.[1]

Calhoun reportedly engaged in a steady campaign to orient the route through Georgia's Rabun Gap and down the Tennessee River, instead of acquiescing to the wishes of fellow South Carolina states-

> *It seems that the concept of connecting eastern seaports with the inland great lakes and major waterways was a high priority among early developers and financiers.*

man Robert Y. Hayne, who wanted to take the line through the mountains near Asheville and down the French Broad River. Calhoun, the fiery South Carolina senator and vice president of the U.S., ultimately had his way.

Hiking The Route

Today, the tunnel at Stumphouse Mountain in South Carolina, and the amazingly massive stone masonry works (which the Blue Ridge RR used instead of trestles) are some of the more visible reminders of this surprising relic from yesteryear. The builders obviously intended for this line to handle a significant amount of freight, and they were building it to last indefinitely.

Despite a huge investment of time and money, the efforts toward this amazing construction project ultimately were all for naught. Though records indicate it was 80% completed by 1859, the outbreak of the U.S. Civil War interrupted funding and distracted the builders, and one tunnel (through Stumphouse Mountain) had been a particularly difficult obstacle. By the time other developers got around to reconsidering the line after the war, the route's usefulness had been circumvented by other railroads.

Two friends and I got the idea of exploring this fabled line after realizing we needed to fill in some gaps on some maps of historic north Georgia railroad grades which the Atlanta Chapter of the National Railway Historical Society (NRHS) keep on file. We partially accomplished this mission on three separate days, the first of which was spent at Walhalla, South Carolina, where the unfinished portion of the line began.

We started our research at the little community of West Union (a suburb of Walhalla), initially searching out and exploring an old siding there leading to a sawmill. This short stretch of rails had been the starting point for the aforementioned unfinished portion of the Blue Ridge line planned across northwestern South Carolina, northeast Georgia, western North Carolina, and on up to Knoxville.

The siding did not appear to have been used in a long time, and the sawmill was closed. However, the rails in the first part of the siding were fairly heavy and there was evidence that this was originally one leg of a "wye" (an arrangement of rails which allowed steam locomotives to reverse direction in earlier days).

The first 300 feet of the siding appeared to have been laid on the original main line grade toward the mountains. There was evidence of this grade across the road from the sawmill and on through a residential area. Attempts to find the grade beyond this point were largely unsuccessful.

We next decided to try to locate the site of the grade coming down from the mountains and around the horseshoe curve as shown on the topo (topographical) map of Walhalla. After a short search, we found a long driveway leading to a house. The drive almost exactly occupied the old grade.

There was a "cut" (a portion of the line where the railroad bed must be excavated through high ground) to the north of the house and a "fill" (a portion of the railroad bed where low ground or a ford across a ditch or chasm must be "filled in") leading to a culvert site to the south.

When we returned to the paved road, we found a deep, apparently unfinished cut which stops at the driveway of the aforementioned home just before the paved road. Next to the cut were little signs marking the grade as an official Boy Scout trail. It follows the old line all the way down from what today is known as Stumphouse Tunnel Park. Little evidence of the line could be found south of that point due to modern development in the area.

Stumphouse Mountain

The next objective on our list of explorations was Stumphouse Mountain Tunnel itself. At the time of its attempted construction (back in the 1850s) it would have been the longest railroad tunnel in the world - 5,863 feet. There are two shorter tunnels leading up to Stumphouse Tunnel: Saddle Tunnel, 616 feet long, and Middle Tunnel, 385 feet long. The approaches to these tunnels have filled in, making them almost unrecognizable today.

Wearing rain gear, boots and carrying flashlights, we walked inside the mountain to the end of the uncompleted tunnel, then reversed direction and measured the distance coming back out. According to our figures, the completed portion of the tunnel in that side of the mountain measured 1,600 feet. The interior dimensions of the tunnel measure 16 feet wide and approximately 20 feet high.

Another characteristic of the tunnel (and the reason for our rain gear) is its continuous rainfall, which is a phenomenon in itself. Heavy moist air sinks down vertical airshafts bored from the top of the mountain, cooling below the dew-point as it sinks, creating rain inside the tunnel. It apparently occurs year-round.

Even more interesting, the original tunnel drilling crews dug a total of four of these vertical shafts from the top of the mountain down to the level of the tunnel. The shafts ranged from 161 to 228 feet deep, and enabled the work crews to dramatically increase their work pace. The shafts also provided vents for steam locomotive smoke.

These "exhaust and breathing holes," however, were not completed without a heavy price. Several workers were killed in accidents. Some fell into the shafts or died after being struck by objects falling through the shafts. One individual was scalded by steam from one of the engines used to hoist the buckets of "spoil" from the digging.

After hiking back out of the tunnel and enjoying a picnic lunch in the crisp spring sunshine, we walked over to the beautiful Isaqueena Falls, where we explored the ruins of the old Walhalla Water Works dam.

Middle Tunnel

We next hiked the old Blue Ridge grade down to what was known as "Middle Tunnel," a shorter tunnel southeast of Stumphouse Mountain.

Middle Tunnel is included in the aforementioned Boy Scout Trail which passes through breath-taking cuts and fills of the old line. Spring wildflowers were blooming at this time and there were many "Jack-In-The-Pulpit" flowers along this portion of the route. There was also a lot of poison ivy, so hikers beware!

Following additional explorations in the vicinity of this site, we next drove around to a spot near the northwest end of Stumphouse Mountain Tunnel and its long approach cut. This site today is flooded by Crystal Lake. The portal of the tunnel is completely full of water, mud and debris so that only the rock face above the portal is visible today.

Walking southeast from the portal along a dirt road which appears to run almost exactly above the tunnel, we finally found a crater in the ground which is probably the remains of shaft #4. We were about 1,200 feet from the portal and there were a few small piles of rock here and there in the woods, but no real evidence that a lot of digging had taken place at this site.

With time running out, we left the tunnel area and tried to locate a place where one of our topo maps had indicated that the grade crossed the road between Mountain Rest and Whetstone. We, however, were unable to locate such a grade.

Blue Ridge RR In Rabun Co.

On a subsequent follow-up trip – once again exploring the former route of the old Blue Ridge Railroad – I re-teamed with Bob Young and fellow adventurer Henry Howell. This time, our goal was to explore the line's remnants in Georgia in Rabun County.

Our first stop was at the site where the historic Tallulah Falls Railroad (TF) and the planned Blue Ridge Railroad were both to have crossed Stekoa Creek north of Clayton.

It is ironic that the TF, which was completed from Cornelia, Georgia, to Franklin,

North Carolina, by 1907, succeeded in reaching Rabun County where the Blue Ridge Railroad failed. The irony of the situation is found in the fact that the 58 miles of the TF included some 42 wooden trestles – all of which constantly required maintenance and repair – a tremendously expensive proposition which ultimately aided in the demise of the little shortline.

The Blue Ridge Railroad by comparison, whose failure was caused by the advent of the Civil War, was being built with solid stone culverts and earthen fills across chasms and streams, and was designed to have no wooden trestles whatsoever. Had it been completed, it might very easily still be operational today.

In crossing Stekoa Creek in the 1890s, the TF built a trestle some 30 feet high. A good 50 years earlier, the Blue Ridge had built stone walls on both sides of the creek about 100 feet long. At first, we were puzzled about the purpose of the walls, because a trestle would not have needed such a structure. It wasn't until sometime later that we realized the Blue Ridge only planned to build bridges over the largest of the creeks. All the smaller streams were going to flow through stone culverts covered by massive earthen fills.

It amazed us to see the extent of these planned fills. All of them had to be built by hand using only animal-drawn carts! We found several completed culverts, all built of large rectangular stone blocks set without any mortar. We found out this was standard procedure in the first-class engineering involved in the construction of the Blue Ridge line.

Our second stop on this day was Warwoman Road at Saddle Gap where we could look down on the eastern approach cut to Warwoman Tunnel. On this day, a local resident was unloading household trash into public dumpsters at this site.

"Are you looking for the tunnel?" he called out to us.

When we replied in the affirmative, we

Researcher Ruddy Ellis pauses at "Observation Point" in Rabun County. Dick's Creek Falls are visible (right foreground), and the Chattooga River in the background. The Blue Ridge Railroad bridge across the Chattooga River would have been just downstream from this site, and would have been an amazing 450 feet long and 100 feet high had it been completed.

The graded road-bed of the Blue Ridge Railroad alongside Warwoman Creek in Rabun County is still visible here. (Photo by Ruddy Ellis)

Located on Warwoman Creek near Houck Road, the old mill pictured here was built by Samuel Beck, a captain in the Confederate Army during the U.S. Civil War. It is located in the general vicinity of the east bridge abutment of the Blue Ridge Railroad in Rabun County.

The west portal of "Middle Tunnel" through a ridge near Stumphouse Mountain is visible in this photo. The Stumphouse Mountain tunnel ultimately proved to be too long and laborious to complete, helping to doom the line to abandonment.

A Blue Ridge Railroad culvert over a small stream alongside Sandy Ford Road just east of the second ford across Dick's Creek. Notice the immensely-fortified nature of this construction accomplished with native stone.

The immense east bridge abutment of the Blue Ridge would have been a portion of the span across Warwoman Creek in Rabun County. This abutment was completed circa 1859, just prior to the outbreak of the U.S. Civil War which halted construction.

discovered this gentleman represented a wealth of information on the remnants of the Blue Ridge line in Rabun County. His name was David Mize, and he lived quite near the old Blue Ridge grade and had even ridden on some recent Atlanta Chapter (NRHS) steam excursion trips.

Mr. Mize spent some three hours that day guiding us to grades and culverts almost as far as the Chattooga River. He also related a long-standing legend that in the late 1850s, some 41 immigrant Italian laborers were buried in a cave-in inside Warwoman Tunnel. He explained that, according to the legend, the bodies were left there since work on the project had ceased at about that same time.

I'm sure there are a lot of colorful stories which have evolved through the 135 years since the railroad's demise.

Following dinner that night, we drove back to Atlanta, knowing that our work was still incomplete; our map still had gaps. Of particular significance was the fact that we still needed to find the place where the Blue Ridge planned to bridge the Chattooga River and fill in a gap north of Clayton. We also had not yet found the east portal of the Wall Mountain Tunnel.

Further Searches In Rabun

Several months later, Henry Howell and I returned to Rabun County to continue our project. We spent the morning once again with David Mize, reviewing the route between Warwoman Tunnel under Saddle Gap and on to Mountain City.

We then drove down Sandy Ford Road (off Warwoman Road) past the massive 94-foot long stone culvert of the Blue Ridge which represents the last known remnant in Rabun County. We, of course, were searching for the spot where the Blue Ridge had been designed to span the Chattooga River gorge.

We parked at a spot where Bartram Nature Trail intersects with the road. Hiking down to Dick's Creek, we followed the stream to where it flows down Dick's

Searching For Clues To The Historic Blue Ridge Railroad — Rabun County

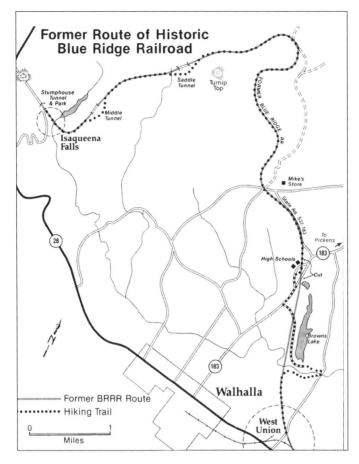

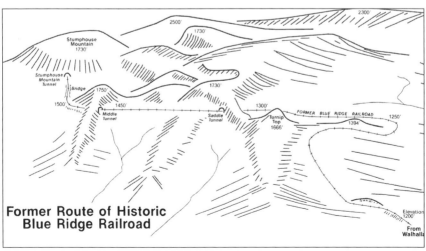

Creek Falls into the Chattooga. As we gazed in awe down this wild scenic river, we realized that a railroad bridge at this spot (which represents the most likely crossing point for the Blue Ridge) would have been a monumental construction project – particularly in the 1850s.

Just judging from the topographic maps, I'd say a bridge 450 feet long and 100 feet above the river would have been required at the very least! I suspect that after the builders got bogged down in the tunnel at Stumphouse Mountain, they couldn't get heavy equipment and building materials around to the Chattooga River gorge, and that's why nothing was ever built there.

Leaving the river, we hiked back up the Dick's Creek Falls spur trail to Bartram Trail and back to our car. We saw no sign whatsoever of any grading or stone culverts in this area, despite the fact we crossed the projected route twice in different spots.

For those readers interested in specifics, the most likely bridge site lies between Earl's Ford and Sandy Ford, but we found absolutely nothing.

It seems fantastic to imagine today that the charter for the Georgia portion of the Blue Ridge Railroad was granted in 1838, the same year the Cherokee Indians were herded out of Georgia on the shameful "Trail of Tears." That was well over 150 years ago!

It also seems almost tragic that the Blue Ridge line was never completed, particularly since virtually all of the culverts – constructed of huge granite stone blocks – are all basically still serviceable today. Seems like a terrible waste in this hugely scenic and historic area – but at the same time, an engineering marvel.

Directions:

To reach Stumphouse Tunnel Park, take Interstate 85 north into South Carolina. Take SC 11 to Walhalla, then SC 28 to the park. The entrance to the park will be on the right prior to reaching the Stumphouse Ranger Station.

To reach the Blue Ridge Railroad remnants in Rabun County, take U.S. 23/441 to Clayton. Turn east onto Rickman Road, which joins Warwoman Road. Set your odometer here to zero, so you can measure your mileage.

Just beyond the Stockton House Restaurant (a good spot for lunch, incidentally) a side road runs north along Norton Creek. There are stone culvert walls (from the railroad) in the creek and the end of a high fill on the other side of the road.

Continue eastward on Warwoman Road, turning right into the park and drive to the end of the park. Walk up the steps to the railroad grade and read the information signage there. A nature trail leads to the rock face which would have been the east portal of the 1,700-foot-long Warwoman (Stekoa) Tunnel.

Continue eastward on Warwoman Road (about six miles from Clayton) and turn right onto Sandy Ford Road. At the point where Sandy Ford Road takes a hard left across Warwoman Creek, continue straight on John Houk Road until you reach the old mill. You will be able to see the old railroad bridge abutment there.

Double back to Sandy Ford Road and continue east. At the 6.6 mile point, you will be driving on the old railroad grade. At the 6.7 mile point, the grade swings off to the north and to the uncompleted 2,300-foot Wall Mountain (Dick's Creek) Tunnel. At 8.3 miles, the grade crosses the road and the adjacent creek over another stone culvert. After fording two creeks, you will see the last stonework at about 9.8 miles from Clayton. Beyond this point is Dick's Creek Falls into the Chatooga River. Good luck!

Endnotes

1/ Sketches Of Rabun County History by Andrew Jackson Ritchie, Foote & Davies, 1948, reprinted 1959.

Railroader David J. Fant and the "Valley of Death"

In 1909, David J. Fant watched helplessly as his friend and fellow engineer Ed Miller died tragically in a train derailment outside Toccoa, Georgia. Approximately one year later near the same spot, Fant himself miraculously escaped injury in a similar derailment. His exciting experiences and compassion for his fellow man eventually earned him a spot in the annals of railroading folklore for all time.

The day of April 10, 1910, was overcast; a pall hanging over the Blue Ridge Mountains as they rose up from the forested terrain along the North Broad River south of Toccoa. Old No. 37 began to shake and vibrate wildly as it approached Toccoa Falls, and Engineer David J. Fant – "the evangelist of the rails" - knew he had a serious problem.

Fant yelled for the fireman to jump clear of the train. The car immediately behind the engine and tender bounced crazily as it left the tracks and began dragging the train down a steep embankment. Fant knew at any moment the huge steam locomotive would turn over, delivering him to the hereafter. He cried out to God, threw on the emergency brake, and breathed a quick prayer, certain he was looking on the Georgia pines around him for the last time.

A railroad accident of almost any size today is statewide if not national news, particularly if it involves fatalities or serious injuries. Before the age of the automobile and practical air travel when railroads were the only real means of quick, long distance transportation, railroad mishaps were much more common, but they were just as big a news item, because they were more dangerous.

Before wooden passenger cars were replaced with metal coaches, any very sudden stop of a train could cause the cars to "telescope," or collapse

Fant knew at any moment the huge steam locomotive would turn over, delivering him to the hereafter.

159

into one another as they collided, crushing each car in succession and mangling the unfortunate travelers inside. Worse than this, however, was a wrecked steam locomotive. It has meant a horrible death for many a brave engineer, often killing and maiming engineer and fireman alike, either by crushing them or horribly scalding them to death with the steam and boiling water from the ruptured tanks around the engine.

A company was formed in 1856, to build a railroad through the Toccoa (Stephens County) area to connect Atlanta and Charlotte, North Carolina with steam locomotive rail transportation. However, according to historian Kathryn Curtis Trogden, a national depression and the Civil War held up this project until sometime around 1873-74.

This route was and still is a heavily traveled line, since it is the shortest route by rail from the Deep South to the North. It became so popular in the late 19th century that the iron rails were replaced with steel from 1878 to 1887, and the line was double-tracked in 1917.

The "Air-Line," as this railroad was known, skirted the edge of the mountains, a dangerous route in the days prior to the safety measures taken by today's rail transportation companies. In the Toccoa area, the railroad had sharp curves, high wooden trestles, steep banks and other characteristics which made it a perilous trip, especially during heavy rains which caused landslides and destabilized trestles.

David Jones Fant, an engineer from Atlanta, earned a place in the folklore of railroading as "the evangelist of the rails," because aside from his employment as an engineer, he was also a Baptist minister, preaching wherever his time and schedule would allow him. While many of the railroad employees in the early 1900s were a rough, tough, profane lot, with a "live for today" attitude, Fant was a family man, close to both his family and his ministry.

While on a short run on this line from Atlanta to Toccoa, he met his future wife. He also often ministered to the students at the Toccoa Falls Bible College, and would blow his engine's whistle as he passed by the school, as a call to prayer for his friends there.

Fant also knew the dangers of railroading on the Toccoa run. His knowledge of the danger this route represented constantly plagued him, and he also knew that he could be the inadvertent cause of the deaths or injuries to others because of this peril.

In addition to the normal dangers of this route, Fant also had to be on the lookout for other steam locomotives on the tracks, as well as the people and livestock which often strayed accidentally onto the rails. Livestock were big enough to actually derail a train themselves, although it was considered good luck (and good eating)for the engineer to catch poultry in the grill of his engine.

Fant witnessed such an accident involving engineer Ed Miller, a friend of his, who only the day before, (through Fant's persuasion) had attended railroad church for the first time. Fant was running a fast freight and had sidetracked at Toccoa to allow the northbound No.36 passenger train under Miller to pass. Miller, however, never arrived. At Ayersville, six miles up the mountainside of Toccoa, a landslide caught and derailed the locomotive of the No 36 at Currahee Crossing.

On learning of Miller's fate, Fant waited only long enough to take on local doctors and nurses, before going to his friend's rescue. The wreck was a terrible one. The engine had been turned over by the force of the landslide, trapping Miller and his fireman beneath it. Unfortunately for them, they were not killed by the impact, but were slowly dying from a complete scalding they had received from their engine. Their skin was sliding off their bodies, and the colors of their eyes had faded by the time Fant reached them.

The dying Miller feverishly asked Fant to pray for him. The evangelist engineer pulled out his worn, grease-stained testament and began to read:

"Yea though I walk through the valley of the shadow of death, I will fear no evil,

Railroader David J. Fant and the "Valley of Death"

for thou art with me. . ." Fant read steadily.

On April 10, 1910, near the anniversary of Miller's death at the site, Fant passed through that same valley of death once again on a run to Atlanta. He was at the controls of No. 37, heading for Atlanta with his friend and black fireman - Rufus Johnson.

After passing through Toccoa, Fant pushed the old engine up to its cruising speed of 50 miles an hour, to accelerate for the climb through the edge of the mountains. Toccoa Falls Bible College rushed by, and it was shortly thereafter, that Fant's world turned topsy-turvy.

Since he was going south on a banked curve at such a high speed, the engine of No. 37 should have turned over on the higher outside rail, derailing it and trapping Fant beneath his engine. Miraculously, however, the engine fell instead over in the opposite direction, and when it finally came to rest seventy feet below, the evangelist of the rails climbed out uninjured from above the wheels. He immediately began to search feverishly for his devoted fireman.

Fant found Johnson a short distance away – also unharmed – but in a state of shock. The conductor and flagman arrived soon afterwards, and not finding Fant and Johnson, assumed they had met their fate trapped beneath the huge engine.

The wreck drew headlines in the Atlanta Journal, and unfortunately, Fant's assumed death was reported therein, a mistake which was not corrected before Fant's young son read it in the newspaper.

Fant's wife, however, was spared some of the shock. She and their three-year-old daughter, Mary, were on a passenger train that ironically was following Fant's No.37. Not only did they get to see that he was alright, but were given a tour of the wrecked engine and cars.

It had been a terrible wreck, but no one was killed. Little Mary was unimpressed, remarking only: "Daddy turned his engine over."

Arriving safely in Atlanta with his family, Fant stopped at the terminus long enough to send a telegram to his friend Rev. R.V. Miller in Hendersonville, North Carolina. It read "Saved from a serious wreck. Psalms 91:9-12. Continue to pray."

Miller's reply was: "Have just learned of your deliverance. Psalms 91:9-12. God answers prayer."

The passage that both these men cited reads as follows:

"Because thou hast made the Lord which is my refuge, even the most High thy habitation;

"There shall be no evil befall thee, neither shall any plague come nigh thy dwelling.

"For he shall give his angels charge over thee, to keep thee in all thy ways.

"They shall bear thee up in their hands, lest thou dash thy foot against a stone."

The late Atlanta historian Franklin Garrett once wrote that the stretch of Southern Railway between Charlotte and Atlanta has never been quite the same since David J. Fant made his last run on September 22, 1939, retiring at the age of 71, after 47 years of service. His narrow escape from the wreck of the Southern Crescent in 1910 made him a legend.

Interestingly, even that train wreck adventure was dwarfed the following year when Fant had the dubious honor of watching his train being robbed at gun-point near Gainesville by one of the last remaining bandits from the old West – Bill Miner. The "Gentleman Bandit," as Miner was dubbed in folklore, had migrated to the eastern United States after numerous robberies and murder in the western United States Canada made him a "Wanted" man in those areas.

David J. Fant died in 1965 at the age of 97. The rails through Toccoa today are not the same in many ways as they were in Fant's day. The trip is now safe, but the old-timers still close their eyes when they hear a train approaching, imagining that it is a steam locomotive about to pass through the Valley of Death. They silently pray that the next sound they hear is not a crash. . . .

The Pigeon Mountain Railroads

It may be something short of a world record that has stood unrecorded and unchallenged for over 80 years. Northwest Georgia's Pigeon Mountain may contain the most railroad tunnels of any such summit in the world.

No less than eight railroad tunnels pierce various ridges and spines of the rugged defile that extends southward from Lookout Mountain across the northwest corner of Georgia. Two railroads in this vicinity owed their existence to an early 20th century iron industry which once flourished in this locale.

This railroad network and the iron mines that gave them life are located about eight miles west of LaFayette in northwest Georgia's Walker County. Pigeon Mountain was once a bustling beehive of iron ore mining and narrow gauge steam railroading activity. All of it was built using little more than black powder, mules, carts, hand tools and back-breaking labor. Insects, snakes and other unhappy disturbed wild creatures no doubt contributed to the miseries of those laboring at this site.

Today, a portion of this mining area – the old Estelle Railroad – is an excellent "Rails-To-Trails" hiking venue. GA Highway 193 twists its way through Dug Gap to reach the Cloudland Canyon area. Unknown to many travelers in this region today, this road passes over the top of an abandoned railroad tunnel once used by the standard gauge Tennessee, Alabama & Georgia Railway – known simply as the TAG line. The north portal of this tunnel is just off the north side of the highway.

Not far from the south side of the highway through Dug Gap is the site of two former ore loading tipples at Estelle, once a company town of the Chattanooga Iron & Coal Corporation (which preferred to be

---

Two railroads in this vicinity owed their existence to an early 20th century iron industry which once flourished in this locale.

162

The Pigeon Mountain Railroads

called "The Corporation" in the 1920s). Diminutive steam locomotives and trains of the Estelle Railway ran over small three-foot gauge track, extending six miles south on the west flank of Pigeon Mountain, to trundle iron ore to these tipples and crushers. The crushed ore was then loaded into cars on the TAG line.

TAG Railway

Although one would be hard-pressed to find it on most maps today, there are two railroad stations just over one mile apart on this line. One is called Kensington and the other is called Hedges which is located near Davis Crossroads. Today, Hedges is the end of the line on a 23-mile branch line of the Chattooga & Chickamauga Railway (C&C), headquartered in LaFayette.

The C&C took over operation of both the old Central of Georgia main line from Chattanooga to Lyerly, Georgia, and the remaining stub of the TAG line from Chattanooga to Kensington and Hedges in 1989.

Until about 1980, the TAG line rails continued unbroken for 92 miles, starting at Chattanooga and continuing through High Point and Kensington to eventually reach Gadsden, Alabama. The first through-train ran on the Chattanooga Southern Railway on June 25, 1891. This railroad was reorganized in 1911 as the Tennessee, Alabama and Georgia.

For nearly 70 years, heavy trains thundered over the TAG line connecting Chattanooga and Gadsden. From the start, the steel mills at Gadsden were the reason for the road's existence.

Interestingly, there was also passenger travel on this railroad too, but it was accomplished in small gasoline-powered motor cars which were referred to derisively as "doodlebugs". It must have been quite a thrill in the 1920s to ride in one of the diminutive gasoline cars as it hurtled through the damp pitch black darkness of the 1,648-foot-long Pigeon Mountain Tunnel.

Several long side-tracks extended off the TAG line near Kensington and Hedges to reach Estelle. From these side-tracks, the Estelle Railway dumped the crushed ore into cars on the TAG line which then took the ore to the steel mills.

Southern Railway purchased the TAG line on January 1, 1971. By then, the iron ore business on Pigeon Mountain had been no more than a memory for nearly four decades.

Changing patterns of railroad activity ultimately doomed much of the TAG line beginning about 1980. Southern Railway had a parallel line to Gadsden via Fort Payne, Alabama. As a result, the track south of Hedges was gradually abandoned in stages. Today, the rails have been removed and a silent road-bed yawns into the distance from Hedges to Gadsden.

TAG Tunnel

The only tunnel on the TAG line is located about two miles south of the current end of the track at Hedges. It is one of the more tangible remnants of this now forgotten railroad. The long curved shaft into Pigeon Mountain is partly filled with water and debris today.

The north portal of the tunnel can be reached by hiking in from Route 193. However, hikers are discouraged from entering this tunnel, particularly in warm weather, when snakes and other wild animals may inhabit its dark and musty recesses.

At one time, the north portal was once the site of a small servicing facility. A water tank quenched the thirst of steam locomotives laboring to the entrance. Some old footings from a former building at this site can still be seen in the tall grass.

Estelle Railway

The little burg of Estelle was located immediately southwest of Kensington, and gave its name to the three-foot gauge railway which extended six miles back along Pigeon Mountain. Estelle was dominated by a large ore crusher and tipple which loaded the iron ore from the ten-ton cars of the Estelle Railway into the cars on the TAG line.

Little remains to mark Estelle today. A few concrete footings from the twin crushers can be found in the undergrowth, and several nearby small hills are really mine tailings. The village was dismantled and virtually erased from the face of the earth when the ore mining ceased.

Iron mining began on Pigeon Mountain as early as 1884, but the Estelle Railway was not built by The Corporation until after 1910. Much of the mining and railway activity appears to have ended sometime around the Great Depression of the 1930s.

The Corporation reportedly went bankrupt about 1927. The scrap drives of World War II, stripping the mountain of all the steel rails and other equipment, kept things going for awhile, but it didn't take long to remove the usable and recyclable raw materials.

Starting at Estelle, the six-mile Estelle Railway extended along the west face of Pigeon Mountain. According to a guidesheet prepared by the Georgia Department of Natural Resources which manages the Crockford-Pigeon Mountain Wildlife Management Area, the railroad followed the mountainside.

Hiking In

On a recent autumn hike along this route, the writer of this article was accompanied by two railroaders experienced with this area – Harold Holiman, general manager, and Randall Magnusson, superintendent of the Chattooga & Chickamauga Railway. These two knowledgeable veterans of the rails pointed out the remains of numerous remnants of this aged line. Today, these sites would be discernible only to experienced eyes.

Much of this roadbed is now known as the Estelle Mine Trail, marked by orange paint splotches on the trees along the route. The trail is passable by hikers, horseback riders and mountain bike riders - but not by motor bikes or motorized vehicles of any type.

Numerous clefts in the mountainside are left from former mining activities. Mining was done both by boring shafts (which have collapsed into the mountainsides as time passed), and by stripping exposed iron ore from the surface.

The Estelle Railway was a private, non-common carrier operation. As a result, it was not required to file reports of its development and/or its activities, so little information exists on it today.

One level area along the steep mountainside between two of the tunnels appears to have at one time been the site of small rail yard, probably about three or four tracks wide. Here, the tiny dinkey steam locomotives of the Estelle Railway marshaled the 10-ton cars of ore into trains to take them to the crusher.

Estelle Railway Tunnels

Then, there are the tunnels. When they encountered an obstructing ridge on the mountainside during construction of the rail line, the road crews simply dug and blasted a short tunnel through it, rather than divert the tracks around it. This practice was repeated seven times as the railway was extended southward from Estelle, and was the reason for the many tunnels in Pigeon Mountain.

Most all of the tunnels are approximately 500 to 1,000 feet in length. Since their abandonment

The village was dismantled and virtually erased from the face of the earth when the ore mining ceased.

The Pigeon Mountain Railroads — Walker County

during the Depression, many have been reclaimed by nature. Some have collapsed along much of their length.

The tunnels were often bored through well-fractured shale rock. Since abandonment, this rock has continued to erode from the walls and ceilings of the tunnels, often nearly completely filling them. Any wood shoring used for support inside the tunnels rotted away years ago.

As a result of the extreme danger of these tunnels, the Georgia Department of Natural Resources strongly discourages exploration inside them. At the site of each tunnel, the orange Estelle Mine Trail markers are diverted around the tunnels by a steep curving trail which climbs and twists over each ridge.

DNR management officials claim that a few of the narrow gauge cars which were used to haul the iron ore from the mines to Estelle Railway are still located inside one partly-collapsed mine at the far end of the Estelle Mine Trail. Due to the thick undergrowth and remote location, this mine is almost impossible to locate today.

Eight tunnels and miles of vacant roadbed aside, little remains to indicate that this once was a bustling industrial area. Mother Nature has reclaimed her own on Pigeon Mountain, but a good hiking opportunity awaits those who wish to venture onto the Estelle Mine Trail.

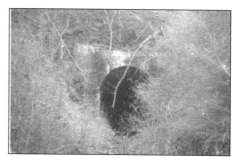

LAST REMNANT - The only tunnel on the Tennessee, Alabama & Georgia (TAG) Railway is still visible today through the undergrowth on Pigeon Mountain. It can be reached by hiking from Georgia Highway 193. The rails on this line, however, were taken up long ago.

GHOST ROAD - Much of the former route of the Estelle Railway is used as a biking trail as of this writing, and is known as Estelle Mine Trail.

The tiny town of Estelle was once located immediately southwest of Kensington, Georgia. It gave its name to the three-foot-gauge railway (photographed here circa 1924) which ran into Pigeon Mountain.

Old mine shafts opened in the 1920s still dot the mountainsides in the vicinity of Pigeon Mountain. Most of the mining activity in this area ceased in the 1930s.

The Gainesville-Northwestern Railroad In Helen, Georgia

Many former residents and current citizens still have fond memories of this little mountain short-line railroad.

Byrd-Matthews Lumber Co., one of the largest lumber mills east of the Mississippi in its day, opened in Helen, Georgia, White County, in 1912. It was a momentous occasion, because with it came the Gainesville-Northwestern Railroad, the transportation link necessary for the shipment of the thousands of board feet of lumber to Gainesville, Georgia.

After reaching Gainesville, the lumber was then transferred to other railroads for distribution throughout the United States as well as to other countries. Lumber production was big business in north Georgia where virgin timber was still abundant in the early 1900s.

The Gainesville-Northwestern Railroad (called G&NW) featured an excursion service from Gainesville to Robertstown, and also provided freight and postal service to these areas. The run began at the Gainesville Depot and made stops at Bradford Street Station, New Holland, Clark, Autry, Dewberry, Brookton, Clermont, County Line, Mossy Creek Campground, Meldean, Cleveland, Asbestos, Mt. Yonah, Nacoochee, Helen, and Robertstown. Gainesville, Brookton, Clermont, Meldean, Cleveland, Nacoochee, Helen, and Robertstown were agency stations, and the train made regular stops at them. The others were known as "flag points" or "flag stops."

Mr. T.B. Henderson owned a general merchandise store next to the Nacoochee Station. This building still stands today (It is the old brick building at the intersection of Hwy. 75 and 17, near the Indian mound). Mr. Henderson's daughter provided the following information:

"The Nacoochee Post Office was located in the general store and Mr. Henderson was postmaster there. He also served as rail agent at the Nacoochee Station. His duties included the issuance of tickets and the posting of freight bills. Most of the merchandise in Mr. Henderson's store came in by rail from Athens or Gainesville.

"Mr. Henderson was one of the few per-

The Gainesville-Northwestern Railroad In Helen, Georgia — White County

Engine #203 of the Gainesville-Northwestern Railroad pulls into Nacoochee Station in the early 1900s. The depot pictured here still stands as of this writing.

sons in the area who owned an automobile. Sometimes passengers coming in on the train would need transportation to one of the "resorts" in the area or to a friend or relative's house. After arriving at Nacoochee Station (which also still stands across Hwy 75 from the old general merchandise store), Mr. Henderson's son - Bon - would drive the travelers to their destination.

Mrs. Davidson helped her father in the store, post office and at the little railroad station. She remembers that in the store, they sold groceries, hardware, men's, women's and children's clothing, seeds and fertilizer, all mostly delivered by rail. She said that Mr. L.G. Hardman (whose beautiful old home also still stands near the intersection of Hwy. 75 and 17) shipped butter and milk from his dairy by rail to Gainesville, and Mr. "Simp" Logan shipped asbestos from his asbestos mine by railroad.

Mr. Henry Davidson, who became the husband of Miss Mary Lula Henderson, was one of the many who helped to build the railroad from Gainesville to Robertstown. His brother, Mr. George Davidson, was engineer on the train and Mr. Paul Westmoreland was fireman.

The railroad brought many visitors to the White County area. Major resorts included the Alley House (present-day Old Sautee Inn), Nacoochee; the Henderson Hotel in Cleveland; and the Mitchell Mountain Ranch in Helen.

The Gainesville-Northwestern Railroad continued its 37-mile run from Gainesville to Robertstown until 1930. Shortly thereafter, when the seeming inexhaustible supply of virgin timber had been depleted almost entirely, the railroad, with its life-blood gone, was discontinued. The tracks were taken up; the railroad rights-of-way reverted back to private ownership, and the Gainesville & Northwestern Railroad disappeared from White County forever.

Tales of the Rails in Georgia

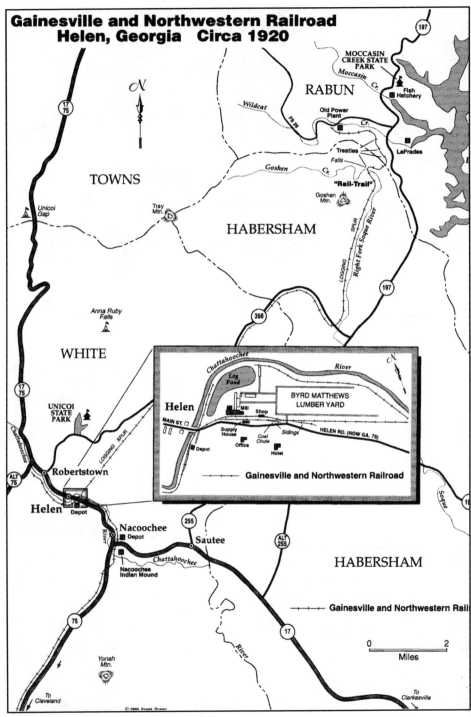

Route of the Gainesville-Northwestern Railroad.

Railroad Landmark: Old Dalton Depot

For over 140 years, the historic structure alongside the railroad tracks in Dalton has withstood the ravages of time and war. Today, railroad buffs can enjoy a meal where Civil War soldiers once trod.

When Mark Thornton sold a plot of land in Whitfield County to the state of Georgia in 1846 for $100, he clearly stipulated the property could only be used for one purpose: to build a railroad station which would provide rail transportation to other sections of the state. Eight years earlier, Georgia's Western & Atlantic (W&A) Railroad had been established to connect the Chattahoochee and Tennessee Rivers in a trade route between the Atlantic Coast and the West, and Thornton wanted to establish the Dalton area as an important stop along the way. It wasn't long before his dream became a reality.

Prior to construction of the Dalton Depot, trains had been rumbling into the area for seven years. When the tracks from Dalton to Atlanta were completed in 1847, town residents celebrated the occasion and the Fourth of July holiday with a barbecue and public speaking.

The first train from Atlanta arrived in Dalton on July 22, 1847, paving the way for the arrival of many more locomotives in future years.

Following the erection of the Dalton depot in 1852, the station quickly became the focal point of life in Dalton. Soon after the depot's completion, the population of Dalton soared from 300 to 1,500.

Today, travelers are still attracted to the Dalton Depot – one of only two surviving original W&A passenger depots in the state. An extensive $1 million renovation in 1990 by two Rome, Georgia, developers – Walter Hackett, Jr. and Mike Wrobel –

The first train from Atlanta arrived in Dalton on July 22, 1847, paving the way for the arrival of many more locomotives in future years.

transformed the 10,550-square-foot building into The Dalton Depot Restaurant and Trackside Cafe.

The one-story brick structure with its shallow-hipped roof, overhanging eaves and arched loading doors, remains typical of nineteenth century depot architecture.

Inside the structure abides some of the area's most significant history. Edward White, an entrepreneur from Massachusetts who named the town after his mother's family, hammered a circle of nails into the depot to mark the center of the town in 1852. Measuring from the nails in a one-mile radius, White established the first city limits from Dalton in a circular fashion.

Although records do not reveal the name of the depot's architect, many believe Eugene LeHardy, a W&A civil engineer and designer of the old Chattanooga depot erected in 1859, served as the designer of the Dalton station.

During the U.S. Civil War, soldiers frequently boarded trains at the Dalton Depot. On June 10, 1861, Private Eli S. Stanford boarded a train in Dalton with his company, headed for Big Shanty in present-day Cobb County's Kennesaw. During the march into Dalton, however, Stanford reported in his diary that his comrades "stopped and took some refreshments about two miles from town. After we got to Dalton, the boys increased refreshment and kept up quite a rucus all night. At 4:00 a.m., boarded train at Dalton for Big Shanty, arriving 2:00 p.m. It was obvious some of the boys had too much of the old Billy Patterson (a local moonshine) in them."

The Dalton Depot also played a role in the wild ride of the "General," the W&A locomotive which was stolen by the Yankee saboteurs known today in historic lore as "Andrew's Raiders." Here at the Dalton Depot, a 17-year-old telegraph operator was dropped off from the pursuing engine, "Texas," to send a message to Confederate forces in Chattanooga to warn of the General's approach.

At the time of this writing a popular eatery - the Dalton Depot Restaurant - operated inside the historic Dalton Depot.

In later Civil War action, railroad officials suspect the depot may have received some damage when Union troops entered Dalton in 1864 and set fire to several buildings. Although the brick exterior remained virtually unharmed, ornamental brackets beneath the overhanging eaves were added during later repairs to the roof, representing stylistic features normally in vogue after the construction of the original building.

Today, trains still rumble down the tracks beside the old depot which is owned by the City of Dalton and leased to private business owners. The Depot Restaurant still contains the station's original freight scales and other railroad memorabilia. Diners can also watch trains zooming by the window from a front row seat in The Trackside Cafe.

Surprisingly, the activity on the tracks outside the depot does not disturb diners and patrons to the facility. The 1852 builders of the depot specially designed the structure to isolate it from ground vibrations.

Placed on the National Register of Historic Places in 1978, the antebellum Dalton Depot still maintains an important role in the heart of the city's downtown district. It is located at the east end of King Street, and is open daily for lunch and dinner, Monday through Saturday.

Northwest Georgia Railroad Disaster
The Wreck Of The W&A

On a sunny afternoon in June of 1912, a large group of picnickers embarked on a special excursion train for a trip they thought would take them to Chattanooga, Tennessee. Instead, it took them on a horror-filled trip into destiny.

"Onward thundered 179, with hundreds of souls on behind.
    Faster and faster it sped the rail, 'Til it reached a place called Willowdale."

(From "The Wreck Of The Willowdale" by T.B. Kendrick)

Train wrecks of yesteryear were as traumatic and compelling as are the news accounts of airline crashes and other natural disasters today. Newspaper headlines dating near the turn of the century detailed the grim accounts of these incidents, usually providing a foretaste of the tragedies which were described in the article with graphic and oftentimes macabre detail.

On the morning of June 12, 1912, another beautiful summer day was unfolding for a group of 400 odd Calhoun, Georgia citizens on board the Western & Atlantic Train No. 179. Unfortunately, the only memories this group would retain of this day would be of suffering and death.

No Inkling Of Disaster

The occasion was a picnic for the Knights of Phythias Lodge, their friends and families. A special excursion train had been retained for the day, and the destination was the Civil War battlefields in Chattanooga, Tennessee.

A cross-section of Gordon County was represented that morning as the train departed the Calhoun station amid much jubilation. Spirits were high. All indications pointed to a memorable day, and it ultimately became that and much more.

The group departed Calhoun

A special excursion train had been retained for the day, and the destination was the Civil War battlefields in Chattanooga, Tennessee.

171

early, and by 8:00 a.m. were on the siding in Dalton – 20 miles north in Whitfield County. A southbound train was due through Dalton at 8:08, and once it had passed, the Chattanooga delegation continued its journey.

Some two miles north of Dalton, in an area known as Willowdale, a work crew was performing routine maintenance on the tracks. At the sound of the approaching northbound passenger train, the three men – Arthur Pilcher, Bill Richards, and John Shuman – quickly ceased working and moved with their tools to an area of safety, while waiting for the train to pass.

Disaster Strikes

Suddenly, as the train reached them, the locomotive erupted from the tracks without warning. The cars which followed gyrated into tangled masses of wood and steel, their crumpled remains scattered about the hillside on either side of the tracks.

The three poor unsuspecting maintenance workers were immediately engulfed in the avalanche of wood, iron, and spewing debris, as was the fireman of the fateful 179, Claud Holcomb of Resaca. Richards and Shuman, amazingly, were not seriously injured by the wreckage. Section hand Pilcher, however, was killed, as was fireman Holcomb, who was completely buried beneath the engine. His death was judged to have been instantaneous.

Follow-up investigations suggested the cause of the accident was a spreading of the rails at the point of derailment. It was speculated that the high temperatures of the week could have been the culprit. Skeptics were quick to point out that the Willowdale curve had been the scene of many serious wrecks in the past. None, however, had equaled the magnitude of this wreck. Others noted that the engine pulling No. 179 had earlier been in a serious accident south of Dalton.

Help On The Way

Eyewitness accounts of the tragedy maintained that immediately following the crash, the passengers showed great calmness and presence of mind. Within minutes, a make-shift emergency ward was assembled on the hillsides adjacent to the disaster site.

Within an hour, as soon as word could reach Dalton, all available physicians were rushed by special train to the Willowdale area. Much of the thanks for this quick response went to the local telephone exchange which voluntarily took the responsibility of locating the doctors and advising them of the needs involved.

Those victims most seriously injured were returned to Dalton on the train which had carried the physicians to the wreck site. Many victims interviewed in later days emphasized that it was the sight of so many injured bodies being loaded that brought the scope and magnitude of the catastrophe home to them.

In Dalton, all available hotel rooms were pressed into service. The First Baptist Church became a hospital, as did the city park downtown, where rows of cots and litters told of the horrors all too graphically. Scores of Dalton ladies volunteered as nurses, babysat the children who had been on board, and

Suddenly, as the train reached them, the locomotive erupted from the tracks without warning.

offered help in any way possible.

One such lady, a Mrs. Statem whose home was in the vicinity of the derailment, donated her entire supply of linens for bedding and bandages. The North Georgia Citizen, Dalton's weekly newspaper, reported that "Mrs. Statem busied herself, despite the fact that she was in a 'delicate condition' (emphasis added), in assisting in caring for the injured, her work and generosity showing the noble woman she is."

The Tragedy Described

In all, four cars jumped the tracks that fateful day. The baggage car followed the engine down the eastern slope of the steep embankment, while the other cars fell to the right.

Engineer Charlie Kitchens was at the throttle and stayed his post, escaping with only a badly bruised and lacerated head and a broken arm. The conductor, A.W. Hill, escaped uninjured.

Those most seriously injured were evacuated to Dalton first, with a second run following shortly thereafter.

Meanwhile, back in Calhoun, word was filtering back via a special long distance telephone line established by the Dalton Telephone Company. This courtesy was extended to the victims without charge, and allowed the two cities to remain in uninterrupted communication.

In Calhoun, rumor was as rampant as fact, and a sense of shock pervaded the town. According to accounts in the next day's Calhoun Times, townspeople were "completely stunned by the news." Later dispatches during the ensuing days detailed how the town seemed unable to come out of the stupor thrown over it by the serious injury to so many of its distinguished citizens. In the aftermath of the disaster, the presence of "ambulance chasers" – those who attempt to turn another's tragedy into their personal gain – abounded.

Tragedy Profiteers

One enterprising photographer filmed stereopticon views of the horror only a few hours after it happened. Calhoun people reportedly turned out in record numbers to see the show – to see how close they themselves had come to serious injury, even death.

Another fortune hunter, who, incidentally was never identified, went about the wreck site collecting edible food items from the many picnic baskets and undamaged items of passengers' personal property. He is reported to have made a tidy sum hawking his bounty around the wreck site and about Dalton during the days which followed.

"Enterprising" individuals seemed to abound at the wreck, unfortunately. One small girl, judged to be about 10 years of age, reportedly busied herself helping those critically injured, and helping herself to their jewelry at the same time.

Two young boys who had escaped unscathed evidently were determined not to miss the picnic they had been promised. Reports indicate that they collected a picnic basket and a blanket and spread their repast on the hillside amidst

In the aftermath of the disaster, the presence of "ambulance chasers" – those who attempt to turn another's tragedy into their personal gain – abounded.

TALES OF THE RAILS IN GEORGIA

Another view of the still smoldering ruins of the W&A Railroad wreck near Willowdale. (Photo courtesy of GA Dept. of Archives & History)

the pallets of the suffering.

More numerous, however, than those who sought to profit from the wreck, were those who gave unselfishly in a time of need. Many deeds of heroism were recorded, and physicians who were first on the scene credited many of the passengers with saving the lives of many who might otherwise have perished.

In all, eight individuals out of a passenger manifest of some 400 people were considered seriously injured. Of those, Mrs. John A. Ray, who sustained a serious back injury, was the only passenger who actually died. Others considered most seriously injured were Dr. G.A. Anderson, a representative to the state legislature from Gordon County, and prominent Calhoun matron Mrs. Kate Littlefield.

Eye Witnesses

First-hand reports from those who experienced the horror tended to be the most reliable. One account was rendered by Captain A.H. Hill, a Civil War (Confederate) veteran: "I was at Gettysburg, but believe me, it was nothing like this. I'd rather go through another such

Photographed June 12, 1912, is a view of the tragic accident at Willowdale. Many passengers who were injured were enroute to a picnic in Calhoun. The engineer and fireman both died in this wreck. (Photo courtesy of GA Dept. of Archives & History)

Photographed in 1990, the site at which the W&A Railroad train wrecked at Willowdale is pictured. Willowdale is just north (2 miles) of Dalton.

battle as that one than to be in another accident like this."

Miss Tilla Rooker, who with her brother Bart and sisters Ola Belle and Maude, operated Calhoun's famous Rooker Hotel, was a passenger on the train. Accompanying her for the day's outing was her brother and Joshua Hamilton, Mr. Rooker's Negro man-servant.

"It (the train) was going too fast around a curve near Willowdale. . . and went off the rails," Tilla explained some 77 years later. "Joshua in the baggage car was killed (and) my brother was injured. I . . was not injured, just scared half to death." That day, Tilla would later testify, was her "most exciting event."

Other accounts were less positive. More often than not, the terror of the wreck was more than most victims wanted to remember or re-hash with outsiders.

Rewarding Angels

Once the initial shock of the tragedy had subsided, Calhoun residents began efforts to repay those Whitfield Countians who had so generously given of their time and resources.

A purse containing nearly $100.00 was collected in Calhoun for Mrs. Statem who had donated all her linens. In addition, Dalton townspeople donated to the cause, as did the W.& A. Railroad which recognized the benevolent lady statewide.

The city of Calhoun, led by Mayor J.F. Allison and the aldermen; Col. J.G.B. Erwin, superintendent of the M.E. Sunday School; H.J. Roff, chancellor-commander of the Calhoun Lodge No. 264, Knights of Pythias; W.L. Hines, superintendent of the Baptist Sunday School; and Mrs. C.C. Harlan, president of the Calhoun Woman's Club, presented the city of Dalton with a formal resolution which concluded that the heroic, benevolent actions of many in Dalton had demonstrated "for us and yourselves, woman in her gentlest and truest and man in his noblest aspects."

Aftermath

Regarding the cause of the accident, follow-up investigations were conducted – such as could be done – but no definite culprit other than spreading rails could be pinpointed as having caused the accident. The tracks northward to Chattanooga were cleared and repaired that same day, and by nightfall, it was "business as usual" for the W & A.

Despite the severity of the wreck, the oft-wrecked engine from the train was judged repairable once again. On Friday following the wreck, the locomotive was raised from the ravine where it lay, and by noon, it was at rest on a side track, awaiting shipment to the factory where it would be overhauled for further service in the W. & A. network.

That same Friday afternoon, the body of fireman Holcomb, having been prepared for burial, was shipped south to his home in Resaca where funeral services were held shortly afterward. Mrs. Ray, died several days later and was buried in a family cemetery in Gordon County. Neither the home nor burial site of the deceased section hand Pilcher is known today.

And of the victims who survived the wreck, their first-hand accounts and written recollections over some three-quarters of a century indicate that the Willowdale wreck was not something that was easily forgotten. It was, in fact, a haunting memory which most of those 400 individuals carried to their graves many years after they first cheated the Grim Reaper at Willowdale on a sunny morning in June, 1912.

Subject Index

A

Adairsville Depot 114
Adairsville, Georgia 115, 117
Air-Line, 160
Air-Line Belle 73
Alley House 167
Alpine Helen 90
Allatoona 13
Allatoona Creek 2
Allatoona Dam 4
Allatoona Pass 2
AM Railroad Company 36
American Polearms 22
Americus 38
Americus and Montgomery Railway 35
Angel of Death 107
Anniston, Alabama 61
Andrews' Raiders, 2, 169
Anheuser-Busch Brewery 12
Apalachia 59
Apalachia Dam 57
Appalachian Trail 93
Aragon Barbecue 134
Aragon, Georgia 134
Armstrong Hotel 64
Asbestos 166
Asbestos Station 91
Atlanta and Charlotte Air-Line 71
Atlanta Chapter of the National Railway 153
Atlanta Constitution 44, 61, 66
Atlanta Journal 102, 107
Atlanta Rolling Mill 15
Atlanta and Richmond Air-Line 71
Atlanta Southern Confederacy 24
Augusta, Georgia 106
Autry, Georgia 166
Azalea Drive/Riverside Road 69

B

Baldwin Locomotive Works 92, 98, 99
Ball Ground, Georgia 54
Banking Company of Georgia 60
Banks County 149
Baptist Fellowship Forum
Barnsley Gardens 12
Bartow County 4, 7, 13, 16
Bartram Trail 158
Battalion Georgia Volunteer Infantry 24
Battle of Allatoona 5
Battle of Brushy Mountain 129

Belton, Georgia 108
Big Raccoon Creek 126
Big Raccoon Trestle 126
Big Shanty (present-day Kennesaw),
 Georgia 3, 22, 116
Billy Carter's Service Station 40
Bill Miner Crossing 107
Birdie Gailey 97
Black Diamond/Blue Ridge 82
Blue Ridge 12, 53
Blue Ridge and Atlantic Railroad 143
Blue Ridge Railroad 69
Blue Ridge Scenic Railroad 48, 53, 55, 57
Bluff Street 138
Boy Scout Trail 154
Bradford Street Station 166
Brookton 91, 166
Brookton, Georgia 92
Brushy Mountain 129
Brushy Mountain Tunnel 129, 130
Buford Dam 68
Buford Highway 75
Bull Durham tobacco 127
Bulloch Hall 69
Burton 91
Byrd-Matthews (later Morse Brothers)
Byrd-Matthews Lumber Mill 93
Byrd-Matthews Lumber Co. 166

C

Camp McDonald 21, 23, 25, 29
Calhoun Lodge No. 264
Callie's Collectibles 38
Canton, Georgia 54
Cardinal's Car 75
Cartersville, Georgia 6, 104
Cartersville Railroad Company
 in Dawson Co., 46
Cass Station 114, 118
Cedar Bluff, Alabama 63
Cedartown, Georgia 13, 131
Central Railroad 60
Chamblee 67, 71, 72
Chamblee Depot 67, 72
Chamblee First United Methodist Church 68
Chamblee-Dunwoody Road 67, 68, 72
Charles C. Davis 106
Charleston, South Carolina 83
Charlotte 71
Charlotte & Atlanta Train 39, 144

177

Chattahoochee High School 95
Chattahoochee River 68
Chattahoochee River 67, 90, 91
Chattanooga, Rome &
Columbus Railroad 60
Chattanooga Iron & Coal Corporation 162
Chattanooga, Tennessee 4, 27, 125
Chattooga & Chickamauga Railway 164
Chattooga River 156
Cherokee Advance 17
Cherokee County, Alabama 63
Cherokee Indians 158
Cherokee National Forest 59
Chickamauga Railway 163
Chief Ladiga Trail 129
Cincinnati, Ohio 16, 19, 83
City of Gainesville 98, 99
City Point, Virginia 122
Civil War 73
Civil War line 83
Civilian Conservation Corps, 149
Clark, 166
Clarkesville, 76, 146
Clayton 76, 81, 82
Clayton House 3
Clean Town, 130
Clear Mountains, 96
Clermont 91, 94, 166
Cleveland 91, 166
Cliff House 89
Crockford-Pigeon Mountain Wildlife,
Currahee Crossing 160
Cobb County 16
Cobb County's Kennesaw 169
Coca-Cola syrup 88
Cochran's Funeral Home 138
Columbus, Georgia 14
Comer Shop 75
Company F, 56th Georgia Regiment 29
Confederacy 115
Confederate Arsenal 22
Confederate War Department 21
Confederate Memorial Day 11
Confederate Memorial Museum of
Coosa River 9
Coot's Lake Rest Stop 130
Cooper's Day Use Area on Lake Allatoona 118
Cooper's Iron Works 113, 118
Coot's Lake 130
Cordele, Georgia 37

Cornelia, Georgia 76, 80
County Line, 166
Cowboy, 142
Curtis Switch Road 50
CSX Railroad 90
CSX Transportation 54

D

Dade County 15
Dahlonega, 41 103
  access to Georgia Power's Morgan Falls
Dahlonega Electric Railway Company, 44
Dahlonega Nugget, 103 104
Dahlonega Railroad Co. 44
Dallas, Georgia 126
Dallas New Era 123
Dalton Depot 114, 118, 168, 169
Dalton Short-Cut Railroad Company 46
Dalton Telephone Company 172
Danville, Virginia 127
Davis Crossroads 163
Dawsonville Mountain Chronicle 45
Dewberry 166
Demores 76
Desoto Hotel 8, 9
Dickey Cemetery 56
Dick's Creek Falls 158
Dictionary Of Georgia Biography 16
Dillard 76, 81
"dinky" 144
"Dip" 95
Disney boxcars 83
Dixie Hunt Hotel 103, 105
Doraville 70, 71
Downtown Marietta Development Authority 34
Ducktown, Tennessee 55
Dug Gap 162
Duke's Creek Falls 91
Duluth, Georgia 74
Durham and Southern Railroad 98

E

Earl's Ford 158
East Side Elementary 136
Ellijay, Georgia 55, 58
Emerson-Allatoona Road 6
Enfield rifles 23
Engine #1219 141
Engine #209 98

Enon Cemetery 18
Escowee Falls 90
Estelle Mine Trail 164
Estelle Railway 162, 163, 164, 165
Etowah Valley Historical Society 3, 5, 6
Etowah River Bridge 113, 118
Etowah Valley Railway Company 47
Etowah, Tennessee 54
Euharlee Creek 132

F

Farill Plantation 64
Farill, Alabama 64, 66
"Father of Rockmart," 133
First Baptist Church 171
Fishing Creek 107
Fletcher House 119
Floyd County 63
Forrest L. Shiver 98
Forrestville Station 66
Fort Donelson 22
Fort Sumter 24
Fort Payne, Alabama 163
Frank & Corn 151
Franklin, North Carolina 76, 81, 88
French Broad River 153
Fried Green Tomatoes 111

G

Gadsden, Alabama 163
Gainesville, Georgia 90, 166
Gainesville & Northwestern Railroad 167
Gainesville and Dahlonega Electric Railway Company 45
Gainesville & North Western Railroad 95
Gainesville & Northwestern 90, 93
Gainesville & Northwestern Railway 99
Gaston County, North Carolina 71
Gainesville Depot 166
"General" 116
Georgia Department of Natural Resources 164
Georgia General Assembly 23
Georgia Institute of Technology 16
Georgia Military Institute 24
Georgia Pike 22
Georgia News-Tribune, 138
Georgia State Railroad, 26
Georgia State Legislature 9
Georgia's Western & Atlantic 168

Georgia 197, 93
Georgia Department of Natural Resources 36, 92
Georgia Department of Transportation 49, 129
Georgia Division Safety Committee of Southern Railway 126
Georgia Highway 3, 56, 91
Georgia Marble Works 46
Georgia Mountains 55
Georgia Mountains Museum 98
Georgia Northeastern Railroad 48, 49 Georgia Power 93
Georgia Power Company 68, 72
Georgia Rural Telephone Museum38
Georgia State Legislature 67
Georgia State Veteran's State Park 36
Georgia Veteran's Memorial Park 37
Georgia Veteran's Memorial State Park 37
Glenbrook Hotel 89
Global Village 38
Goodyear Mill 138
Goshen Creek 92
Grand Canyon 82
Great Depression 110
Great Locomotive Chase 10, 115
Great Locomotive Chase Festival 115
Great Locomotive Chase Marker 114
Great Locomotive Chase 115
Grey Fox 105, 107
Greystone Hotel 66
Grim Reaper at Willowdale 174

H

Habersham, 91, 92
Habitat for Humanity's Global Village and Discovery Center 38
Hall County 108
Hall County Police Office 102
Hazel Creek 77
Heart of Georgia Railroad Company 36
Helen, Georgia 91, 166
Henderson Hotel in Cleveland 167
Historical Society, 153
History of Bartow County 16
History Of The Roswell Railroad 67
Hiwassee Loop 55, 57, 58
Hiwassee River 57, 59
Hogback Bend 56
Hometown Foods IGA, 51

"Hook & Eye" 54
Howard Street 60, 64, 66
Holly Springs Depot 17, 20
Holly Springs 16, 17

I
Interstate 28 68
Interstate 75 12
Interstate Commerce Commission 137, 139

J
Jimmy Carter National Historical, 39
Juliette, Georgia, 111

K
Kennesaw Civil War Museum 113
Kennesaw House 26, 27, 32, 115, 120
Kennesaw House/Marietta Museum of
"King Cotton" 110
Kingston 11, 114
Kingston Inn 8
Kingston Depot 116
Kingston Station 119
Kingston Times 12
Kingston Women's History Club 120
Kingston, Georgia 116
Knights of Pythias 174
Knights of Phythias Lodge, 170

L
L&N Railroad Depot 49
Lacy Hotel 22, 116
Lake Allatoona 15
Lake Blackshear 35
Lake Blue Ridge 56
Lake Burton, 92
Lake Lanier 68
Lakemont 76, 82
LaPrade's Fish Camp 92
Laurel Mill 73
Leather's Ford, 43
Leslie Drug Company, 38
"Little Mary," 52
Long Branch Road, 105
Lost Mountain, 129
Louisville & Nashville Railroad 48, 54, 115
Louisville & Nashville, 48
Louisville & Nashville Railroad, 52
Lumber Mill 90
Lumpkin County, 91, 103

Lumpkin County Jail, 106
Lyerly, Georgia, 163

M
Macon and Cincinnati Air-Line Railroad 45
Management Area 164
Maranatha Baptist Church 40
Marietta, Georgia 70
Marietta & North Georgia Railroad 52
Marietta Daily Journal 31
Marietta: The Gem City Of Georgia 5
Masonic Lodge 19
"Ma White's Bottomlands" 131
McCaysville 51, 57
Meldean 166
Memory Hill 107
Middle Tunnel 154
Milledgeville, Georgia 106
Mineral Bluff 50, 52, 55, 56
Mitchell Mountain Ranch in Helen 167
Moccasin Creek 91
Montgomery Railroad Company 35
"Moon's Station Road" 117
Moon's Station 113, 122
Morgan Falls Dam 68
Morgan Falls Dam and Power Plant 68
Morgan Falls Junction 72
Morgan Falls Station 69
Morganton 52
Morse Brothers Sawmill 91
Mossy Creek Campground 90, 166
Mountain City 76, 81, 147
Mountain Chronicle 45
Mount Hope Cemetery 20
Mt. Yonah 166
Murphy Junction 50, 53, 56

N
Nacoochee 91, 103, 166
Nacoochee Station, 166
Nancy Creek 68
Nathan Dean Sports Complex 133
National Park Service's Vickery Creek 69
National Railway Historical Society 49
National Register of
Historic Places 8, 66, 169
New Holland 166
Newton County 106
Niagara Falls 85
Norfolk-Southern Railroad 136

Normal School 86
North American Railcar Owners
 Association 54
North Carolina 71
North Carolina Transportation Museum 99
North Georgia Citizen 172
North Georgia Electric Company 45
North Peachtree Road 72
Northeastern Railroad 109
Northern Pacific Railroad 49
North Shallowford 72

O

"Old Buck" 68, 72
"Old Line" 54, 59
Old 97 127
Oostanaula River Bridge 114, 117

P

Panic of 1857 15
Panther Creek 78, 80
Passover 81
Pat Calhoun 65
Paulding County 131
Peachtree Industrial Boulevard 72
Peachtree Road 67
Pennsylvania 71
Peru, Indiana 16, 17
Pigeon Mountain 163
Pleasant Hill Road 75
Polk County 131
Polk County Chamber of Commerce 134
Ponce de Leon 125, 135
Post Office Department 146
Powers's Branch 68
Primrose Cottage 69
Pulaski County 19
Pullman cars 138
Pumpkinvine Creek 123, 127
Pumpkinvine Creek Trestle 123

R

Rabun 92
Rabun Counties 91
Rabun County 69
Rabun Gap 81
Rabun Gap Junction 152
Rambo 129
"Railroad Festival Days" 110
"Rails-To-Trails" 129

Rails-To-Trails Conservancy 81
Railway Historical Society 74
Railway Mail Service 144
Railway Post Office 144
Railroad Street 8, 12
Ranson Mercantile building 9
Raynes' Station 64
Reynolds House 10
Richmond & Danville Airline Railroad 109
Richmond & Danville Railroad 108
Ringgold Depot 114, 122
Ringgold, Georgia 4, 29
Ritter Lumber Company 148
Riverwalk 132
Riverwalk and Seaborn Jones
 Memorial Park 134
Roberts Drive 69
Roberts Road 72
Robertstown 90, 166
Robinson Annex 87
Rockmart Slate Quarry 132
Rockmart's annual Homespun Festival 132
Rome & Columbus Railroad Company 64
Rome & Decatur Railroad 66
Rooker Hotel 174
Rose Hill Cemetery 133
Roswell Bank 73
Roswell, Georgia 69, 70
Roswell Manufacturing Company 67, 70
Roswell Railroad 67, 68, 69
Roswell Railroad Depot 67
Roswell Road 69
Royal Palm 135
Rufus Tilman "R.T." Davis 106
Russian Decapod 99
Russo-Japanese War 99
Rutherford "Ruddy" Ellis 75
Rylander Theater 39S

S

Saddle Gap 155
Saddle Tunnel 154
SAM Shortline 35, 39
Sandy Ford 158
Sandy Ford Road 156
Santa Fe Railroad 49
Santa Claus 77
Seaboard Airline Railroad 99, 128
Seaboard Depot 132
Seaboard Railroad 128

181

Second Avenue 66
Seminole War of 183 14
Silver Comet 128
"Silver Comet Trail" 128
Southern Banner newspaper 22
Soque River 91
South Marble Street 133
Southeastern Railway Museum 74
Southern Appalachians 92
Southern Museum of Civil War and
 Locomotive History 117
Southern Railway Company 67, 68, 71,
 73, 112, 145
Southern Railway and Express 103
Southern Railway's Train #36 101,
 104, 106
Southern States Portland Cement Plant 135
Southwest Georgia Railway
 Excursion Authority 36
Spartanburg, South Carolina 71
Spencer, North Carolina 99
State Prison Board 106
Stekoa Creek 154
Stewart and Jones Company and
 Doubletrack 76
Stumphouse Mountain Tunnel 153
"Superb" 75
Sylva, North Carolina 145

T

Talking Rock 54, 56
Tallulah Falls Depot 82, 147
Tallulah Falls Gorge 82, 88
Tallulah Falls Railway 76, 85, 88, 143
Tate City 91
Tennessee Copper Company 55
The Corporation 163, 164
The Dalton Depot Restaurant and
The Depot 121
"the Dinkey" 72, 73
The Eagle 44
"The Great Locomotive Chase" 29, 118
Thomas Van Buren Hargis home 10
Tiger 82
Toccoa, Georgia 104
Toccoa & Elberton Line 150
Toccoa Electric Power Company 56
Toccoa Falls Bible College 160
Toccoa River 48, 50
Trackside Cafe 169

Train Number 59 126
Train Number 81 123
Train Order #92 142
Trans-Siberian Railroad 99
Tunnel Hill 114 122
Turner's Corner 41
Turtletown Creek 57

U

Union Army 115
Union Recorder 107
Union Station in Atlanta 62
U.S. Army Corps of Engineers 6
U.S. Civil War 67, 69, 115, 129
U.S. Highway 4, 11, 41, 88
U.S. Supreme Court 51
U.S. Civil War 9

V

Van Wert 131
Varnell, Georgia 127
Veterans' Memorial Walk 133
Vickery Creek 69

W

W&A Railroad, 9
Wabash Railroad Company 17
Wabash Railroad Hospital 17, 20
Wall Mountain 158
Warwoman Road 155
Warwoman Tunnel 155, 156
Washington 73
Washington, D.C., 125
Western & Atlanta Railroad 5, 8, 15, 115, 120
Whistle Stop Cafe 111
White Sulphur, Georgia 104, 106
White Sulphur Road 103
White Sulphur Station 102
White Sulphur Springs 110
Wildcat Creek 91, 92
Windsor Hotel 39
Woman's History Club 11
Wolfpen Ridge 93
World War II 99
"Wilson's Mill" 721903

Y

Yonah 15, 91

Full Name Undex

A

Abercrombie, Una 97
Adams, Cary 97
Addington, Bob 144
Allen, John 57
Allison, Mayor J.F. 174
Anderson, George 103, 104
Andrews, General, James J. 29
Andrews, James 116
Andrews, James J. 3, 10, 24
Armstrong, Don 3, 5
Armstrong, Jack 57
Armstrong, John 3
Arnold, Craig R. 47
Ayers, Vernon 8, 12

B

Bailey, Irene 96
Banks, Richard 109
Barnwell, W.E. 96
Bateman R.L. 140
Barrett, E.W. 61, 66
Barrett, Frank 17, 20
Battey, Dr. Henry 62
Beck, Samuel 155
Beck, Samuel 155
Bell, Harold 143, 149, 150
Bell, Major Madison 109
Belle, Ola 174
Bennett, Chesley 96
Bennett, Wallis 97
Blance, Joseph 133
Bleckley, James 152
Bogle, Col. Jim 10, 58
Bowen, Price 97
Bowen, Valera 97
Brewer, Henry 145
Brewer, W.H. 139
Brice, Annie 97
Brice, Hugh 97
Broady, Steve 127
Brookshire, H.T. 96
Brooksner, J.M. 47
Broom, C.J. 96

Brown, Edward 97
Brown, Governor Joseph E. 5, 21, 22, 23
Brown, Jim 80
Brown, Joseph Emerson 29
Brown, Mary 97
Brown, Rodney 22, 237
Bruffey, Edward C. 61
Bryson, Clifton 97
Buell, General Don Carlos 25
Buffington, H.E. 96
Buffington, Ralph 97
Buice, D.T. 97
Buice, Lee 97
Buice, Madison 109
Buice, Matt 109
Bullis, H.E. 140

C

Cain, Andrew 42
Cain, Frank 97
Cain, Jeff 116
Calhoun, John C. 60, 152
Camp, Charles 126
Campbell, William 26
Carmichael, Pete 103
Carroll, John 151
Carruth, Bonnie 97
Carruth, Jarnet 97
Carter, President Jimmy 36, 39, 40
Carter, R.L. 96
Catlett, Nita 97
Chandler, Callie 97
Chandler, Etta 97
Chandler, Winnie 97
Christopher, Nell 97
Clayton, Luther F. 17
Clements, Hal 138
Coffee, Gussie 109
Coker, Lunie Mae 97
Cole, Henry Green 34
Cooper, Mark Anthony 13, 15
Cooper, Mark David 118, 122
Cooper, Glenn 9
Corrie, Arthur M. 135, 136, 138

Cox, Dan 31
Cox, Dr. Carey 33
Cox, John 126
Crawford, Ruth 97
Culpepper, Laura Belle 97
Culpepper, Lillie Mac 97
Culpepper, Pink 97
Cunyus', Lucy J. 16

D

Dalton, Beecher 76
Dalton, Catherine 76
Davis, Elizabeth L. 73
Davis, Gordon 106
Davis, Herschel 97
Davis, Jim 103, 106
Davidson, George 167
Davison, Robert E. 106
Delong, Hortense 97
Delong, Kelsey 97
Dillard, Alec 80
Dillard, Hughes Denton 16, 19
Dobbs, Annie Lou 104Dotson, Earl 148
Dosser, J.W. 140
Dowie, W.I. 140
Dyer, Otis 97
Dynes, W.L. 140

E

Eberhart, A.B. 96
Elder, Mary 97
Ellis, Ruddy 56
Ernest Abercrombie 97
Evans, W.T. 96
Erwin, Col. J.G.B. 174

F

Fant, David J. 160, 161
Finlay, J.J. 140
Flagg, Fannie 111
Fletcher, Dix 32
Fletcher, Eliza 34
Forrest, General Nathan Bedford 64
Forrester, Avie 97

Frost, J.E. 140
Fuller, Captain William A. 4, 23, 25, 27, 116
Furlough, Benjamin 16, 19
Furguson, Spencer 57

G

Gailey, Birdie 97
Gailey, Sylvia 97
Garnett Keith 97
Garrett, Franklin 161
Garley, H.D. 47
Garrison, Harry 96
Gearin, George, 96
Gilliam, Emery 57
Gillespie, Jesse 98
Gilstrap, Seaborn 97
Glenn, G.R. 47
Glover, John Heyward 32
Gordon, John B. 61
Goulding, Dr. Francis Robert 10
Grant, Lee 97
Grant, Mae 97
Greer, Beulah 96
Grier, Hoke 97
Griffin, Lucas 97
Grill, Impala 134
Grindle, Claude 96
Grindle, W.C. 96
Grizzle, J.E. 97
Groga, Josephine 96
Grogan, Elmira 96

H

Hale, P.T. 140
Hamilton, Joshua 174
Hampton, Ralph 96
Handford, James 102, 105
Haney, Henry 121
Harbin, O. Wiley 120
Harlan, C.C. 174
Hardy, George 140
Harper, Mary Lee 7
Harrison, Fairfax 73
Harve, Gussie 87

Haynes, Annie Mae 97
Haynes, Emma 97
Haynes, Hubert 96
Haynes, Idell 97
Haynes, John 96
Haynes, Mabel 97
Haynes, Myrtle 96
Hawkins, Charles E. 96
Hawkins, Richard 96
Hawkins, Samuel H. 35, 36
Head, Adele 97
Head, Brown. B.J. 96
Head, Chester 96
Head, Exer 96
Head, H. 47
Head, Lillie 97
Head, Minnie 96
Head, Joe F. 3, 5
Head, Ruth 97
Henderson, Mary Lula 167
Hendrix, Floyd 97
Hicks, Dr. Thomas J. 51
Higgins, Henry E. 32
Highsmith, Ada 96
Hill, A.W. 172
Hill, Captain A.H. 173
Hillhouse, David 85
Hilty, Robert 140
Hines, Bobby 38
Hines, W.L. 174
Hitt, Michael 67
Holcomb, Claud 171
Holliday, John Henry "Doc" 36
Hood, Lt. Gen. John G. 2
Hooper, Mae 97
Holton, Byron 67
Houston, Private Andrew Jackson 5
Howell, E.C. 56
Howell, Henry 154
Hudgins, Beulah 96
Hudgins, Clyde 97
Hudgins, Daisy 96
Hudgins, David 97
Hudgins, Essie 97

Hudgins, H.G. 96
Hudgins, James Zacheus 94, 97
Hudgins, Lena 96
Hudgins, Marilu 97
Hulsey, Edgar 97
Hulsey, Ernest 96
Hulsey, Mary 96
Hulsey, Vallie 97
Hughes, Jane 16
Hughes, James Louis 16, 19
Hughes, Dewey 16
Hunter, Charlie 102, 105
Hughes, Julian M. 16, 17
Hurtel, Gordon N. 61
Hyman, Mac 38

I

Iix, Sallie 97
Imboden, Jacob P. 46

J

Jackson, Burke 19
Jackson, Edwin 51
Jackson, Captain Henry 61, 63
Jackson, Mary Belle 97
Jackson, Olin 75, 95, 104, 123, 131, 132, 134, 136, 137
Jarrard, C.C. 96
Jarrard, Ethleen 96
Jarrard, Salena 96
Jarrard, Vivian 96
Johnson., Hon. J. Lindsay 61
Johnson, Rufus 161
Johnston, Joe 129
Jones, J.B. 42
Jones, Seaborn 132, 135
Jones, Y.D. 97
Juliette, Lake 112

K

Keene, Grant 92
Keith, A.B. 96
Keit, C.H. 96
Keith, Homer 97

Keith, H.W. 96
Keith, Jewell 97
Keith, J.L. 96
Keith, Nina 97
Keith, S.J. 141
Keith, Vassie 97
Keith, Vera 97
Kelley, Lawson, E.B. 96
Kent, Frank 81, 162
Kichens, Charlie 172
Kimbrell, Goldman 147
King, Jack 61
King, John Pendleton 9
Kuhn, Will 140
Kurtz, Wilbur G. 120
Kurtz, Wilbur G. , Sr. 29
Kytle, A.S. 96
Kytle, Gertrude 97

L

Lackey, J. Henry 97
Lancaster, Carl 96
Lancaster, Cora Belle 97
Lancaster, O.G. 96
Lancaster, U.S. 96
Langford, Esther 97
Lanier, Sidney 241
Lathem, Joyce Denton 16
Lawson, D.T. 96
Lawson, H.L. 96
LeHardy, Eugene 169
Levingston, Bunnie 16
Little, Deputy Sheriff 102
Littlefield, Kate 173
Lobrugh, Dan 140
Lockhart, Anna Belle 96
Lockhart, F.P. 96
Logan, Escoe 97
Logan, Henry 97
Logan, R.C. 57
Logan, Maude 97
London, Merritt M. 104
Lord, D.W. 97
Lord, W.H. 96

Lyon, Mattie Harris 24

M

Maddox, Clyde 97
Maddox, Iris 96
Malone, Debbie 66
Malone, Deborah 122
Marlow, Russell 97
Martin, Albert 97
Martin, Roy 9
Marlowe, Mozelle 97
McCollum, Jane 19
McGee, Herschel 97
McKinney, Colonel Mike 52
McNeal, Michael 97
Meaders, J.A. 96
Miller, Bertie Mae 97
Miller, Ed 160
Miller, Grover 96
Miller, J.T. 96
Miller, Mike 43
Miller, Ralph 97
Miller, Walter B. 101
Miner, Bill 104
Mintz, Duane 127
Mitchell, General Ormsby 25
Mize, David 156
Mintz, Leonora (Mrs. Robert Henry) 136
Moere, John H. 47
Mooney, Diane (Mrs. Dennis) 1
Mooney, Walter T. 101
Moore, Fred 97
Moore, Myrtle 97
Moore, Tom H. 106
Mozeley, Henry T. "Colonel" 152
Mullinax, Cordia 97
Mullinex, Martha H. 120
Murphy, Anthony 116
Murphy, June 97
Murphy, Ralph 97

N

Nichols, Jim 123

O
Owen, Ethel Hughes 16

P
Parks, Joseph E. 23
Patten, Dewey 97
Patrick Calhoun 60, 61, 63
Payne, Liccie 96
Payne, Lillie 96
Peck, Y.W. 96
Pennington, John 148
Peter, Bracken, 120
Pettyjoh, W.P. 96
Peyton, H.H. 96
Phillips, Colonel William 23, 25
Phillips, Ida 42
Phinizy, Lula (or Lulah) 110
Pierce, Maudelle 97
Pierce, Nellie Mae 97
Pierce, Robert M. 138, 139, 142
Pikes, Joe Brown 23
Pilcher, Arthur 171
Pinkerton, William 106
Pittenger, William 26
Poole, Howard 97
Price, Col. W.P. 44
Price, W.P. 43
Price, William P. 44
Puckett, Clarence 97

Q
Quinby, William T. 15

R
Ragsdale, Theron E. 143
Ray, John A. 173
Reed, Henry 97
Reed, M.D. 96
Reeves, Dan 39
Richards, Bill 171
Ripley, Robert 56
Roark. Agnes 97
Roark, Ethel 96

Roark, Lucile 97
Roberts, Ike 72
Roberts, Isaac Martin 68, 71
Roberts, John Morgan 71
Roberts, Lucinda White 7
Robinson, William A. 15
Roff, H.J. 174
Rogers, Carl 81
Rogers, Eugenia 97
Rooker, Tilla 174
Roosevelt, U.S. President Theodore 69
Ross, Marion 34
Ross, Sergeant Major 27
Russell, William 118
Rusts, Corporal Gus 140

S
Sargent, J.F. 47
Seay, Tom 61
Seibert, Evans, L.B. 140
Shaw, Ray 104
Sherman, Gen. William T. 2, 32, 116
Shoemaker, Bob 12
Shope, Roy 81
Shuman, John 171
Simpson, Cladith 97
Smedlund, William 22
Smith, Harry 142
Smith, Maggie 97
Smith, T.J. 47
Smith, William R. 119, 120
Sorrells, Henry 142
Spencer, Inez 96
Spencer, Colonel Thomas 5
Standridge, Pink 96
Staton, Charlie 97
Staton, F.C. 97
Staton, Lola 96
Staton, M.K. 96
Staton, Willie 97
Staton, Adelia Joe 97
Stringfellow, Bill 56
Snyder, John B. 145, 151
Swann, F.W. 140

T

Tanner, Hester 97
Temple, Sarah 22
Tench, Rev. Hoyt 76
Thomas, R.H. 96
Thompson, Ralph 97
Thornton, Mark 168
Truelove, Pearl 97
Truelove, Laurie 97
Turley, Nancy 69, 72
Turner, Nath 142
Turner Quillian 97
Turpen, Drucy 87
Tyner , G.F. 96
Tyrie, James 16

Y

Young, Bob 154

W

Walker, Clarence 97
Walker, Tony 97
Walker, W.L. 97
Wall, Mack 57
Wallace, Texas 97
Walker, Brawner 80, 145
Walton, C.R. 52
Ward, Noah 80
Waters, Bertha 97
Waters, Ruth 96
Watts, John B. 106
Westmoreland, Paul 167
Whelchel, Nellie 96
Whisenhunt, J.W. 140
White, Isaac 71
White, Polly (Mary) Falls 71
Whitmore, Paul 97
White, Sarah Mary Givens 71
White, Robert 5
Whitley, Henry 29
Whitmire, Nell 97
Whitmire, Hassie Mae 97
Whitmire, Julius 97
Whitmire, W.A. 96

Whitaker, J.W. 140
White, James 71
Whittle, J.W. 106
Wiggins, W.M. 107
Wilber, Al & Karen 56
Wilder, Dr. Daniel 32
Wiley, L. M. 14
Willie, Lewis, 42
Willie, Meaders, 97
Wilson, Joe Mack 34
William, Sherman, T. 10
William, Vineyard, 57
Williams, Alice 140
Williams, Academy, 131
Williams, Goldie   140
Williams, Jerie Lynn 112
Williams, Travis 115
Williamson, Captain John D. 60, 61, 64, 66
Wilson, Joe Mack 34
Windencamp, W.J. 107